T0376610

Grief and Addiction

Grief and Addiction illuminates the role of grief work in addiction counseling, encouraging counselors to be more comprehensive in their treatment, and to increase empathy for what the treatment process is asking of clients.

Acknowledging that entering recovery includes a loss of coping skills, and that it requires building a new identity, this book focuses on addiction-specific grief work. *Grief and Addiction* integrates concepts like complicated grief, nonfinite loss, trauma, family grief responses, and treatment suggestions in one place—all with a focus on the application to addiction work.

Featuring appendices with information and examples for clinicians, *Grief and Addiction* provides treatment strategies drawn from both the addiction and grief world for professionals and counselor educators.

Julie Bates-Maves, PhD, LPC, is an associate professor in the Department of Rehabilitation and Counseling at the University of Wisconsin–Stout. Her teaching and research interests are centered on trauma, addiction, and reducing stigma.

Grief and Addiction

Considering Loss in the Recovery Process

Julie Bates-Maves

Routledge
Taylor & Francis Group

NEW YORK AND LONDON

First published 2021
by Routledge
52 Vanderbilt Avenue, New York, NY 10017

and by Routledge
2 Park Square, Milton Park, Abingdon, Oxon, OX14 4RN

Routledge is an imprint of the Taylor & Francis Group, an informa business

© 2021 Julie Bates-Maves

Library of Congress Cataloging-in-Publication Data
Names: Bates-Maves, Julie K., author.
Title: Grief and addiction: considering loss in the recovery
process / Julie Bates-Maves.
Description: New York, NY: Routledge, 2021. | Includes
bibliographical references and index.
Identifiers: LCCN 2020016722 (print) | LCCN 2020016723
(ebook) | ISBN 9781138587434 (hardback) |
ISBN 9781138587458 (paperback) | ISBN 9780429468001
(ebook) Subjects: LCSH: Addicts—Counseling of. |
Addicts—Rehabilitation. | Grief. | Drug abuse counseling. |
Substance abuse—Treatment.
Classification: LCC RC564 .B3654 2021 (print) | LCC RC564 (ebook) |
DDC 362.29/186—dc23
LC record available at https://lccn.loc.gov/2020016722
LC ebook record available at https://lccn.loc.gov/2020016723

ISBN: 978-1-138-58743-4 (hbk)
ISBN: 978-1-138-58745-8 (pbk)
ISBN: 978-0-429-46800-1 (ebk)

Typeset in Bembo
by codeMantra

Contents

Acknowledgments

To my past clients:
Over the years I have been transformed by my profession and there are no words that adequately describe all that it has meant for me personally and professionally. I am incredibly grateful for all you have taught me and I am honored to have been trusted with your stories. It is never lost on me how much responsibility there is in hearing someone's pain and someone's joys. I am grateful for your trust, vulnerability, endurance, and strength. I am better for having known you all.

To my husband:
Thank you for putting up with me during this process, and pretty much always. Even though it may not always seem so, I do know how lucky I am to have a partner who supports and encourages me. I love you (to prove it, I won't make you read this cover to cover)!

To my boys:
You two are the loves of my life and I am so lucky to be your mom! I hope that someday you can read excerpts of this book and know a side of me I rarely bring home. This, as most things are, was an exercise in persistence. I did it because I believed it mattered. I hope that you persist when you find something that matters to you. I love you forever, and ever, and more.

Part I
Setting the Stage

1 Introduction

Intent

As a counselor and now a counselor educator, I am fascinated by clients' stories and the ability of humans to withstand great pain. More than that, it's the ability to endure great pain and *still keep moving* that catches my attention. Addiction is not simple, and yet we often simplify the narrative; that is, addiction is often equated to being stuck, moving backwards, and/or the erosion of a life. I have worked with many clients who would agree that for them, addiction meant just that—being stuck, becoming a different person, losing sight of the larger world, and sometimes even death. Yet, many of the same clients *also* described relief and/or the added ability to cope (or avoid) intense emotions or circumstances through use or other behaviors. Still others described addiction as offering a distraction, optional numbness, perceived action against problems, community or a sense of belonging, a sense of control or identity, and/or physical relief; in short, a way to sustain and cope with life—even if it was a crappy life. Other clients described enhanced creativity or social prowess, a sense of power (over self and others), and feelings of security or certainty. For others, addiction added deceit, abuse, trauma, self-deception, fear, pain, and strained or failed relationships. Ultimately, I have found that in many stories, addiction added to life as much as it took away.

Addiction is about both presence and absence. In considering how to help people end an addiction, we need to consider the whole picture of what the behaviors brought, produced, or were intended to produce (the presence) and what they took away or diminished (the absence). An examination of the elements that were purposeful and functional and those that eroded purpose and ability. In the larger world (particularly in popular media) and sometimes even in the counseling relationship, addiction is framed as something that's *only* killing you, rather than something that's helping you survive. I believe addiction is both—it's running toward and away from death at the same time. The irony never escapes me that counselors so often combat all-or-nothing thinking, and yet we sometimes engage in it ourselves when working with clients.

When faced with severe consequences, especially death, humans can search for a solution *before* they search for understanding. That urge is understandable and one I certainly experience myself—I want to fix something that seems broken so there is less pain (for me and others). Yet, my training and professional understanding tell me that simple fixes may do no better than a band-aid over a gaping wound. They provide the appearance of protection or action but offer no actual healing.

To treat and heal our wounds, we need to examine them to determine the damage that's been done, clean them and stabilize our body, take medication if needed, and give our body time to sort things out so that we recover. Last, we need to assess how we were hurt in the first place to avoid the same injury in the future. I see addictions treatment following a similar path.

We need to examine what's inside the addiction, determine the damage that's been done (as well as what's still intact), stabilize the body and the mind, medicate if needed, and allow the body and mind time to adjust, and sometimes acquire a different level of functioning. At times, we deal with scars that are left—lasting effects of a deep wound. My goal with this text is to further explore the so-called wounds of addiction and to discuss some options for beginning to heal them. As stated earlier, grief and the grieving process will play a central role, as well as examining the impact of loss and the opportunity for reconstruction of meaning.

When clients enter recovery, some begin to grieve what was lost during the addiction and celebrate the beginning of sobriety, of recovery. But what about grieving the loss of the addiction itself? In my own clinical work and in speaking to other counseling professionals, I have noted little discomfort or objection to exploring the "negatives" of an addiction with clients. Notably, I *have* encountered hesitation or overt avoidance of the "positives" of addiction, that is, "don't speak of the glory days" or "don't encourage clients to focus on what they miss, instead focus on what they have to look forward to in recovery."

The more I think about this idea of avoiding the so-called "good stuff" for fear of the session spiraling into a celebration of addiction or complete focus on the past, the more confused I become. Largely the confusion stems from two places:

1   Counselors have skills that are intended to shape and influence the direction and depth of conversations. We need to lean into our skill set to initiate and navigate difficult conversations.
2   What if the "glory days" were the only time the client felt powerful, or noticed, or admired, or skillful? That's significant. We risk missing meaning when we avoid talking about the perceived high points of use/patterns.

When entering recovery, a client such as this would not only contend with the addition of a new set of behaviors, thoughts, and feelings, but an absence of "glory." That speaks to identity work, to connection, self-esteem, and potential social skill deficits. Further, inviting reflection on the "glory" of it all is a chance to observe a client reminisce about a time when they felt more worthy. If self-worth is centered on the addiction or a component of it, we need to know so we can help them redefine and reconstruct *who they are*, not just *what they do*.

Please note that I am not advocating that addictions are healthy or preferable, but they **are** purposeful. As stated earlier, for many, addictive behaviors add to life as much as they take away. Addiction and the associated behaviors meet needs and we cannot underestimate how important that is.

As a counselor and counselor educator, I firmly believe in the power of grieving as a healing agent. Examining the meaning of loss and its impact on a life is valuable. Though many counselors acknowledge the importance of grief, it seems that at times, we miss opportunities to broaden concepts and address grief from multiple angles, particularly in addictions. The focus instead can go straight to behavior change and changing a client's environment. For example, asking or mandating that clients stop use and find a new social group. As healthy as that sounds, both ending use and finding new friends represent major life changes and are inherently filled with loss (and reactions to loss).

This text will emphasize the importance of understanding and processing grief in the context of addiction and recovery. Ideas for how to adapt existing bereavement models to this context will also be included. I sincerely hope that the information presented will encourage counselors to be more comprehensive in their approach and to increase empathy for what the process of treatment is asking of clients; that is to change their internal and external worlds.

Introducing Ben

When I teach, I find that information is more useful when applied to cases. Ben* will serve that purpose here as we move chapter to chapter. This will serve as an introduction to Ben's story; it will be continued throughout the book as we cover additional concepts.

Name and details have been altered to maintain client anonymity; case examples are designed for learning purposes and application of concepts.

Ben was a 34-year-old male who identified as Hispanic. He was seeking treatment to end his use of both heroin and cocaine. This was his fourth attempt at recovery; he had tried twice on his own and attended court-mandated outpatient treatment once. His demeanor was quiet and calm. What struck me upon meeting him was how tall he was, and yet, he felt so small. He was bent at the waist, his shoulders were forward, and he had his arms wrapped around his upper body. He looked at the floor with occasional fleeting eye contact and he spoke softly.

Metaphorically, he reminded me of an armadillo. As odd as that might sound, consider this: the outer shells of armadillos project a tough appearance to outsiders, and yet their belly is soft and vulnerable to attack. To counter this vulnerability when faced with a threat, armadillos will first stand still and see if the threat simply passes them by. If that doesn't work, they run and attempt to hide. If that still doesn't work, they roll up into a ball and protect themselves; they fold in half and essentially assume the fetal position. They are trying to minimize the damage of an attack by protecting their insides (Conger, 2008). This was Ben. During that first encounter, it was like he was trying to shrink himself to take up less space in the world. Like he was protecting his insides by curling up to buffer any attack he might encounter.

Ben had a 16-year history with heroin and a three-year history with cocaine; this amounts to him initiating heroin use at 18, and cocaine at 31. He primarily injected both substances intravenously and made it clear that this was a complication he ran into in previous quit attempts; he reported "missing" the needle and being drawn to that method of use. He briefly described the "mesmerizing" visual of drawing the plunger back and seeing blood swirl in the barrel. This allure will be discussed in more depth in a later chapter. At the beginning of our work, he was using cocaine and heroin each between three and five times a day.

His initial heroin use came after a football injury during his senior year in high school. His dad injected him with heroin after a severe knee injury and subsequent surgery. Ben said, probably three or so times throughout our first meeting, that the medications were not adequate for his level of pain and "my dad was trying to help me." He described his dad's "dedication and support" while growing up and recalled his first experience with heroin.

> He would come to every practice, every game. He wasn't one of those parents who forced their kids ... he wanted it [football] because I wanted it. I never doubted he'd be there; he never gave me reason to doubt.

When asked about his thoughts on his dad's solution to his pain, namely heroin, he said,

> At the time, I didn't even know what it was really. He didn't tell me it was heroin until I asked for another dose and he didn't have any more. I trusted my dad and so when he told me, it seemed weird, but I honestly didn't think too much about it. We never talked about it after that. Years after my accident I learned that we didn't have good insurance when I got hurt and that my dad had to pay off about $7000 for my surgery. That's why I didn't go back to the doctor for my pain; my dad didn't think he could afford it.

Ben grew up without a second parent. His birth mother did not want children and when she became pregnant, she told Ben's dad that she would carry the baby to term but "after that, he's all yours. I'm not meant to be a mother." As I listened to him, I felt a sadness for him and was curious about his reactions to this. He appeared rather flat and matter of fact while describing his mom and that didn't really change upon further discussion. Ultimately, he said,

> She didn't really want a kid. I don't think it was personal—she didn't know who I'd become or anything. Thinking about it doesn't really feel good, but she's never been there for me, so kind of just had to move on, I guess.

Overall, Ben's basic needs were largely met growing up and he had fond memories of his youth.

> We had what we needed and sometimes what we wanted. My dad never really told me how much money we had or didn't have, and I never thought to ask really. My dad did good most of the time; I know he loved me.

Listening to Ben describe his parents and initial use led me to believe several things about him: (1) He believed himself worthy of love and felt love from his dad; (2) He believed himself capable of loving another; (3) He trusted his father and saw the positives in him even when his behavior was questionable; (4) He was dedicated to preserving his father's memory and did not want his struggle to reflect poorly on his dad.

At age 18, Ben moved out to attend a trade school for welding. He moved into an apartment with a friend and started using heroin periodically (approx. two or three times per month).

> We would party and when people brought it [heroin] over, we just kind of did it. I never really worried too much since I had it once and it honestly didn't seem like a big deal to not have it after that first dose…. so I figured, what the hell.

A more regular pattern of use emerged at age 19 (two–three times per week); daily heroin use (two–three times per day) emerged later that same year.

> One time in [welding] class I burned my hand pretty bad. I remember using that night to numb the pain so I could try and sleep. I knew it would work—I mean the pain from my hand hurt way less than my knee had a couple years before. Just made sense. It [use] got away from me after a while. My roommate started selling to make his tuition money. We both started using more after that and it wasn't really that

fun anymore, but it was just what we did. After a while, I'd get sick if I stopped, so I just kept going.

Ben finished up his schooling and bounced around between part-time jobs before landing his first full-time welding position at age 22. He first attempted to go cold turkey a year later at 23 years of age.

> I think some people there [at work] wondered about me. The first time I tried to stop using, I got dope sick and people just assumed I had the flu or something. I gave up on day 4 (and used) and went back to work after that. I flew under the radar or maybe not, I don't know. Sometimes I wonder if I was on people's radar and they just never thought or cared to ask if I was ok. I still wonder about that sometimes.

Aside from that isolated attempt at sobriety, daily use continued for the next four years.

> It wasn't that hard to hide. I'd use at home before work, take a drive for lunch and use, and then usually once or twice more when I got home. It was a maintenance dose at that point—I didn't feel high anymore. I don't even remember when I stopped feeling high, but it was gone for a while. I kept using because I couldn't handle withdrawal; it was just too damn hard.

At age 27, he was pulled over and heroin was found in his car. He pled no contest and was sentenced to treatment and six months' probation. After his arrest, Ben informed his employer about his addiction.

> That was embarrassing [to tell his boss]. Thankfully he didn't fire me but told me if it [arrest] happened again, I was out. Telling my dad was the really hard part. He knew that I had used every now and again after I moved out, but never knew that I had developed a solid habit. I think he thought I stopped messing around with it by the time I was 20 and for sure after I got my welding job. I hid a lot of things from him, so to sit in front of him and tell them who I really was … it sucked. I didn't know what to say. I remember him crying though. He blamed himself. I've basically tried to wipe that conversation from my brain. It sucked.

Three weeks after the arrest, his father was diagnosed with lung cancer. Ben completed ten outpatient sessions as mandated by the court around this same time.

> Counseling was ok. My use decreased during that time [in treatment], but it never went away. And my dad's diagnosis hit me like a brick.

To be honest, it scared the absolute hell out of me. My dad was always the strong guy, and now he was sick—he looked like it too. A couple months after my counseling ended, I tried to get sober again on my own. The withdrawal kept me going back though. I had a lot on my mind, and I remember thinking that this was probably the best time to try [to stop using] because of my dad, but the worst time for the same reason. Part of the reason I even tried was so that I wouldn't die before him. I didn't want that for him; to have his son die before him. I didn't want him to feel like a failure.

Approximately four years later, around Ben's 31st birthday, his father died; cocaine use started in the weeks after the funeral.

We had known for a while this was probably going to kill him, but it's like I couldn't accept it and I was so wrapped up in my own life that I was able to distract myself from it. I was never actually prepared for him to die. His death crushed me. I needed, or at least I thought I needed, cocaine to get out of bed so I could show up for work and get through the day. I really don't think I would have gotten out of bed without it.

Cocaine became part of his life; use ranged from three to five times per day. Heroin, enough to stave off withdrawal symptoms, also continued. After injecting heroin, he would follow with cocaine to *"get a boost of energy."* He boiled down the concurrent use as *"the only way to function without being sick in my body or sick in my head."* Over time, as with heroin, he described it becoming something *"I just did."*

Ben sought treatment about three years after his father's death. During the intake interview, he said, *"I don't want to do this forever. I should have stopped a long time ago. I can't do it alone I don't think, and I'm pretty much alone at this point. Please help me."* Ben stared at the ground as he said this. Then he raised his head to look me straight in the eye as he said, *"please help me."* I don't think I'll ever forget that moment; you could feel the weight of the request. As I reflect now, it strikes me that by asking for help, change had already begun to happen in his life—he wasn't alone anymore.

Reference

Conger, C. (2008). *How do armadillos roll into a ball?* 10 November 2008. Retrieved on February 23, 2018 from https://animals.howstuffworks.com/mammals/armadillo-ball.htm

2 Definitions and Concepts

The labels we apply to our lives shape our perceptions of them. Words matter. As such, let's explore some definitions.

Addiction

The American Society of Addiction Medicine (ASAM, 2011) briefly defines addiction as the inability to consistently abstain from a substance or behavior, impairment in behavioral control, craving, diminished ability to recognize its negative impact on one's life and relationships, and a dysfunctional emotional response. This idea of addiction as compulsion, lack of control, and continued use originated with David Smith in 1988 and continues to factor into current definitions and diagnostic criteria. For instance, in discussing substance use disorders (SUD), the Diagnostic and Statistical Manual of Mental Disorders, 5th Edition (DSM-5) highlights risky use, social impairment, and lack of control as well as tolerance and withdrawal. Importantly, while tolerance and withdrawal may be present, they are not absolutes for all addictions. That is, they may be present, but they do not have to be for diagnosis.

A more formal definition from ASAM centers on the disease nature of addiction in the brain. It is understood as a "chronic disease of brain reward, motivation, memory, and related circuitry" (ASAM, 2011, p. 1); the relapsing nature of addiction is also noted. Essentially, someone keeps using or engaging in behavior even when they don't want to and even when it is hurting their life. And if a person tries to stop, the body rebels and demands more of the substance or behavior. They go on to note that addiction also impairs executive brain functions resulting in distorted perceptions, problems with impulse control and judgment, impaired learning and problem-solving, and compulsivity. ASAM also notes that addiction has "avolitional aspects" (2011, p. 1). Basically, this means that people with addiction often struggle with low motivation or loss of drive.

Recognizing the variability in individual presentation of addiction, Miller, Forcehimes, and Zweben (2011) broke addiction down into seven dimensions. The first six are familiar: use, problems resulting from use, biology and physical adaptation to a substance (specifically tolerance and withdrawal), behavioral dependence on a substance or behavior (i.e. priorities shift and other areas of life are neglected), cognitive impairment, and medical harm (i.e. aggression, overdose, diseases resulting from chronic use like cirrhosis). The seventh, however, motivation for change, echoes ASAM's point on the avolitional nature of addiction. Miller and colleagues also note [client] hesitance to acknowledge the extent of an addiction and the low internal drive towards treatment and/or change as common for some.

The National Institutes on Drug Abuse (NIDA; 2016) defines addiction as a chronic brain disease, with features of compulsion, continuance despite negative consequences, and relapse. NIDA also emphasizes that willful use or engagement erodes as the addiction progresses; essentially, the brain changes with addiction and the ability to exercise self-control is hampered. Unsurprisingly, NIDA and ASAM's definitions are not worlds apart. While I greatly value the biological foci of ASAM and NIDA, I equally value their acknowledgment that addiction is more than that. Gabor Maté (2010), William Miller and colleagues (2011), and others not only agree, but strongly advocate for a broader definition of addiction.

In defining addiction, attention must be given to the relational disruptions that can occur within the self and in relation to others, cognitions, emotional responses, spiritual connectedness, and more. It's also important to move beyond the assumption that addiction is always about use of a substance like alcohol or heroin. Behaviorally, according to ASAM, addiction is seeking out something to either produce a reward (i.e. get high) or provide relief from pain. Substances can provide either of these, but many other behaviors can too. Maté (2010) sees the hallmarks of addiction, substance-related or not, as compulsion, impaired control, continued use or engagement despite negative outcomes, and dissatisfaction, irritability, or intense craving when the object is not available. Nonsubstance addictions can be as problematic as substance-related ones, and so, this text will reference both.

Recovery

Addiction is multifaceted and complex. Recovery is as well. The most comprehensive definition I have found to date is the one by the Substance Abuse and Mental Health Services Administration (SAMHSA, 2012). SAMHSA emphasizes the individual nature of recovery and states repeatedly that self-determination is key. Put simply, clients should have a voice in their recovery, and we should encourage them to use it. In working to define recovery, SAMHSA considered multiple perspectives including those of clients, family members, advocates, politicians, medical and mental health and Alcohol and Other Drug Abuse (AODA) providers, and others. This multidisciplinary definition is especially useful when considered through the lens of comprehensive care and treatment. Recovery is not singular and *just* about the person attempting it; it's about our collective efforts to help and support someone through a major life change.

Importantly, SAMHSA's definition covers not only recovery for substance abuse disorders, but for mental health disorders as well. SAMHSA (2012) briefly defines recovery as "a process of change through which individuals improve their health and wellness, live a self-directed life, and strive to reach their full potential" (p. 1). Within this rather simple definition, however, are several layers of life. Four dimensions are identified by SAMHSA in particular: health, home, purpose, and community. *Health* encompasses sobriety and abstinence from either the substances or behaviors that are problematic. Physical health, wellness, and disease are also included here. The self-directed nature of recovery is further highlighted in this dimension with emphasis on healthy decision-making that supports a whole, healthy life. *Home* equates to stability and safety. *Purpose* is fairly apparent, having a meaningful existence. Learning to find, or regaining, purpose and meaning in the day-to-day activities like work, school, family life, hobbies, and social involvement. Emphasis is also placed on freedom and independence, both internally and practically (i.e. adequate income and resources). Finally, *community* notes the importance of relationships and connection. Relationships in many ways, enable purpose, aid in stability (or instability), and can impact our physical wellness. Therefore, we cannot discuss recovery without also discussing meaningful connections.

These four dimensions set the stage for a deeper discussion of what recovery is. The guiding principles developed by SAMHSA (2012) delve deeper into the facets of recovery and the collective effort needed to initiate and sustain it. As you're reading, remember that *abstinence and recovery are not the same thing.* Abstinence is part of recovery for many, but it is not recovery-defined. Solid recovery efforts can be made as use continues or subsides. One has to look at the bigger picture that this definition lays out and apply it in one's work.

Principle 1: Recovery Emerges from Hope

Essentially the idea here is that we must believe that recovery is possible, that people can heal (internally and externally). It's fitting that SAMHSA lists this as criteria number one, as hope is everything. Consider making a financial investment with no expectation or dream that it would pay out … would you still make it? I'm not sure I would. Generally, I've found that people are risk-averse and that we prefer certainty over uncertainty—even if the certainty is a painful one. That is, people do not always move toward a "better" future unless they have a sense of the road it would take to get there, and some guarantee that the road is less painful than the one they are currently on. The quote, "pain is real, but so is hope" fits within this principle for me. I value this idea very much, mostly because it's realistic. Life is full of both—addiction can make it seem like that's not true, and therein lies a challenge. It's noted that fostering hope is a collective effort; family, providers, friends, peers, etc. have a role here. I often picture the idea of hope as training wheels—others hold the individual up with their hope until the individual gains the ability to hold themselves. Believing inside oneself that a different way of life can be achieved, and not just being told by others it's possible, is essential to a recovery attempt.

Principle 2: Recovery Is Person-Driven

The idea of self-determination is central here. This principle is all about believing in the client's ability to choose and contribute to their own recovery and resilience; keeping that in mind as providers, we do not know better than clients, we *know different*. Clients will have, or develop, goals for themselves that will be more meaningful than externally imposed ones (i.e. our goals *for* them). Allowing and encouraging clients to use the information provided to them to make decisions about their lives and providing guidance when needed is important. As is apparent, this is a strengths-based principle. It's about believing in the capabilities of the people we work with, even when they are struggling. Seeing the beauty and strength in the storm, so to speak. The uniqueness of individuals is the capstone of this principle and it makes the point that since clients are not standardized, we should not expect one treatment approach to fit all. I often say that "people are not cookies." Therefore, cookie-cutter approaches will not often work because they do not account for the different ingredients in the "recipe" that make up a life. As providers, we must cater to the individual "recipe" of a client and encourage them to do the same.

Principle 3: Recovery Occurs via Many Pathways

This principle centers on the practical nature of catering to the uniqueness described above. Individuals will have unique needs, preferences, hopes and goals, cultural considerations, backgrounds, living environments, social circles, etc., that will shape their road to recovery. Trauma and other co-occurring mental health issues will also factor into the recovery process for some. The key message here is that recovery is a destination that can be reached from many roads. For some people it may include professional counseling services and more formalized treatment, for others it may include faith-based or peer-support approaches, still others may rely on family support and school-based systems. Medication-assisted treatment and solo attempts at recovery are also options exercised by some. There are as many roads to recovery as there are people traveling on them. No road to recovery will be identical to another, and for me, that's lovely. It deflates statements like *"I know the way to do it"* or *"I know what's best,"* or *"This is what I (or someone else) did, so you should do it too."* Recovery from this perspective rests on the strengths, coping skills, resources, abilities, desires, potentials, and value of each individual person.

One caveat that SAMHSA included here is that adolescents and children may not yet be developmentally (or legally) able to choose the best course, so additional guidance may be warranted. Abstinence from the problematic substance or behavior is also endorsed from SAMHSA's perspective due to the risks of continued use or behavior.

The non-linear nature of recovery is also noted within this principle. Namely, the road to recovery is sometimes a bumpy one. I picture a road riddled with potholes. Until those holes can be filled in and repaired, or an entirely new road paved, one must learn how to avoid the bumps. Even if you're a skilled avoider, from time to time you might still hit a huge pothole and rip the wheel off your car, so to speak. Point being, don't be surprised if people hit potholes sometimes; it happens. The task is then to keep moving forward as we're also simultaneously working on the road to improve the conditions; this is resilience and helping people recognize its existence is crucial.

Principle 4: Recovery Is Holistic

This principle captures the gravity of recovery. Moving from an addiction toward recovery requires movement to some degree in multiple areas of life: mind, body, socially, spiritually, how one copes with joys and stresses, housing, employment/education, schedules, time management, family interactions, mental health more broadly, medical care, transportation, social engagement and making contributions to the world locally and more globally. Moreover, in moving away from addiction, a lot changes and the recovery approach should account for that and provide appropriate supports. Treatment coordination is also stressed here; again, it's a collective effort to help someone enter and stay in recovery.

Principle 5: Recovery Is Supported by Peers and Allies

As previously stated, you cannot talk about addiction and recovery without also talking about relationships and connection. The general idea here is that by helping others, we are helped. There's gain in giving. Helping people find ways to engage, or re-engage, in the world is a part of recovery.

Thinking back to some of the people I've worked with, this idea hits my heart. All of my former clients have added to my life. On occasions when I would bring this up in a session and elaborate on the value they added to my world, some smiled, some were surprised, and others flat out rejected the idea and I was met with "you're just saying that because it's your job." Reconnecting people with their inner value is integral to the reconnection with the social world. Remembering, or realizing for the first time, that they matter to others in ways that are helpful, positive, significant, and unique to them, can play an important role in the recovery process—particularly around the feeling of self-worth and believing one deserves a different life. It goes back to the first principle, hope; hope that one can add to the good in this world and that one can receive good in return.

Finding your new place and beginning to discover your purpose are important aspects for some and peer groups and mutual support groups can be helpful here in fostering this sense of connection. The emphasis on belonging and contributing to society are evident within this principle. Later in the text, we'll talk about attachment theory and addiction, and the significance of these areas will be discussed further.

Principle 6: Recovery Is Supported through Relationships and Social Networks

Following a path similar to the previous principle, the power of presence is detailed here. This principle boils down to the idea that clients need to have people in their lives who believe in their capacity to change. Recall the analogy presented earlier about making a financial investment with little guarantee of payout … we need to stack the deck a bit and provide some risk abatement—essentially a safety net so that if one falls, they will be supported. Family members, providers, peers, community members, employers, faith leaders, and others can contribute to a sense of belonging, inclusion, and purpose. Being present during a change attempt and believing in their ability to persist, even if they fall, supports recovery efforts.

Principle 7: Recovery Is Culturally Based and Influenced

Culture and cultural presentations can vary, and yet it matters for all of us. Values, traditions, and beliefs shape how people move in the world; they will also have a hand in shaping one's recovery. Services and approaches should strive to be curious about culture and its impact on the client's life. SAMHSA notes that providers and services should be culturally congruent, competent, and attuned. This is another connecting point between the principles as cultural attunement further supports individualized care.

Principle 8: Recovery Is Supported by Addressing Trauma

Trauma will be defined later in this chapter, yet within the principles put forth by SAMHSA it centers on experiences like physical or sexual abuse, domestic violence, war, and disaster. Trauma and addiction go hand in hand for some. It's a chicken or the egg type of question. What came first? Did trauma act as a precursor to addictive patterns? Or did addictive patterns give rise to traumatic experiences? Whichever is true, it's important to recognize the impact trauma can have on the recovery process. Trauma-informed services will add to safety, appropriate care determinations, and ultimately increase the chances of effective treatment. Empowering disempowered clients is good practice, and yet it feels even more pressing when trauma is involved. Helping clients reestablish their ability to choose and to determine what comes next is significant. Encouraging autonomy and placing emphasis on counselor-client collaboration can go a long way toward hope and increased self-efficacy.

Principle 9: Recovery Involves Individual, Family, and Community Strengths and Responsibility

This principle comes back to the idea that going it alone is not as good as going together. Essentially, this is yet another reminder that people attempting recovery need the rest of us. Support from families and loved ones are often elemental to recovery and the greater community must also play a role. Creating supportive environments that allow for second, third, fourth, or more chances and allowing people to try again (after a lapse or relapse) without stigma, discrimination, or prejudgment are important aspects of recovery attempts. Finally, the individual is tasked with taking responsibility for their recovery and working to get what they need. It's a collective effort, yet the client is understood to have a lot of say here. Encouraging clients to find and use their voice, and believing it is worthy of being heard, are foundational to recovery.

Principle 10: Recovery Is Based on Respect

This principle further advocates for freedom from discrimination, stigma, and shame for people attempting recovery. Wonderfully, SAMHSA reminds us "that taking steps towards recovery may require great courage" (p. 1). Communities, providers, and others can add to a respectful dialogue by appreciating the experiences and resilience of people with addiction. Self-acceptance, reconstructing a meaningful life and identity, and recapturing one's self-esteem and efficacy are central to recovery. Such areas are more manageable if the world does not reject you. Not surprisingly, self-acceptance and other-acceptance tie together for many people.

Taken together, the ten principles create a recovery picture that emphasizes the development of internal and external supports, fostering of hope and respect, reconnection, and holistic care. Considering holism, recovery attempts should account for culture, individuality, personal preference, and trauma. Surrounding all the areas of recovery and necessary supports is the idea that people with addiction have voices that deserve to be heard. *There is hope.* Part of our job as providers is to help people find the light in the darkness and decide where to go once, they can see…. what a privilege.

Loss

My favorite definition of loss comes from Winokuer and Harris (2012). The authors simply describe it as "the real or perceived deprivation of something that is deemed meaningful" (p. 40). I like their definition in the context of this book because it is so broad. They do not reference socially acceptable losses only (like death) but leave it open for interpretation and individual perception. What's meaningful to one may not be meaningful to another. What's easy for one person to let go of and move on from may feel impossible to another. In the context of addiction, societal opinions about the meaning, or lack thereof, of a loss often enters the conversation, that is, "Just stop using. Be strong. Your life will be better in recovery." In trying to encourage, we sometimes devalue and discourage instead. Let's keep an eye on that as we progress through this text.

Primary Loss

The initial loss is referred to as the primary loss. It simply comes first. For example, if I lose my job, that is the primary loss.

Secondary Losses

Secondary losses come in the wake of the primary loss. So, if I lose my job (primary loss), I also lose my income, my identity as a counseling professor (at least temporarily), my daily routine, my health insurance, my coworkers, etc. All of these are secondary to the primary loss; put very simply, they come second. Worth noting is that sometimes the secondary losses are as or more impactful than the primary loss. Order does not equal importance. Keep that in mind for later.

Grief

Rando (1993) defined grief as psychological, behavioral, social, and physical reactions to the perception of loss. Weiss (2001) described grief as distress that is a response to the loss of an emotionally important figure. At its core, grief is a natural reaction to losing something. Take note that these depictions do not limit grief to the loss of a person; grief is applicable to much more than death.

Also understand that the brain is impacted by grief and the physical symptoms of grief are a function of stress hormones. When a significant loss occurs, the brain interprets that as a stressor, triggering the pituitary gland to release adrenocorticotrophin (ACTH) (Shulman, 2018). This release sends a signal to the adrenal gland to release cortisone (a stress hormone). With significant loss, this is not a short-lived hormonal response, rather a prolonged one. With prolonged stress comes a prolonged stress response. Grief is a persistent stressor for many. When the body is flooded with high levels of cortisone, that can compromise the immune system. This can translate to physical symptoms of grief like persistent colds, physical exhaustion/fatigue, and unspecified pain (among others) (Shulman).

Depending on the nature of the loss (traumatic or not), the brain might also be operating in a way that's often referred to as bottom-heavy (Siegel & Bryson, 2011). This means that the more primitive structures of our brain (limbic system, survival functions) are overactivated and the thinking centers (anterior cingulate cortex) are under activated. This means people may become driven by their emotions and be less capable of long-term planning, reasoning, emotional regulation, and impulse control. Grief changes the way we function for a period of time. It's not an imagined state. It's quite real and normal.

In fact, one central point across many definitions of grief is how normal it is (Centre for Clinical Interventions (CCI), 2015; Park & Halifax, 2011; Winokuer & Harris, 2012; Worden, 2009). Individuals experience a broad range of reactions and there's no exact recipe for what grief *should* look like. Some characterizations of grief are narrow in that they are only referencing adjustment to death. Others, as mentioned in the DSM 5, focus on predominant feelings of emptiness and loss (APA, 2013). Consider this description: *"Grief, of course, is a profound and often complex response for those who have been left behind by the dying"* (Park & Halifax, 2011, p. 355). The same authors go on to acknowledge that survivors…

> are often broken apart by the knowledge that they cannot bring back that which has been lost. The sense of irrevocability leaves them often helpless and sad, sometimes cognitively impaired, and sometimes socially withdrawn.
>
> (p. 355)

Worden (2009) categorized grief into four areas: feelings, physical sensations, cognitions, and behaviors. Feelings linked to grief include sadness, anger, guilt and self-reproach, anxiety, loneliness, fatigue, helplessness, shock, yearning, emancipation, relief, and numbness. Physical sensations range from tightness in the body to a sense of hollowness. Weakness in the muscles, low energy, nausea, dry mouth, feeling breathless, anxiety, and a sense of detachment or "this isn't real" are also noted (Worden).

Cognitions will of course vary in response to a loss, yet, some common experiences include disbelief, confusion, preoccupation, a sense of presence and hallucinations (i.e. seeing or hearing things that aren't really there) in the wake of a loss. Behaviorally, Worden (2009) noted several symptoms that evidence grief. First, sleep and appetite disruptions were common, along with being absentminded or forgetful. Social withdrawal, dreams centered on what's been lost, avoidance (specifically reminders of the loss), and general restlessness. Internal or external calling out (i.e. "please come back, please"), as well as sighing and crying are common. Finally, visiting places or carrying objects that remind the person of what's been lost, and treasuring objects connected to the loss are discussed. Worden refers to this combination of experiences as *uncomplicated grief*, also referred to as *normal grief*.

The CCI; 2015 largely mirrors Worden's points, but they add three additional symptoms: guilt about not initially feeling pain or sadness about a loss, worry about grieving "wrong"—feeling like one is grieving off-script from what's expected, and guilt about getting on with life and not dwelling on the past. Please remember that Worden (2009) is speaking specifically to grief that results from the death of a person; that's important, as I am not. Keeping this in mind as you read, start to consider how these concepts and symptoms are connected to addiction and recovery.

Consider here for a moment the similarities between some symptoms of normal grief and substance withdrawal. For example, symptoms of opiate (i.e. oxycontin, heroin, fentanyl) withdrawal include restlessness and/or anxiety, increased pain, sleep disruptions, nausea and other gastrointestinal upset, sweating, drowsiness, tremors, increased heart rate, confusion, muscle spasms, and/or hallucinations (Mayo Clinic, 2018). Similarly, symptoms for stimulant (i.e. Adderall, cocaine, methamphetamine, Ritalin) withdrawal include fatigue, low mood, sleep disruptions, apathy, and overall low energy (The Recovery Village, 2018). Add in potential social withdrawal, guilt, self-reproach, helplessness, confusion, yearning, disorientation, fear, and loneliness and a clear distinction between the experience of grief and substance withdrawal becomes a bit hazy.

I have two points here: (1) For clients who are withdrawing, be sure to assess for grief as well. Talk to your clients about the losses they have experienced. If a loss is recent or recently resurfaced in relation to the withdrawal attempt, be aware that they may be experiencing a combination of withdrawal and grief symptoms. (2) Discuss the potential triggers that come with grief. Since the symptomatology of grief and withdrawal can be so similar, it's advisable to educate clients about what to expect from their bodies and minds in the wake of current or future losses. Further, arm them with coping skills to reduce the likelihood of a lapse or relapse.

Please be aware that depression and grief symptomatology can also overlap. As I'll discuss in a bit, our current DSM does not define grief as a diagnosable disorder, and the bereavement exclusion that previously existed in the DSM-IV-TR (American Psychiatric Association (APA), 2000) is no more. This means that a diagnosis of depression can co-occur with a grief response. Distinguishing between depression and grief is possible. Here's what to look for: grief happens in response to an often-identifiable loss. Depression, while it may follow a loss, is not tied to it; meaning it can occur at any time. Depression is also tinged with a more general sense of worthlessness, hopelessness, and loss of happiness/zest. Grief is more specific—bereaved individuals can often tell you what they are distressed about related to their loss. Bereavement does not typically result in reduced self-esteem or self-regard, whereas depression might. Moreover, pain can manifest in a variety of ways and for a variety of reasons. Be sure to assess rather than assume.

Park and Halifax (2011) noted that the process of grieving can either strengthen us or be a cycle that can trap us and lead to perpetual suffering. From this view, grief can be understood as a natural process that can lead us toward growth, emotional adaptation, new understandings, insight around internal strengths, a push toward connection, and meaningful reconstruction. It can also hurt like hell.

One of my favorite descriptions of grief comes from the introductory pages of Worden's (2009) book:

> Grieving allows us to heal, to remember with love rather than pain. It is a sorting process. One by one you let go of things that are gone and you mourn for them. One by one you take hold of the things that have become a part of who you are and build again.
>
> (Attributed to Rachael Naomi Remen)

What resonates here is the emphasis on feeling sad for what is lost, just as much as rebuilding with what remains. As I stated earlier in the text, recovery is about both presence and absence. Grief, in many ways, can be understood in the same light.

Complicated Grief (CG)

At the most basic level, CG can be described as the inability to integrate pain. Uncomplicated grief, while it can hurt terribly and can cause a myriad of symptoms, is manageable in time and most people find a way to integrate the pain into life—a life that continues in meaningful ways after a significant loss. With complicated grief, life can stay at a standstill. Shear, Boelen, and Neimeyer (2011) describe a painful and impairing state where acute grief symptoms are prolonged, and one struggles unsuccessfully to rebuild a meaningful life after loss. Other symptoms include persistent feelings of intense preoccupation or yearning for the person that's been lost, shock, disbelief, and anger about the death. Further, Shear et al. (2011) note difficulty in both caring for and trusting in others and avoiding reminders of the loss. Shear et al. (2011) noted that in addition to avoidance, one might engage in "compulsive proximity seeking" (p. 140) as a way to manage pain; essentially, some people run from what's been lost, and some continue to search desperately for it. It's worth noting here that avoidance is a natural protective behavior and it can be very helpful in modulating the emotional onslaught a major loss can bring. However, when avoidance goes too far and we disengage from our experience (both internal and external) almost entirely, we also lose the ability to learn from what's happened and to draw meaning from our new reality. The Center for Complicated Grief (2019) echoes these points.

Rumination, or intense focus, on circumstances of the death, including one's own feelings and reactions to it, is not uncommon in complicated grief.

Getting caught in a tailspin of *"what if"* thoughts (i.e. what if I had said this…. or what if I had done something differently…) is also common (Aldao & Nolan-Hoeksema, 2010; Shear et al., 2011; The Center for Complicated Grief, 2018). CG can also impair our ability to regulate intense emotions. This could show up as someone being harshly self-critical about their emotional response to a loss or fearing one's emotions. Consider how some people believe they are feeling too much or feeling too little—the inability to regulate, and to some degree accept, intense emotions can impair the natural flow of a grief process. An analogy offered by Shear et al. (2011) sums it up nicely: *"Similar to inflammation following a physical wound, complications interfere with healing and tend to intensify and prolong pain"* (p. 140).

Interestingly, researchers are working (and have been for several years) to more fully integrate the complications of grief into our diagnostic manuals. Prigerson and colleagues (2009) proposed diagnostic criteria for Prolonged Grief Disorder (PGD) for inclusion into the DSM 5. While it was ultimately not included, a working group for the International Classification of Diseases (ICD) recommended its inclusion in the eleventh edition of the ICD (Jordan & Litz, 2014; Maercker et al., 2013). The ICD-11 was slated for release in 2018 and as of April 2018, it seems that PGD made the cut under the *Disorders Specifically Associated with Stress* category. The ICD-11 Beta draft described PGD as:

> Prolonged grief disorder is a disturbance in which, following the death of a partner, parent, child, or other person close to the bereaved, there is persistent and pervasive grief response characterized by longing for the deceased or persistent preoccupation with the deceased accompanied by intense emotional pain (e.g. sadness, guilt, anger, denial, blame, difficulty accepting the death, feeling one has lost a part of one's self, an inability to experience positive mood, emotional numbness, difficulty in engaging with social or other activities). The grief response has persisted for an atypically long period of time following the loss (more than 6 months at a minimum) and clearly exceeds expected social, cultural or religious norms for the individual's culture and context. Grief reactions that have persisted for longer periods that are within a normative period of grieving given the person's cultural and religious context are viewed as normal bereavement responses and are not assigned a diagnosis. The disturbance causes significant impairment in personal, family, social, educational, occupational or other important areas of functioning.
>
> (World Health Organization, 2018)

Though not PGD, a reminiscent experience was included as a condition for further study in the DSM 5 (APA, 2013): Persistent Complex Bereavement Disorder (PCBD). One significant distinction between the two disorders is the time frame: PGD notes a grief response persisting at least six months might qualify a person for diagnosis, PCBD extends that period to a minimum of 12 months (six months for children). An additional set of criteria for CG have been suggested by Shear, Simon, et al. (2011). CG criteria specify a minimum time frame of one month of symptoms and impairment and extend that to say that the changes in functioning should exceed what is expected in the individual's cultural context. For full listings of the proposed criteria for PGD, PCBD, and CG, see boxes 1–3.

One final note before I move on. I have noticed that while the counseling profession often notes that grief is a natural process with no specific end point or road map, we have a habit of putting time limits on grief in

---

BOX 1. PROPOSED CRITERIA FOR PGD (Prigerson et al., 2009, p. 9)

A   Bereavement (loss of significant other)

B   Separation distress—chronic and persistent yearning, pining, longing for the deceased, reflecting a need for connection with the deceased that cannot be satisfied by others. Daily, intrusive, distressing, and disruptive heartache.

C   Cognitive, emotional, and behavioral symptoms: The bereaved person must have five or more of the following symptoms experienced daily or to a disabling degree:

  1   Confusion about one's role in life or diminished sense of self (i.e., feeling that part of oneself has died).

  2   Difficulty accepting the loss

  3   Avoidance of reminders of the reality of loss

  4   Inability to trust others since the loss

  5   Bitterness or anger related to the loss

  6   Difficulty moving on with life (i.e., making new friends and pursuing new interests)

  7   Numbness (absence of emotion) since the loss

  8   Feeling that life is unfulfilling or meaningless since the loss

  9   Feeling stunned, dazed, or shocked by the loss

D   Timing: Diagnosis should not be made until at least six months have elapsed since the death.

E   Impairment: The disturbance causes clinically significant impairment in social, occupational, or other important areas of functioning (i.e., domestic responsibilities).

F   Relation to other mental disorders: The disorder is not better accounted for by Major depressive disorder (MDD), generalized anxiety disorder, or Post-traumatic Stress Disorder (PTSD)

**BOX 2. PROPOSED CRITERIA FOR PCBD
(APA, 2013, pp. 789–790)**

A   The individual experienced the death of someone with whom he or she had a close relationship.

B   Since the death, at least one of the following symptoms is experienced on more days than not and to a clinically significant degree and has persisted for at least 12 months after the death in the case of bereaved adults and six months for bereaved children:

    1   Persistent yearning/longing for the deceased. In young children, yearning may be expressed in play and behavior, including behaviors that reflect being separated from, and also reuniting with, a caregiver or other attachment figure.

    2   Intense sorrow and emotional pain in response to the death.

    3   Preoccupation with the deceased.

    4   Preoccupation with the circumstances of the death. In children, this preoccupation with the deceased may be expressed through the themes of play and behavior and may extend to preoccupation with possible death of others close to them.

C   Since the death, at least six of the following symptoms are experienced on more days than not and to a clinically significant degree, and have persisted for at least 12 months after the death in the case of bereaved adults and six months for bereaved children;

Reactive distress to the death

1   Marked difficulty accepting the death. In children, this is dependent on the child's capacity to comprehend the meaning and permanence of death.

2   Experiencing disbelief or emotional numbness over the loss.

3   Difficulty with positive reminiscing about the deceased.

4   Bitterness or anger related to the loss.

5   Maladaptive appraisals about oneself in relation to the deceased or the death (e.g., self-blame).

6   Excessive avoidance of reminders of the loss (e.g., avoidance of individuals, places, or situations associated with the deceased; in children, this may include avoidance of thoughts and feelings regarding the deceased).

Social/identity disruption

7 A desire to die in order to be with the deceased.
8 Difficulty trusting other individuals since the death.
9 Feeling alone or detached from other individuals since the death.
10 Feeling that life is meaningless or empty without the deceased, or the belief that one cannot function without the deceased.
11 Confusion about one's role in life, or a diminished sense of one's identity (e.g., feeling that a part of oneself died with the deceased).
12 Difficulty or reluctance to pursue interests since the loss or to plan for the future (e.g., friendships, activities).

D The disturbance causes clinically significant distress or impairment in social, occupational, or other important areas of functioning.
E The bereavement reaction is out of proportion to or inconsistent with cultural, religious, or age-appropriate norms.

Specify if:
  With traumatic bereavement: Bereavement due to homicide or suicide with persistent distressing preoccupations regarding the traumatic nature of the death (often in response to loss reminders), including the deceased's last moments, degree of suffering and mutilating injury, or the malicious or intentional nature of the death.

BOX 3. PROPOSED CRITERIA FOR COMPLEX GRIEF (Shear et al., 2011, p. 23)

A The person has been bereaved, that is, experienced the death of a loved one, for at least six months
B At least one of the following symptoms of persistent intense acute grief has been present for a period longer than is expected by others in the person's social or cultural environment
  1 Persistent intense yearning or longing for the person who died
  2 Frequent intense feelings of loneliness or a feeling that life is empty or meaningless without the person who died

3 Recurrent thoughts that it is unfair, meaningless, or unbearable to have to live when a loved one has died, or a recurrent urge to die in order to find or to join the deceased

4 Frequent preoccupying thoughts about the person who died, for example, thoughts or images of the person intrude on usual activities or interfere with functioning

C At least two of the following symptoms are present for at least a month:

1 Frequent troubling ruminations about circumstances or consequences of the death, for example, concerns about how or why the person died, or about not being able to manage without their loved one, thoughts of having let the deceased person down, etc.

2 Recurrent feeling of disbelief or inability to accept the death, like the person can't believe or accept that their loved one is really gone

3 Persistent feeling of being shocked, stunned, dazed, or emotionally numb since the death

4 Recurrent feelings of anger or bitterness related to the death

5 Persistent difficulty in trusting or caring about other people or feeling intensely envious of others who haven't experienced a similar loss

6 Frequently experiencing pain or other symptoms that the deceased person had, or hearing the voice, or seeing the deceased person

7 Experiencing intense emotional or physiological reactivity to memories of the person who died or to reminders of the loss

8 Change in behavior due to excessive avoidance or the opposite, excessive proximity seeking, for example, refraining from going to places, doing things, or having contact with things that are reminders of the loss, or feeling drawn to reminders of the person, such as wanting to see, touch, hear or smell things to feel close to the person who died. (Note: sometimes people experience both of these seemingly contradictory symptoms.)

D The duration of symptoms and impairment is at least one month

E The symptoms cause clinically significant distress or impairment in social, occupational, or other important areas of functioning, where impairment is not better explained as a culturally appropriate response.

our diagnostic manuals. While I understand the need to delineate who qualifies and who doesn't for any given diagnostic classification, I hope that client experiences are not undervalued because they haven't met the specified time frame. Pain is subjective and timelines are objective. Rely on your clients to inform you about their experiences and the difficulties they bring. "By the book" doesn't always pan out when people and pain are involved.

Bereavement

Bereavement is *"the state or fact of being bereaved or deprived of something or someone"* (Merriam-Webster, 2018, p. 1). While this is a standard dictionary definition, it hits the nail right on the head and captures the expansiveness of loss. Put simply, it's not just people we mourn.

Mourning

I often tell my students that bereavement is the state we are in, grief is our internal response (emotional and cognitive), and mourning is what we do (behaviors). Merriam-Webster (2018) captures that in their definitions of mourning as well: *"the act of sorrowing,"* *"an outward sign,"* and *"a period of time during which signs of grief are shown"* (p. 1).

Disenfranchised Grief

Put simply, disenfranchised grief is grief that is not acknowledged or valued by society (DiBase, 2012). Losses that are not seen as legitimate or worthy of our sadness or grief fit here.

Doka (1989, 2002) introduced the concept and expanded our understanding by detailing five categories of losses that can result in disenfranchised grief:

1 *Loss is undervalued or seen as less worthy of grief.* Examples include loss of pets, miscarriage and/or infertility, changes in identity, changes in jobs, shifts in life stage, changes in physical health and/or functioning, loss of hope or potential, loss of language or culture, loss of income or status, loss of faith or religious identity, mental illness in self or loved one, the loss of a substance or behavior pattern, loss of coping skills deemed "unhealthy" by others, etc.
2 *Stigmatized relationships.* Examples include: death or loss of an ex-partner, loss of an abusive or "unhealthy" partner or relationship (i.e. friends who use or engage in unhealthy behaviors one is trying to move on from), death of a valued person in prison, same-sex relationships ending or a partner dying, deportation of a family member or loved one, etc.

3   *When death is involved, the method of death is stigmatized.* Examples include death from overdose (intentional or not), death by suicide, homicides, drunk driving related deaths, HIV/AIDS, abortion, etc.

4   *The individual experiencing grief isn't recognized as deserving.* Consider coworkers, acquaintances, ex-partners, grieving old friends, death or loss of clients, and children, among others. Children are often short-changed; that is, some in the world do not believe kids have the developmental capacity to grieve. They certainly do, and like all of us, they will do it in their own way and in their own time.

5   *How someone grieves is seen as unacceptable.* This is essentially bucking the trend of what's expected in one's culture. Examples include not crying or emoting "enough" or at all, throwing oneself into a task (i.e. work, cleaning, organizing for a cause, etc.), stopping altogether and embracing nothingness for a while, isolating versus reaching out, reaching out versus isolating, anger, etc.

Disenfranchised grief is often in the air when the world tells someone *how* or *what* to grieve, and/or when the world judges or questions the validity of someone else's pain. As I'm writing this, our country is experiencing turmoil around immigration law and especially around the separation of families at the border. The arguments in favor of separation result in disenfranchised grief. For example, someone saying that parents are the ones doing this to their children (i.e. bringing them illegally into the country) and so the sadness and distress of the children doesn't matter. The experience, sadness and immense grief felt by the children (and parents), is dismissed, or disenfranchised, by a segment of the population. This example captures both the undervaluing of the loss and not seeing the individuals as deserving of grief. Although I'm not referencing death in this example, stigma most definitely plays a part, particularly around the criminality of entering a country without documentation. Disenfranchised grief is not often talked about in larger culture and may not be a term that many are even familiar with, but if you pay attention, you'll see it. I'm asking that you pay attention and as counselors, do more than notice. Label it, discuss it, and help diminish the sense that only *some* pain is worthy of grief.

Nonfinite Loss

This concept is particularly relevant to this text as we consider both tangible and non-tangible losses. Nonfinite loss can best be understood as loss that has enduring effects in everyday life. Winokuer and Harris (2012) differentiated nonfinite loss from death-related loss in three ways:

1   The loss and the reaction to the loss (aka grief) are ongoing and might follow a particular event or period of life like an arrest, health event or scare, deployment, childhood trauma, assault, and/or addiction.

2   The loss interferes with normal development and prevents expected growth in some aspect of life, such as not having children, feeling unsafe in public, struggling to hold steady employment, having to quit one's job, inability to attend school, etc. More specifically, physical, cognitive, social, emotional, or spiritual losses might get in the way of meeting life expectations.

3   The consideration and valuing of intangible losses such as loss of identity, loss of status, loss of certainty or safety, loss of coping, loss of hope or potential, loss of excitement for life, loss of joy, etc.

Researchers (Bruce & Shultz, 2001; Jones & Beck, 2007) identified five hallmarks of nonfinite losses:

1   Ongoing uncertainty about what will happen next.

2   Feeling disconnected from the larger world and what is considered "normal."

3   The size and impact of the loss is often unacknowledged by others—it's overlooked or ignored.

4   An enduring sense of powerlessness and hopelessness connected to the loss.

5   Chronic despair and dread as people try to reckon with what I call the pre and post bubbles. That is, what the world was before the loss(es) occurred, and what the world now is after the loss (after our bubble of what we thought the world was has been burst). Basically, what we thought the world was…. we now question that: that is, *"I thought I was safe, and I now realize that no one is truly safe. What do I do with that?"*

In sum, nonfinite loss is about adaptation and accommodation to a loss that doesn't end. Consider an expanded example:

> Peter worked at the same company as a civil engineer for 24 years. He was well-regarded by his peers and had been the lead on multiple projects. He enjoyed this lead role on projects and valued the knowledge he was able to pass down to newer employees. He had hoped to one day become a member of the management team. His relationships with co-workers were enjoyable and he felt contentment when at work, both professionally and socially. He felt important, wanted, and capable. His salary provided a comfortable, financially secure life for his family.
>
> During the recession in 2008, Peter's company laid off 10% of its workforce and unfortunately, he was one of the 10%. Despite being provided a severance and early retirement package, he was devastated. He noted that when he told his partner and children about his job loss, he was supported and *"well-loved"*, but he *"felt like a failure. For*

so many years I had been valued and a needed member of the team, and now I was out the door, just like that." Peter knew himself, for 24 years, as a respected, valued member of a skilled team. The team was now gone, along with the projects, and over time he began to feel *"less useful, less needed."* He also saw himself as a provider for his family and as a role model for his children. His self-perception changed following the lay off and he stated on more than one occasion that he felt ashamed that his daughters knew he was laid off. Additionally, the leadership roles he valued were gone, and with that, the opportunity to mentor new engineers. He stated that he "missed feeling important".

He no longer had the build-in socialization that the work environment provided. He noted that *"it turns out that work friends were just work friends. I didn't hear from most of them after I left."* He lost his routine. During his career, he had a set waking time, working time, and a set end to the workday. While working, he had a definition to his life that he now lacked. He did not find the flexibility comfortable and preferred the structure he once had. His dreams of promotion within the company were now dashed, and he grappled with the idea that after his 24 years of work, he was selected for termination. He questioned the value of his efforts and his professional worth. Peter described feelings of aimlessness and confusion. He did not believe that he any companies would hire an "old engineer that was canned" and so he did not look for work even though he wanted it. Essentially, he went from a purpose-filled daily life, to one that was predominantly sitting in front of the TV.

Peter perceived his status as a former engineer to be less than. He described a vague, persistent sadness that centered on the question of *"Who am I now?"* and the frustration at his inability to clearly answer that for himself. He balked at the "encouragement" from others that *"life is good now—you can do whatever you want!"* Ultimately, the finite loss of a job triggered a series of nonfinite losses that disrupted Peter's life and hopes for his future, coupled with uncertainty about his own identity and path forward.

Ambiguous Loss

Ambiguous loss is just that, ambiguous; we can't quite put a finger on these losses. They are hard to pinpoint, name, or describe because it might be unclear exactly what's missing or been lost (Boss, 1999; Boss, Roos, & Harris, 2011; Winokuer & Harris, 2012). Think of losses that don't necessarily fall on a timeline. For instance, a death or job loss might occur at a certain time or date. Losing the identity of a wife or worker, however, might take longer to set in. The impact of such a loss isn't seen outwardly by others. This intangible nature can make it harder for others (and oneself) to not only acknowledge a loss has occurred, but to value it.

Within this type of loss are two specific types: *physically absent* and *psychologically absent* (Ali, 2010; Boss et al., 2011). *Physically absent* refers to when a person is physically absent but psychologically present. Basically, this means that someone is missing and there's no way to know if they are alive or dead. As a result, then, valued people in this person's life are left in an emotional limbo, uncertain of what to feel and unsure of when (and if) the emotional turmoil will resolve. Some examples include military members who are missing in action, instances of kidnapping, runaway cases, individuals who are lost at sea, and unexplained disappearances.

One example that made national news was of a Center for Disease Control employee, Timothy Cunningham, who vanished for two months after leaving work early due to reportedly feeling ill (Stack, 2018). Consider the family's experience for the months of absence when no trace of their loved one could be found. The uncertainty and confusion of whether one should grieve or hold out hope for reunion would be ever-present. The word that comes to my mind when thinking about this experience is *aching*. It would ache to not know and simultaneously want to know (and hope for good news) and perhaps not want to know (for fear of bad news). Ultimately, Mr. Cunningham's body was found in a river, yet the circumstances of his death remain a mystery (Stack, 2018).

Psychologically absent refers to when a person is physically present but psychologically absent. Essentially, the body of a person is with you, but the personality you once knew is no longer there. A client whose husband had sustained a serious traumatic brain injury in a car accident described this as *"the shell of my husband is here, but the Adam I knew is gone. I have his body, but I feel like I lost his soul."* In addition to traumatic brain injuries, this type of ambiguous loss can occur with dementia or Alzheimer's, addiction, autism, infertility, depression, PTSD, and other chronic mental health issues (Boss et al., 2011).

Consider the experience of sending a loved one overseas on a military deployment. Upon their return home, the once easy-to-talk-to person is now snippy and short in their answers. They prefer isolation over socialization and engage in less physical affection than before. Communication becomes more surface-level and less intimate. A feeling of disconnection and confusion enters the relationship. Some people in the world will celebrate the return home of the individual and presume that it's a happy, smooth transition back to "normal" life (aka life before deployment). As a result, the losses can be missed or overlooked. A family may regain their member, but life is different now—a difference that was not anticipated or necessarily welcome.

Unconventional Grief

This type of grief is very similar to psychological absence in ambiguous loss. The term unconventional grief is used to describe the grief caused by "a loved one becoming someone that you no longer know or recognize" (American Academy of Bereavement, 2015, p. 1). Think about grieving over someone who's still living. As with ambiguous loss, this might include people with dementia, addiction, chronic illness, or depression.

Essentially, the individual changes from who you always knew them to be into some other version. With addiction, for example, behavior may move from caring, considerate, and responsible to self-serving, erratic, and even illegal. For an individual with depression, behavior and mood may shift from upbeat, positive, and engaged to isolated, hopeless, and absent. People may grieve the life that is no longer being lived, or the life that can't be regained. Consider someone with dementia who will not regain memories, or a person with an addiction that now has a criminal record. Certain possibilities for their life are now off the table and both the individual and their loved ones can grieve those losses.

Anticipatory Grief

As the name implies, this type of grief *occurs* before the loss. This form of grief can show up when there is a "significant, impending loss or death" (Overton & Cottone, 2016, p. 430). Symptoms of anticipatory grief are like those of normal grief: strong emotional reactions, isolation, poor concentration, absentmindedness, appetite and/or sleep disruptions, etc. People might also feel tired (emotionally and physically) if acting as a caregiver or protector (American Academy of Bereavement, 2018).

In anticipating a loss, a person might be afraid that each phone call could bring bad news. If a person's abilities and health are expected to deteriorate as an illness progresses (i.e. addiction, cancer, or other illness) one may experience hopelessness and grieve the loss of stability, one's independence, and/or future (American Academy of Bereavement). Essentially, this is grieving the losses as they appear on the horizon, not just after they've occurred.

Some researchers argue that anticipatory grief can help people prepare for their upcoming loss and buffer the impact when it finally arrives (Costello & Hargreaves, 2008; Reynolds & Botha, 2006; Rogalla, 2018; Zilberfein, 1999). This buffering effect is attributed to *proactive coping* (Rogalla, 2018; Schwarzer & Luszczynska, 2008). Essentially, this means that stress, in moderation, is seen as an adaptive response that produces energy in a person. If one can learn to grab hold of that energy and use it, they are more equipped to handle stress when it first arises, rather than waiting until it overwhelms them. A recent study by Rogalla (2018) found that in advance of an anticipated death, people who proactively coped by reframing the upcoming loss as a challenge versus a threat and developed and accepted social supports experienced more growth than those who didn't. It remains, however, that research around whether or not this type of grief is adaptive for everyone—that is helpful to our health and eventual adjustment—is mixed and continued study is needed (Reynolds & Botha, 2006; Rogalla, 2018).

Trauma

Defining this term is slightly tricky due to the arguably subjective nature of trauma. Basically, it's hard to box up—what's traumatic to one, may not be traumatic to another (SAMHSA, 2014a, 2018a) and so nailing down an all-encompassing definition is hard. An additional complication is that the larger, non-clinical world sometimes thinks of PTSD and trauma as the same thing, seeing no distinction. PTSD is a significant, powerful experience that has trauma at its roots, but it is not the only way to understand trauma. In class I say that *PTSD is one fish in the trauma sea.*

According to Merriam-Webster, trauma is

> *an injury (such as a wound) to living tissue cause by an extrinsic* (aka outside) *agent, a disordered psychic or behavioral state resulting from severe mental or emotional stress or physical injury, or an emotional upset (i.e. the personal trauma of not living up to one's own expectations).*
>
> (2018, p. 1)

A more concise definition is *"an experience that produces psychological injury or pain"* (Dictionary.com, 2018, p. 1). SAMHSA (2018a) defines trauma as resulting

> *from an event, series of events, or set of circumstances that is experienced by an individual as physically or emotionally harmful or life threatening and that has lasting adverse effects on the individual's functioning and mental, physical, social, emotional, or spiritual well-being.*
>
> (p. 1)

The DSM-5 defines trauma within the diagnostic criteria for PTSD (specifically criterion A; APA, 2013, p. 271):

A   *Exposure to actual or threatened death, serious injury, or sexual violence in one (or more) of the following ways:*
  1   Directly experiencing the traumatic event(s).
  2   *Witnessing, in person, the event(s) as it occurred to others.*
  3   *Learning that the traumatic event(s) occurred to a close family member or close friend. In cases of actual or threatened death of a family member or friend, the event(s) must have been violent or accidental.*
  4   Experiencing repeated or extreme exposure to aversive details of the traumatic event(s) (e.g., first responders collecting human remains; police officers repeatedly exposed to details of child abuse).

Note: Criterion A4 does not apply to exposure through electronic media, television, movies, or pictures, unless the exposure is work-related.

The diagnostic features section for PTSD (APA, 2013, p. 274) elaborates as to what types of events qualify under criterion A:

A1: Direct experiences may include, but are not limited to exposure to war as a combatant or civilian, threatened or actual physical assault (e.g., physical attack, robbery, mugging, childhood physical abuse), threatened or actual sexual violence (e.g., forced sexual penetration, alcohol/drug facilitated sexual penetration, abusive sexual contact, noncontact sexual abuse, sexual trafficking), being kidnapped, being taken hostage, terrorist attack, torture, incarceration as a prisoner of war, natural or human-made disasters, and severe motor vehicle accidents. Medical events that are sudden and catastrophic qualify, but not necessarily life-threatening, debilitating conditions.

A2: Witnessed events may include but are not limited to observing threatened or serious injury, unnatural death, physical or sexual abuse of another person due to violent assault, domestic violence, accident, war or disaster, or a medical catastrophe in one's child.

A3: Indirect exposure through learning about an event is limited to experiences affecting close relatives or friends and experiences that are violent or accidental. Examples include violent personal assault, suicide, serious accident, and serious injury. Death due to natural causes does not qualify.

As I mentioned earlier, some people mistakenly do not distinguish between trauma and PTSD and use the terms interchangeably. The primary risk of lumping PTSD and trauma into a false equivalency is that people and experiences get left out. Notably absent from the PTSD criteria are events that may not threaten death but are still highly distressing. For instance, major losses or separations like divorce or loss of custody, humiliation, sexual coercion, non-combat military trauma, bullying, forced displacement, prolonged emotional abuse, and life-threatening illnesses and/or debilitating medical conditions that change one's functioning or life expectancy (Briere & Scott, 2013, SAMHSA, 2018b). Such experiences may not qualify someone for a diagnosis of PTSD, but they may still be swimming in that trauma sea.

Briere and Scott (2015) echoed the limitations of the diagnostic criteria noting that people will consider experiences traumatic beyond actual or threatened death, serious injury, or sexual violence. In short, *perception matters*. Talk to your clients. Listen to their stories. Learn about the impact the stressor has had on their lives and how they are (or are not) coping. Learn how they self-identify or define their experience.

Trauma has been associated with substance use, mental health disorders, and other significant behaviors (i.e. non-suicidal self-injury) and it is a relatively common experience; particularly so for people with mental health and SUD (SAMHSA, 2018a). Traumatic events and the associated loss, grief, and mourning also impact identity development (Bernsten & Rubin, 2007). A person who has encountered traumatic experience can start to view the world through the traumatic lens; it may influence their understanding and expectations of self, others, and the world. For some clients, trauma, grief, and substance use (and therefore recovery) will fit together.

Culture

Culture is a system of beliefs, values, and assumptions that drive behavior and are shared by a group of people (Peace Corps, 2018). The customs and language shared by a group are included as are the artifacts (aka things) they value. We cannot underestimate the importance of culture in life more broadly, but also in terms of addiction and recovery. Everyone has a culture, yet not everyone is aware of how it has shaped, who they are, and what they do. The impact of culture will be considered in more depth in future chapters. In addition to racial, ethnic, and regional/geographic cultural influence, we will also consider *drug culture*.

Drug Culture

Drug cultures also organize around shared beliefs, attitudes, customs, and languages and are shared by a subgroup of people. Though research is rather limited in this area, SAMHSA adds that drug cultures often have rituals and behaviors that evolve over time, as well as socialization patterns that may not be shared by the larger community (2014b). Social hierarchy may also play a role in some groups, with more seasoned members guiding and teaching newer members (Jenkot, 2008; SAMHSA, 2014b). Drug cultures related to alcohol use are sometimes widely known. Consider a fraternity that is known for heavy drinking and uses that image for recruitment. I pledged a sorority in my undergrad and there was an expectation around alcohol use; more than that there were rituals that supported the expectation. For example, pledges were tasked with preparing the "punch" for parties (it was almost entirely vodka). If a pledge expressed hesitancy to prepare or consume, there were social consequences to be paid. Of course, this is not true of all Greek life, but it is true for some.

Encouraging use, support for binge drinking in some cases, and rituals that are said to foster community could certainly be considered a drug (or drinking) culture (Gordon, Heim, & MacAskill, 2012). In short, drug cultures grow out of drug and alcohol use (SAMHSA, 2014b) and they can be powerfully influential to participants. Worth noting is that some people may use or engage in behaviors in relative isolation and as such, may not participate in a drug culture (SAMHSA, 2014b; White, 1996). A term that describes such individuals is *acultural addict* (White, 1996).

Acultural "Addict"

First, let me say that I'm not a fan of the term "addict"; White (1996) originated this term. I prefer person-first language that emphasizes the humanity of people dealing with SUDs. In line with this preference, I will omit the "addict" label and simply say "acultural" when discussing this classification. So, an acultural individual uses or engages in behaviors in near isolation from others (White, 1996). One example offered by SAMHSA (2014b) includes a medical professional with access to medications and therefore less reliance (if any) on purchasing from a dealer. In this case, there is less need to interact with other people engaged in a drug culture. There may also be layers of more traditional cultural expectations that overlay this instance. For example, an individual with a high-status job and increased socioeconomic status may be more hesitant to engage with street-level dealers for fear of losing face and status. A second example is someone who moves from doctor to doctor seeking prescription medications (SAMHSA, 2014b) or an individual who steals medications from family or friends. A person who uses or engages in behaviors alone and works to hide it may also be considered acultural.

Cultural Identity

Cultural identity is the "identity or feeling of belonging to a group" (Moha, 2005, p. 19). It's a part of our self-concept and it's rooted in how we perceive ourselves and how others perceive us (Groen, Richters, Lagan, & Deville, 2017; Ibrahim & Heuer, 2016). Importantly, our cultural identity centers on our own definition of who we are and what that looks like (Groen et al., 2017). It also centers on the racial, ethnic, and/or cultural reference group characteristics that influence our relationships, resources, conflicts, and our reactions to them (think coping skills) (APA, 2013). Not surprisingly, the culture(s) we live in shapes our cultural identity. This concept and our clinical responsibilities related to the cultural identity of our clients are detailed in the Cultural Formulation chapter in the DSM-5. Five areas are outlined: cultural identity of the individual, cultural conceptualization of distress, psychosocial stressors and cultural features of vulnerability and resilience, cultural features of the relationship between the individual and the clinician, and overall cultural assessment.

Cultural identity of the individual: Asks clinicians to describe the person's racial, ethnic, and cultural groups that might influence their relationships with others, their access to care, developmental and current challenges, as well as current predicaments. For immigrants and racial or ethnic minorities specifically, it's recommended that the degree and kinds of involvement with both the culture of origin and the majority culture be detailed. Language preference and abilities and how one uses language may help in identifying barriers like access to care, interpretation needs, and one's ability to socially integrate. Other areas to explore under this heading include religious or spiritual affiliation, socioeconomic status (current and past), place of birth and where someone grew up, migrant status, and sexual orientation and identity (APA, 2013, pp. 749–750).

It begrudges me that this section of the diagnostic manual is tucked in the back; people miss it, and yet it's integral to proper diagnosis and care. The cultural formulation chapter intends to provide a framework for clinicians as they consider a person's life and problems. It guides us in determining the role of culture in a client's life and problem set. In addition to cultural identity, four additional categories are included.

Cultural conceptualization of distress: Examines the cultural constructs that impact how the person views and understands their problems. It also considers how culture influences communication of concerns; do they keep them to themselves or do they communicate them to others (and if so, how they do that)? Additionally, this encourages examination of origin; that is, where do they think their problems come from—what's their source or cause? The severity of symptoms and the meaning attributed to their symptoms should be considered against their respective cultural norms. My favorite part of this subsection is the encouraged emphasis on professional help and treatment, but also on traditional, culturally specific, alternative, and/or complementary care. Essentially, this is saying that there are many options for helping and our clinical opinion and treatment strategies may not be the most efficacious one all the time (APA, 2013, p. 750).

Psychosocial stressors and cultural features of vulnerability and resilience: Instructs clinicians to assess for both sources of stress and support with particular emphasis on one's social environment (current and past events both included). Additionally, how family, religion or spirituality, and broader social networks provide emotional and informational support during these times. What's considered stressful and what's considered supportive are likely to vary based on cultural group, developmental stage, family structure, and context. Because of this variation, it's important to find out what's true for each client. Levels of functioning, ability or disability, and resilience should also be assessed against the cultural reference groups standards—essentially, what's considered normal and expected within their cultural group(s)? (APA, 2013, p. 750).

Cultural features of the relationship between the individual and the clinician: Examine the differences between the counselor and client in the following areas: culture, language, and social status. Specifically, explore areas that may impair communication, diagnosis, or treatment. For example, experience with discrimination, sexism, or racism may interfere with forming a trusting, safe relationship. In short, rapport may suffer if differences go unnoticed or are ignored. Additional complications that might arise include difficulty in understanding the extent of, or meaning attributed to a client's symptoms, and missing the cultural significance they may hold (APA, 2013, p. 750).

Overall cultural assessment: This brings the information from the previous sections together and uses it to inform diagnosis and treatment planning (APA, 2013, p. 750).

Following the outline for cultural formulation detailed above, there is also a Cultural Formulation Interview offered in the DSM-5 (CFI; APA, 2013, pp. 750–757). The CFI is a set of 16 questions for clinicians to use during assessment about the impact of culture on clinical presentation. I strongly suggest that readers become familiar with the CFI and integrate it into practice. Back in 1999, Bhugra et al. noted the importance of cultural identity and argued that mental health practitioners underestimate the connection between cultural identity and mental health. To not perpetuate the mistakes of the past, I'll work to highlight the potential connections between culture, grief, addictive behaviors, and recovery.

References

Aldao, A., & Nolen-Hoeksema, S. (2010). Specificity of cognitive emotion regulation strategies: A transdiagnostic examination. *Behavior Research and Therapy, 48*(10), 974–983.

Ali, J. I. (2010). *Mourning me: An interpretive description of grief and identity loss in older adults with mild cognitive impairment (MCI)* (Unpublished doctoral dissertation). University of Victoria, Victoria, BC, Canada.

American Academy of Bereavement. (2015). *Unconventional grief: Grieving someone alive*. Retrieved on October 8, 2018 from http://thebereavementacademy.com/unconventional- grief-grieving-someone-alive/

American Academy of Bereavement. (2018). *Grieving before a death: Understanding anticipatory grief*. Retrieved on October 8, 2018 from https://whatsyourgrief.com/anticipatory-grief/

American Psychiatric Association. (2000). *Diagnostic and statistical manual of mental disorders* (4th ed., Text Revision). Washington, DC: Author.

American Psychiatric Association. (2013). *Diagnostic and statistical manual of mental disorders* (5th ed.). Washington, DC: Author.

American Society of Addiction Medicine (ASAM). (2011). *Definition of addiction*. Retrieved on March 8, 2018 from https://asam.org/resources/definition-of-addiction

Bereavement. (2018). In *Merriam-Webster.com*. Retrieved on May 11, 2018 from https://www.merriam-webster.com/dictionary/bereavement

Bernsten, D., & Rubin, D. C. (2007). When trauma becomes a key to identity: Enhanced integration of trauma memories predicts posttraumatic stress disorder symptoms. *Applied Cognitive Psychology, 21*, 417–431.

Boss. (1999). *Ambiguous loss*. Cambridge, MA: Harvard University Press.

Boss, P., Roos, S., & Harris, D. L. (2011). Grief in the midst of ambiguity and uncertainty: An exploration of ambiguous loss and chronic sorrow. In R. A.

Neimeyer, D. L. Harris, & H. R. Winokuer (Eds.), *Grief and bereavement in contemporary society: Bridging research and practice* (pp. 163–176). Routledge: New York.

Briere, J. N., & Scott, C. (2006). *Principles of trauma therapy: A guide to symptoms, evaluation, and treatment* (1st ed.). Thousand Oaks, CA: Sage Publications.

Briere, J. N., & Scott, C. (2013). *Principles of trauma therapy: A guide to symptoms, evaluation, and treatment* (2nd ed.). Thousand Oaks, CA: Sage Publications.

Briere, J. N., & Scott, C. (2015). *Principles of trauma therapy: A guide to symptoms, evaluation, and treatment* (2nd ed.). Thousand Oaks, CA: Sage Publications.

Bhugra, D., Kamaldeep, B., Rosemarie, M., Manisha, D., Jayshree, S., & Julian, L. (1999). Cultural identity and its measurement: A questionnaire for Asians. *International Review of Psychiatry, 11*, 2–3.

Bruce, E. J., & Schultz, C. L. (2001). *Nonfinite loss and grief: A psychoeducational approach.* Baltimore, MD: Paul H. Brookes.

Costello, J., & Hargreaves, S. (2008). Anticipatory grief: Some implications for social work practice in working with families facing impending loss. *Practice: Social Work in Action, 10*, 45–54.

DiBase, R. J. (2012). *Disenfranchised grief: Oncology nurses facing the challenge.* Retrieved on May 11, 2018 from http://www.cancer.org/acs/groups/content/@ greatlakes/documents /image/acspc-036055.pdf

Doka, K. (1989). *Disenfranchised grief: Recognizing hidden sorrow.* Lexington, MA: Lexington Books.

Doka, K. (2002). *Disenfranchised grief: New challenges, directions, and strategies for practice.* Champaign, IL: Research Press.

Gordon, R., Heim, D., & MacAskill, S. (2012). Rethinking drinking cultures: A review of drinking cultures and a reconstructed dimensional approach. *Public Health, 126*(1), 3–11.

Groen, S. P. N., Richters, A., Laban, C. J., & Deville, L. J. M. (2017). Cultural identity among Afghan and Iraqi traumatized refugees: Towards a conceptual framework for mental health care professionals. *Culture, Medicine, and Psychiatry, 42*(1), 69–91.

Ibrahim, F. A., & Heuer, J. R. (2016). Cultural and social justice counseling. *International and Cultural Psychology.* doi: 10.1007/978-3-319–18057-1_2

Jenkot, R. (2008). Cooks are like gods: Hierarchies in methamphetamine-producing groups. *Deviant Behavior, 29*, 667–689.

Jones, S. J., & Beck, E. (2007). Disenfranchised grief and nonfinite loss as experienced by the families of death row inmates. *Omega, 54*(4), 281–299.

Jordan, A. H., & Litz, B. T. (2014). Prolonged grief disorder: Diagnostic, assessment, and treatment considerations. *Professional Psychology: Research and Practice, 45*(3), 180–187.

Mate, G. (2010). *In the realm of hungry ghosts: Close encounters with addiction.* Berkeley, CA: North Atlantic Books.

Miller, W. R., Forcehimes, A. A., & Zweben, A. (2011). *Treating Addiction: A guide for professionals.* New York, NY: The Guilford Press.

Moha, E. (2005). *Multilingualism, cultural identity, and education in Morocco.* Springer Science & Business Media. doi: 10.1007/B104063

Mourning. (2018). In *Merriam-Webster.com.* Retrieved on May 11, 2018 from https://www.merriam-webster.com/dictionary/mourning

National Institute on Drug Abuse (NIDA). (2016). *The science of drug abuse and addiction: The basics* (Media Guide). Retrieved on March 12, 2018 from https://www. drugabuse.gov/ publications/media-guide/science-drug-abuse-addiction-basics

Overton, B. L., & Cottone, R. (2016). Anticipatory grief: A family systems approach. *The Family Journal: Counseling and Therapy for Couples and Families, 24*(4), 430–432.

Park, C. L., & Halifax, R. J. (2011). Religion and spirituality in adjusting to bereavement: Grief as burden, grief as gift. In R. A. Neimeyer, D. L. Harris, & H. R. Winokuer (Eds.), *Grief and bereavement in contemporary society: Bridging research and practice* (pp. 355–364). Routledge: New York.

Peace Corps. (2018). *Defining culture.* Retrieved on June 25, 2018 from https:// www.peacecorps.gov/educators/resources/defining-culture/

Prigerson, H. G., Horowitz, M. J., & Jacobs, S. C. Parkes, C. M., Aslan, M., Goodkin, K., … Maciejewski, P. K. (2009). Prolonged grief disorder: Psychometric validation of criteria proposed for *DSM-V* and *ICD-11. PloS Medicine, 6*(8), e1000121.

Rando, T. (1993). *Treatment of complicated mourning.* Champaign, IL: Research Press.

Reynolds, L., & Botha, D. (2006). Anticipatory grief: Its nature, impact, and reasons for contradictory findings. *Counseling, Psychotherapy, and Health, 2*(2), 15–26.

Sanders, M. (2011). *Slipping through the cracks: Intervention strategies for clients with multiple addictions and disorders.* Deerfield Beach, FL: Health Communications, Inc.

Schwarzer, R., & Luszczynska, A. (2008). Reactive, anticipatory, preventive, and proactive coping: A theoretical distinction. *Prevention Researcher, 15*(4): 22–24.

Shear, M. K., Boelen, P. A., & Neimeyer, R. A. (2011). Treating complicated grief: Converging approaches. In R. A. Neimeyer, D. L. Harris, & H. R. Winokuer (Eds.), *Grief and bereavement in contemporary society: Bridging research and practice* (pp. 139–162). New York: Routledge.

Shear, K. M., Simon, N., Wall, M., Zisook, S., Neimeyer, R., Duan, N., Reynolds, C., Lebowitz, B., Sung, S., Ghesquiere, A., Gorscak, B., Clayton, P., Ito, M., Nakajima, S., Konishi, T., Melhem, N., Meert, K., Schiff, M., O'Connor, M-F., First, M., Sareen, J., Bolton, J., Skritskaya, N., Mancini, A. D., & Keshaviah, A. (2011). Complicated grief and related bereavement issues for DSM-5. *Depress Anxiety, 28*(2): 103–117.

Shulman, L. M. (2018). *Before and after loss: A neurologist's perspective on loss, grief, and our brain.* Baltimore, MD: Johns Hopkins University Press.

Siegel, D. J., & Bryson, T. P. (2011). *The whole-brain child: 12 revolutionary strategies to nurture your child's developing mind.* New York: Random House.

Smith, D., & Wesson, D. (1988). *Treating cocaine dependence.* Center City, MN: Hazelden Foundation.

Stack, L. (2018, April 5). Body of missing C.D.C. employee found in Atlanta river. *The New York Times.* Retrieved on July 18 from https://www.nytimes. com/2018/04/05/us/cdc- employee-missing.html

Substance Abuse and Mental Health Services Administration (SAMHSA). (2012). *SAMHSA's working definition of recovery updated.* Retrieved on March 12, 2018 from https://blog.samhsa.gov/2012/03/23/defintion-of-recovery-updated/#. WqaR1eSWyUk

Substance Abuse and Mental Health Services Administration. (2014a). *Trauma-informed care in behavioral health services* (Treatment Improvement Protocol [TIP] Series 57; HHS Publication No. SMA 13–4801). Rockville, MD: Author. Retrieved on June 22, 2018 from http://store.samhsa.gov/shin/content/SMA14-4816/SMA14-4816.pdf

Substance Abuse and Mental Health Services Administration. (2014b). Improving cultural competence. (Treatment Improvement Protocol (TIP) Series, No. 59. Center for Substance Abuse Treatment). Rockville, MD: Author. Retrieved on June 25, 2018 from https://www.ncbi.nlm.nih.gov/books/NBK248421/

Substance Abuse and Mental Health Services Administration. (2018a). *Trauma and violence.* Retrieved on June 22, 2018 from https://www.samhsa.gov/trauma-violence

Substance Abuse and Mental Health Services Administration. (2018b). *Types of trauma and violence.* Retrieved on June 22, 2018 from https://www.samhsa.gov/trauma-violence/types

The Center for Complicated Grief. (2018). *Complicated Grief Overview for Professionals.* Retrieved from https://complicatedgrief.columbia.edu/professionals/complicated-grief- professionals/overview/

The Mayo Clinic. (2018). *How opioid addiction occurs.* Retrieved on February 18, 2018 from https://www.mayoclinic.org/diseases-conditions/prescription-drug-abuse/in-depth/how- opioid-addiction-occurs/art-20360372

The Recovery Village. (2018). Stimulant withdrawal and detox. Retrieved from https://www.therecoveryvillage.com/stimulant-addiction/withdrawal-detox/#gref

Trauma. (2018a). *Dictionary.com.* Retrieved on June 22, 2018 from http://www.dictionary.com/browse/trauma?s=t

Trauma. (2018b). *Merriam-Webster.com.* Retrieved on June 22, 2018 from https://www.merriam-webster.com/dictionary/trauma

Weiss, R. S. (2001). Grief, bonds, and relationships. In M. S. Stroebe, R. O. Hansson, W. Stroebe, & H. Schut (Eds.), *Handbook of bereavement research: Consequences, coping, and care* (pp. 145–167). Washington, DC: American Psychological Association.

White, W. L. (1996). *Pathways: From the culture of addiction to the culture of recovery. A travel guide for addiction professionals, 2nd ed.* Center City, MN: Hazelden.

Winokuer, H. R. & Harris, D. L. (2012). *Principles and practices of grief counseling.* New York, NY: Springer Publishing Company.

Worden, J. W. (2009). *Grief counseling and grief therapy: A handbook for the mental health practitioner* (4th ed.). New York: Springer.

Worden, J. W., & Winokuer, H. R. (2011). A task-based approach for counseling the bereaved. In R. A. Neimeyer, D. L. Harris, & H. R. Winokuer (Eds.), *Grief and bereavement in contemporary society: Bridging research and practice* (pp. 57–68). New York: Routledge.

World Health Organization. (2018). *The ICD-11 beta draft: Prolonged grief disorder.* Geneva: World Health Organization. Retrieved on April 19, 2018 from https://icd.who.int/dev 11/l-m/en#/http%3a%2f%2fid.who.int%2ficd%2fentity%2f1183832314

Zielberfein, F. (1999). Coping with death: Anticipatory grief and bereavement. *Generations, 23*(1), 69–75.

3 The When and What of Loss

When a loss happens is often as important as what the loss is; we need to consider the context in which the loss occurs to fully realize its impact. Consider a client example: Alicia* was actively using (heroin and oxycontin); unbeknownst to her, she had become pregnant. She found out she was pregnant when she had abnormal bleeding, went to the doctor, and discovered she was in the process of miscarrying (*name and details have been altered to maintain client privacy). During our sessions, she identified three losses: loss of freedom, loss of pregnancy (with the added layer of miscarriage), and loss of motherhood/loss "of a way out."

Here's what she meant (and loosely said)…

1   Loss of freedom: *"I can't really say that it [use] only hurts me anymore; I don't have that freedom to not care in the same way as before. I'm not sure what to do with that."*
2   Loss of pregnancy through miscarriage: *"I was pregnant and now I'm not. The doctor said that I might have miscarried because of my use and it might also be unrelated. So basically, I might have helped my baby die without knowing it."*
3   Loss of motherhood and loss of "a way out":

> *I want to be a mom. I didn't plan to get pregnant now, but I can't stop thinking about how I lost a chance at it and it feels like I killed a better future. I'm not even sure if that makes sense. I just always thought that when I had kids, I'd get out of this life and into a better one. Like they'd be worth the effort to stop and live better. Like I'd be worth the effort…. I don't know. I never even got the chance to be called 'mom'.*

She connected her use to the loss, believing the drugs contributed to the miscarriage. This connection extended to the circumstances surrounding the miscarriage as well as she began acknowledging her use impacted others, and she drew on a larger meaning for her future recovery attempts. Primarily, that she could do it one day and saw motherhood as a meaningful reason to enter recovery. Following the miscarriage, we had insightful, emotion-filled conversations in session around these points and meaning specifically. She also overdosed (and thankfully survived). Her insight and awareness brought pain, guilt, and shame to the surface. Her other coping skills were (at that point) unmatched to the level of pain she was experiencing. Please note that I said *other* coping skills—*her use was an attempt at coping* (numbing and disconnecting in particular) and I don't want that to be missed or undervalued.

It's worth noting a couple terms that applied to Alicia's case: *meaning-making* and *meaning finding* (Attig, 2000, 2001). *Meaning-making* is a conscious and active process of reinterpreting. The idea here is to find new meaning in experiences, pain, loss, and related behaviors. There's active effort to create new meaning through reframing, reflection, and action. *Meaning finding* is more focused on awareness and acceptance of spontaneous meaning that can come out of grief and pain.

For Alicia, she and I searched for the meaning in her overdose and miscarriage. One meaning we found (i.e. meaning finding) was that her behavior mattered in the world; she did not live in a bubble. What she did mattered to and for others. As obvious as that might sound, it was a revelation of sorts to her; she had become so insular during use that she no longer made that connection. One meaning we made (i.e. meaning-making) is that this loss could help her toward recovery. Out of loss could come growth. Out of pain, hope. The idea of finding or creating meaning will apply to many others who experience loss. In fact, the search for meaning after loss appears to be universal and an important component of grief (Winokuer & Harris, 2012).

I do still wonder what it would have been like had she been in (or closer to) recovery, had a social network that was healthy and present, had the ability to forgive herself, and believed she was deserving of a different life (baby or not). Now honestly, she may have still overdosed. The pain may have still overwhelmed her ability to cope in a way that did not involve drugs … but maybe not. It's prudent that we consider the interaction between where a client is (i.e. pre-addiction, active addiction, in treatment, recovery, etc.) and how that might impact the way a loss is processed, as well as their ability to cope.

When thinking about loss related to an addiction, consider losses that occurred prior to the addiction. Addictive behaviors and substances may be used as an escape or cover for past events or unaddressed, unresolved pain. All clients have lives before addiction. It can be useful to explore the connections between prior events or periods of life to their current use and/or behavioral patterns. Essentially, explore the perceived origin story of one's addiction. Some clients draw a clear line of sight. For instance, one client was raped at 17 and reported using heroin as a means to escape the memory and "to force myself to relax when I'd freak out." There is not always a significant event that clients will tie to their addiction, but sometimes there is. It might be a death, sexual assault or abuse, loss of safety and/or certainty, loss of control, losing a job or failing in school, a fractured or terminated relationship, growing up in addicted or abusive homes, domestic violence, feeling like an outcast, etc.

For some clients, the initial stages of use (or behaving) are an attempt to solve one problem with another. For example, the pain of chronic social exclusion might compel someone to use meth if it brings a social connection with it, or if it might reduce the awareness that one is so alone. Inevitably though, in running from something, we run toward something else. We can get so focused on escaping the monster that's chasing us that we don't realize we're running toward a cliff. For clients that incur losses before an addiction or problematic patterns are present, explore them. Talk about the potential connections to their current circumstances and how some skills from the past (even if not currently being used) might aid their recovery efforts.

Here are some options for discussion questions around these points:

- *Is it possible that the addiction, while quite a headliner, is not the actual problem but rather an attempt at coping? Let's talk about that. What purpose does the use/pattern have? How does it help you? How does it hurt you? Is it working (is the pain different, more manageable, or gone when using/doing)? What's still missing that you need or want?*
- *Are you giving yourself credit for the fact that you've survived/coped or blaming yourself for surviving/coping this way? What's it like to carry those feelings (either way)?*
- *Is the prospect of having to remember something you've been actively trying to forget getting in the way of recovery? Is there anything that haunts you from the past that you're scared might come back to life in sobriety? How confident are you that you can deal with it without your use/pattern? Let's talk and work on adding some more ways to cope to your toolbox.*
- *What skills or memories do you have that might help you move forward toward recovery? What isn't broken that we can start using again or what can we start rebuilding to help you move forward toward recovery?*

Additional interventions and options for talking about loss and grief will be discussed in future chapters. Keep reading for now.

Losses

The ability to be aware of, acknowledge, and sit with the accompanying emotions of loss varies from person to person. People typically do what's worked for them in the past—that is what's made the pain more manageable. For people that numb emotions, they will likely try to numb. For people that respond with anger, they will be angry. For those that isolate, they will isolate. Those that find comfort in connection will seek it out or work to provide it to another. And so on. The same is true for people with addictions (alas—people really are people).

If the addictive behaviors or substances are a central coping skill for unpleasant emotions—think numbing, isolation, distraction, or chemically induced euphoria, you may see an uptick in use, or a return to use following a loss. If the addictive behaviors are directly connected to a loss, such as with Alicia's example earlier, you may see increased use as well, and you may also see an entry point into (or a return to) recovery or a period of less or no use. In the next chapter, we'll discuss the mediators of mourning (Worden, 2009) and how our relationship to a loss will impact our response to it. For now, let's consider some losses that a person may encounter and begin to acknowledge the secondary losses that may follow.

Sanders (2011) noted several losses that can impact both addiction and recovery and at times, add a secondary layer of shame; I've also added to the list based on my own clinical experience:

Pregnancy, Abortion, Miscarriages, and Stillborn Births

Substance use during pregnancy is associated with both negative pregnancy and child health outcomes (Louw, 2018). Varner et al. (2013) found that cannabis use, smoking, illicit drug use, and exposure to second-hand smoke during pregnancy were associated with an increased risk of stillbirth. If health complications do arise, guilt and shame can be induced or compounded. One client said, *"It's the I knew better, but didn't do better scenario."*

Pregnancy is both exciting and scary for many; the addition of a child brings a near tidal wave of change. A pregnancy may have been unplanned and a surprise. The surprise may be welcome or unwelcome; it may be scary if use is still occurring, and/or a motivator to work toward sobriety and recovery more urgently. A planned pregnancy while actively using carries stigma and judgment from the outside world, and perhaps internally as well (i.e. *"How could I do this to a child? I can't even care for myself"*). The joy of the pregnancy for some may be tarnished or diminished by the opinions or concerns of others.

I recall two clients who expressed guilt and shame upon learning they were pregnant—one had an unplanned and the other a planned pregnancy. Both worried about their ability to parent while addicted. Both worried that they would pass their problems down to their children. For the planned pregnancy, the guilt centered on not telling her partner she was trying to get pregnant. She feared he would say no; she carried a sense of selfishness and guilt *"for cheating him out of a choice."* She would talk about how this guilt would transform into shame-filled questions like *"If I can't be honest with my husband, should I even have a child with him? Will he still love me? What's wrong with me? I'm such a liar—am I even fit to be a mom?"*

For the unplanned pregnancy, the guilt centered on *"bringing this kid into the world with two dope-head parents."* She felt broken and guilty for sporadic use throughout the pregnancy and struggled with whether or not to abort early on. Her questions centered on

> *are they better alive with me, or to never be born at all? I honestly don't know the answer to that. I don't want to torture a kid, I really don't. Some days it seems like living with me would be torture. I don't want another person to suffer because I can't get my shit together.*

Ultimately, she decided to move forward with the pregnancy at the urging of her family. Both clients also hoped for some redemption via their children—the idea that they could *"put some good back into the world after taking so much."*

In these two cases, several losses are present: loss of routine, loss of freedom in some ways. One client remarked, *"I'm glad to lose my freedom to do whatever I want, but it's still scary. It's a big adjustment to have to think about what I do to my body and how it affects their body now too."* Additionally, losing the ability to disconnect from the consequences of their use; this idea is reflected in the previous statement and even more so in the following:

> *It really isn't just about me anymore. My recovery or my failure impacts another life now. I used to be able to say F-off—this is my body and my life, and I can do what I want. I feel like that's not as true now. It's hard because I don't know if I can do it* [recovery].

Miscarriage or stillbirth are associated with depression and anxiety and also losing one's sense of self. Pregnancy-loss is painful no matter when or why it occurs. The future a mother or father envisioned is now different. Another layer here is that the grief and sadness of the partner are often forgotten. Researchers have found that the sadness and grief of fathers and non-pregnant lesbian partners are mostly ignored or dismissed (Rinehart & Kiselica, 2010; Wojnar, 2007).

I can recall one client who felt pressured into an abortion by family *"because I was a junkie and they told me that a junkie can't raise a kid. That I'd be doing it a favor."* The client felt incapable of deciding for herself and listened to those external voices more than her own. Following the procedure, she experienced several months of increased use and a depressive episode. The lack of control, the belief she couldn't trust her internal voice, and the idea that she was not capable of doing a role she had longed for (being a mother) became too heavy a load to bear; she returned to her primary coping skill—heroin.

Consider the range of emotions tied to pregnancy and/or pregnancy-related loss in the context of a SUD or compulsive pattern. Shame, guilt, sadness, anger, confusion, uncertainty, hopelessness, powerlessness, relief, hope, excitement, happiness, fear … all or some combination may be present. This is a tall emotional order even for someone with adequate coping skills and support. This is an even taller task for someone still working to find consistent, solid coping skills.

Death of Child, Parent, Sibling, Friend, Pet, Significant Other

Depending on the nature and quality of relationship, the impact will vary. For instance, losing a child that lived at home will impact one's daily routine in a different way than one living outside the home. Losing a partner or spouse may mean a secondary loss of income or housing. It doesn't matter whether it's a child, parent, sibling, friend, pet (for some people, pets are family), or significant other, losses are likely to reverberate. Again, depending on the role this person or being fulfilled in life, death may bring changes in routine, support, companionship, financial stability, laughter and joy, consistency, hope for the future, and identity (i.e. mother, wife, partner, son, etc.). Consider that not all losses here will be sad. For example, an abusive partner's death may be met with relief, joy, hope, and a sense of freedom. Death does not always bring sadness, and as counselors, we need to be careful of our assumptions and be open to exploring all reactions. Remember, grief is a reaction to loss—not *just* a sad one.

Removal of Children/Loss of Custody

Losing custody of children, whether temporary or permanent, is hard, for children and parents alike. I recall one client describing it as "only I can love them right. Others might be able to give them more things, but only I can love them right." Some clients may see this as a significant failure and others may struggle with the idea that they are not meeting the needs of their children. The heartache that can come when there is genuine love for a child and the realization that sometimes that's not enough can be intense. A host of emotions may arise including guilt, shame, anger, shock, defensiveness, sadness, and remorse. Further, confusion and uncertainty may be present if the allegations or terms of reunification are unclear. Consider also that some adult clients may have been removed from their own homes as children; old memories may be triggered and produce their own emotional responses.

Separation, Divorce, or Other Failed Relationships

The loss of a significant relationship, romantic or not, brings change. Some are welcome, like losing arguments, stress, and unhealthy patterns. Some are of course unwelcome, like loss of companionship, routine, love, comradery, and stability. If a partner or friend was a primary means of coping and support, this may present additional recovery challenges. Loneliness and boredom can be powerful and for some, triggering.

Relationships with "healthy" people may be lost when use or patterns begin or continue. Likewise, when one enters recovery, "using" friends can be lost. It seems the world often underestimates the importance of connection, particularly when connections are deemed unhealthy. For instance, when individuals are mandated (by courts or loved ones) to stay away from "using" friends—that's far easier said than done for some people. If the choice on the table is being alone or being with people who have unhealthy behaviors but other redeeming qualities (i.e. kindness), many of us would opt for the latter. Remember to appreciate the impact of relationship losses; even if the relationships were largely unhealthy, they still mattered and are worthy of grief.

Financial Stress or Ruin and/or Loss of Housing

The literal costs of addictive behaviors can be significant. I recall one client who reported spending $700 per month on cocaine alone. Another client with gambling disorder accumulated $30,000 in slot debt. An additional layer was that the credit card carrying the debt was co-signed by her father; he ultimately paid the bill and took a second mortgage to do it. Yet another client was a dealer who relied on his sales to feed his family. The goal of getting a "regular job" and making far less was a hard reality he felt unprepared for financially and emotionally. He didn't want to seem like a failure to his kids and in some ways, he quantified his love—the amount of money spent equaled the love felt.

Securing safe, supportive housing for those in or entering recovery can be challenging and emotionally taxing. For clients living in halfway or sober houses, one lapse may mean homelessness. Another unfortunate reality is that "sober houses" are not always drug or alcohol-free. Other challenges may include job or financial instability, ultimatums by roommates or family, and probation requirements (think location and other occupants).

Legal Problems/Arrest or Incarceration

Legal problems often intersect with other areas of life. If someone is arrested and acquired a record, loss of freedom or incarceration is one obvious concern. Time away from home, family, and friends is another layer of loss. Disruptions to working life or future aspirations may factor in as well. A former client had hoped to join the marines but found that recruiters were uninterested following brief incarceration for cocaine possession and distribution. Employment and housing searches become more complicated, particularly with felony convictions. The impact of challenging job and housing searches may impact financial stability, compromise one's ability to care properly for children or others in the household, and reduce hope. Identity may also shift. I recall another client who reported a shifting sense of self during incarceration, *"I always saw myself as a nice, regular person. But there I was sitting in jail for possession and theft; it shook me. Maybe I wasn't who I thought I was. That's a trippy thought."*

Loss of Control

Losing one's freedom may be more metaphorical for some; think beyond incarceration. Being stuck in an emotional-behavioral pattern can sometimes feel like imprisonment. Losing control and being tied to a pattern of behavior that brings temporary euphoria, release, relief, numbing, what have you, can be maddening. Depending on something outside yourself to feel okay on the inside can be a challenging way to live. Some clients have described losing choice and control,

> *I didn't get to decide what I wanted my life to look like anymore. At least not totally—I had to have oxy otherwise I'd get dope sick. A ton centered on finding and affording it. Fear of withdrawal was constantly on my mind. I lost control of my life, not just my use.*

Losing control may also result in diminished hope; the idea that if we're no longer driving our car, we don't get to decide where we're headed. Keep that on your clinical radar and be curious about it in sessions.

Loss of Safety

Loss of safety can come in many forms. For those that experience trauma this perspective shift can be profound. I have memories of several clients who reported rapes or attempted sexual assaults and other abuses; some coped with substances or behaviors, others' experiences came after the addictive patterns were already established. Overdosing or witnessing the overdoses of others, particularly those considered to be seasoned users, can bring home the reality that use can be fatal. Loss of safety can be concrete—ingesting substances that may kill you depending on what they're cut with. It can also be more abstract—no longer trusting your own judgment.

One client who will never leave my memory is Carlos (name has been changed). Normally punctual, he was late for his 6 am appointment; when he walked in around 6:20 am, his face was drained of color, and he appeared detached from the moment. Turns out that during his walk to the clinic he witnessed an attempted murder—one man stabbing another in the chest. He described the visuals—blood and lots of it, one man falling to the ground the other fleeing, screaming and *"quiet chaos"*—he elaborated saying that the neighborhood was largely quiet (it was about 5:45 am), and the screams of the injured man broke that silence. He described feeling paralyzed by the shock of what he saw. Carlos had been going through the motions of a normal Monday; getting up, showering, and walking to the standing appointment. Having such a mundane and consistent routine upended with such a dramatic event resulted in a loss of safety. His once peaceful walk was now filled with reminders of terror and violence. He feared the route and the people on it. He also struggled with the question, *"If I never used to begin with, and never had to go to treatment, would I have ever seen something like that?"*

Loss of a Substance, Behavior (i.e. Shopping), and/or Process (i.e. Readying a Syringe)

Facing and accepting that substances or behaviors can no longer be relied on maybe a painful loss experience. Ending the process of use or behaving can resemble ending a relationship. Consider what's involved in an addictive pattern: time, money, attention, physical sensations and emotional aspects (numbing or enhancing feelings/sensations), social components, and culture (i.e. language, community, shared knowledge). In many ways, this echoes the loss of a romantic relationship. One is left to rebuild a life without all the pieces they're used to having; it can be emotionally and physically taxing.

Loss of Identity

This is typically a secondary loss and can result from a number of circumstances. For instance, losing a job or career may bring questions of "who am I without it?" I've heard clients commiserate in group settings over how they aren't sure they know how to be "straight." Many clients have echoed this sentiment over the years—that they just aren't sure who to be without the parameters of their addiction. A client who also happened to deal once asked, "Am I still powerful without my money? People need me right now; they depend on me to deliver. I'm good at my job [dealing]. I'm not sure I want to walk away from it just yet."

This idea can manifest in a variety of ways: loss of status, losing the parent identity if kids are removed or otherwise absent, leaving behind the label of "addict," etc.

Yet another example is Andy★. When I knew him, he was 56 years old and working to end his injection heroin use. While having a fair amount of success with reducing the frequency of use, he kept injecting (even when methadone precluded the high). He eventually disclosed that he *"liked helping new people to figure that shit out."* He liked teaching new injectors how to do it properly. He felt skillful and competent. He thought that if he let go of injecting, he'd also be letting go of feeling competent. "I'm an old f-er and I don't want to be f-ing useless. This is all I got."

Loss of Physical Appearance and/or Self-Esteem

The erosion of one's physical appearance over the course of an addiction can represent additional layers of loss. Now having said this, not all clients deteriorate in their physical appearance. Sometimes few, if any, changes occur on the outside. But for those that do notice a change in appearance, it can be a significant adjustment during recovery. Consider the potential for long-term reminders of one's addiction; for instance, track marks that become scars, or lack of dental care that results in extractions. Some physical changes are not reversible, and once in recovery, may present challenging triggers or shame points for those that are reminded of their past. A client once told me, *"It feels like I've died on the inside a little bit, but damn when I look in the mirror, I realize that damage hasn't been contained."* He was 28 years old at the time and had smoked methamphetamine for so long that his dental health was dire. He had several front teeth removed and discovered that his gums were also so damaged that they would have a hard time fitting a denture.

I remember another client who had significant scarring from injection use. She had a fair skin and the purple-dark reddish scars ran up and down both arms. She had dreamed of becoming a hairstylist and so entered cosmetology school. She dropped out two months later after being bullied for never wearing short sleeves, and then for her scars when she did. The physical reminders of her past were worn like a badge she couldn't remove. She religiously applied vitamin E and scar creams to reduce the visibility, but since the scars were so numerous, her arms would never be totally clear. She grieved the loss of *"normal arms"* and the ability to be in public and not be judged. She had lost her *"beauty"* as she said, and that loss brought fear. She feared a lack of acceptance or being triggered back to use. She was scared she'd never again consider her body beautiful. This was particularly significant for her as she had primarily used cocaine and had a very thin frame, even in recovery. She worried that her very slim, scarred body would not be appealing to a potential partner. She had a hard time looking in the mirror and respecting what she saw. This was unfortunately echoed by the world (school mates in particular). Ultimately, there were layers of loss, layers of sadness, and they all deserved to be grieved.

Other Losses

Be open to other losses; ask your clients simple questions like, *"Is there anything else you've lost here that we haven't talked about? Anything that seems to be lingering?"* As you likely know, there's no way to fully account for the human experience. We are all unique beings with individual experiences, even when facing the same event. Explore their world and rely on your clients to inform you about what matters in their life and recovery.

Keep in mind that losses can occur anywhere on the addiction/recovery spectrum: prior to addictive behaviors, during addiction, in detoxification, treatment, initial, mid-or advanced recovery, prior to a lapse or relapse, and/or after a lapse or relapse. Some losses may be directly connected to the addictive pattern (i.e. loss of appearance, loss of children/custody) while others may not be (i.e. the death of a parent)—either way, the losses will interact with either the client's addiction or recovery. Depending on the context and surrounding life circumstances, losses may land differently and have distinct meanings because of *when* they happen. Be open to heavy losses and also to one's that are manageable and simply "okay."

Considering Ben

Let's take time to explore some of the losses in Ben's story. First, and most prominently from his view, was his dad's illness and subsequent death. Going through the process of the cancer diagnosis and seeing his once *"strong"* father deteriorate took a toll on Ben. During his quit attempt after his father's diagnosis, he lost a reliable coping skill. Heroin is unhealthy, no doubt about it, but it works. He wanted to numb his emotions and for a time, no longer had heroin as an option. That's a significant loss—he lost his pain management strategy at a time when his pain was huge. He once noted that *"I missed the anticipation. I missed knowing that in just a few seconds, the world would fade away."* Essentially, he missed knowing that he could make his pain more manageable on command.

Along with the actual substance and its effects, he lost his method of use—injection. This may seem like a side note, but for Ben it mattered. He considered the preparation of the syringe and dose relaxing. It was such an automatic process at that point in his addiction that he could do it without much thought. He lamented, *"After we found out it was cancer, I really missed those few minutes of nothingness. Just going through the motions; I missed the mindlessness of it."* For a person wanting to escape their thoughts and emotions, having a mindless routine disappear stung.

Our conversations about his father's death centered on two themes: strength and abandonment. He once said something to the effect of *"strength doesn't always look strong."* He would also talk about feeling alone in the world, believing his dad was his only true, unconditional support person. He felt abandoned; he resented the cancer. After his father died, he began reflecting on the early loss of his mother. The sense of abandonment from both parents (one by choice, the other by death) brought sadness, anger, and shame to the surface. He started to wonder if his mother had made the right choice by leaving him; he felt broken and wondered out loud if his father would have been better off without him too. *"I know I put him through hell, even after he got sick. He worried about me a lot and that couldn't have been good for him. That kind of stress can f-ing mess with a person."* Guilt and a loss of self-respect were now present in the conversation. He believed he had tarnished his father's reputation because of his own use and worried that his father's legacy would be that of a *"junkie son."*

Additional losses in Ben's story included his arrest and subsequent criminal record. The sense of disappointment he felt stayed with him, mostly centered on disappointing his dad. For Ben, this loss was noted, but never explored in depth; he didn't think it was as important as the other losses. The process Ben and I took in addressing his loss and grief will be detailed in future chapters. For now, remember that the client is the driver of their car; a loss can be present, but it does not mean it demands exploration. Listen to your clients and let them guide you.

Summing Up

Practitioners and treatment programs (and family) sometimes ask clients to give up something (i.e. drug, friends, ways of thinking) without considering how massive a loss it is. By examining losses and grief reactions, we can help clients gain awareness of their pain, both fresh and unresolved, and their resilience amidst such pain. Also, be open to the idea that clients may not find pain, but relief and sometimes even joy in the aftermath of loss. Acknowledging, exploring, and sometimes uncovering losses builds awareness. From awareness, we can build insight and with that, help people either better survive their addictions or move toward recovery. We all learn from the past. Help clients learn and draw meaning from theirs.

References

Attig, T. (2000). *The heart of grief: Death and the search for lasting love*. New York: Oxford University Press.

Attig, T. (2001). Relearning the world: Making and finding meanings. In R. A. Neimeyer (Ed.), *Meaning reconstruction and the experience of loss* (pp. 33–53). Washington, DC: American Psychological Association.

Louw, K. A. (2018). Substance use in pregnancy: The medical challenge. *Obstetric Medicine, 11*(2), 54–66. Retrieved from https://www.ncbi.nlm.nih.gov/pubmed/29997687

Rhinehart, M. S., & Kiselica, M. S. (2010). Helping men with the trauma of miscarriage. *Psychotherapy: Theory, Research, Practice, Training, 47*(3), 288–295. Retrieved from https://www.ncbi.nlm.nih.gov/pubmed/22402086

Varner, M. W., Silver, R. M., Rowland, H. C. J., Willinger, M., Parker, C. B., Thorsten, V. R., et al., Eunice Kennedy Shriver National Institute of Child Health and Human Development Stillbirth Collaborative Research Network. (2014). Association between stillbirth and illicit drug use and smoking during pregnancy. *Obstetrics Gynecology, 123*(1), 113–125. Retrieved from https://www.ncbi.nlm.nih.gov/pubmed/24463671

Winokuer, H. R., & Harris, D. L. (2012). *Principles and practices of grief counseling*. New York, NY: Springer Publishing Company.

Wojnar, D. (2007). Miscarriage experiences of lesbian birth and social mothers: Couples' perspectives. *Journal of Midwifery and Women's Health, 52*(5), 479–485.

Worden, J. W. (2009). *Grief counseling and grief therapy: A handbook for the mental health practitioner* (4th ed.). New York: Springer.

Part II

Models and Theories of Grief and Loss and Considerations for Addiction and Recovery

Introduction and Background

Several models of mourning, grief, and bereavement exist, and I will provide an overview of many. Most theories laid out will be written with death as the primary loss. Following each original iteration, I will work to translate and apply these theories to the addictive and recovery context, connecting the ideas to the addiction treatment world. This layout is meant to help readers bridge the gap between losses involving death and the loss of an addiction (i.e. substance, pattern, or addictive behavior) and/or other addiction-related losses.

A cautionary note before we begin: some models may convey a sense of ordering to clients, even if none is intended. There are pros and cons to that. For some, it may convey a "correct" way to grieve. Some clients may find the implied structure comforting, others may be disturbed by it. For example, some conclude that 'to grieve correctly, you need to progress through these steps…' Essentially, the risk lies in mapping what grief *should* look like versus what it *could* look like. Even if clinicians know better than to adopt this narrow view, clients may end up taking them at face value.

Also consider the Google and Pinterest-related searches, particularly image searches, that may be done before clients ever step foot in your office—that is, searches such as *"how to grieve,"* or *"what does grief look like,"* or *"best way to grieve"* etc. may yield literal maps of how to grieve 'properly.' If clients find they are taking a different path, some may feel like they're doing it wrong or that they're broken somehow. Talk with your clients about their expectations and cultural assumptions around grief: what do they expect, hope for, and fear?

Finally, it's important to consider the compatibility of any approach across cultures. Sue (2001) laid out a multidimensional model of cultural competence which specified three layers of personal identity: *individual* (that is, what makes us unique and unlike anyone else), *group* (the values and beliefs we share with others), and *universal* (common traits among all humans). Notably, he argued that the group level is often neglected by helping professionals. This neglect is significant, as group membership can exert considerable influence over how we see ourselves and others as well as our behaviors and responses to loss. This applies to general life and it also applies to groups tied to an addiction or recovery. Shared values and beliefs are often the common thread of peers who also engage in the addictive behavior and make up the circle supporting the addiction. Likewise, shared value and belief systems run through peer groups which support recovery.

Sue believed that the overall individualism in the United States, that is, the pull yourself up by the bootstrap mentality, was to blame for the neglect of the group level's contribution to one's identity. When relating this information to the realm of grief, this overlays with the grief-work hypothesis in some ways—the idea that the past is the past and one should move on (this idea will be discussed further in the coming pages). The traditional emphasis on autonomy and independence also support this notion. Reliance on continuing bonds, and/or engaging others in the process of newly constructing mental representations, etc. may not always jive with this cultural preference/bias for emotional autonomy.

Additionally, the difficulty that our society often has in discussing issues of discrimination, oppression, and personal bias may stifle critical thought around this level of identity (Sue, 2001) and may also reduce discussions around the varying ways in which people grieve; some prefer to do it alone, others prefer the presence of others. A deficit-perspective also seems to permeate some discussions around race and ethnicity, according to Sue, and I would extend that to people with SUDs. The world at large, and some counselors for that matter, focus on what a person with a SUD is missing, rather than what they bring to the table. Hence, caution is warranted as you read and consider applying these theories and strategies. Not all theoretical approaches will fit a client's view of the world. Learn about your client's beliefs, values, and perspectives on loss. Engage with the client's world and take caution not to force their grief into a theoretical box that simply doesn't fit.

Remember, people are not cookies. As such, do not expect (or train your clients to expect) that grief processes will fit into a cookie-cutter, standardized mold. The same loss can produce varied grief reactions that call for different interventions; use these models to guide your practice rather than dictate it. Same goes for recovery. People find success (or failure) with different paths; be open to that and remain flexible both in thought and approach.

The chapters contained in Part II present several existing models of grief, mourning, loss, and/or bereavement and discuss how those ideas can help process the loss of an addiction and other addiction-related losses. Before doing so, however, it seems prudent to provide a little history. I am certainly not the first person to recognize the importance of processing grief in the context of recovery efforts or the inherent grief in losing an addictive substance or pattern.

Beginning in the mid-1970s, research and arguments emerged as to why and how grief factors into the recovery process. In 1976, Hirschberg, Lewis, and Vaughan talked about the connection between positive treatment outcomes for alcohol and other drugs and adequately addressed grief. They largely focused on grieving, the idea that one is addicted, and working on the acceptance of that reality so that one could grapple with it and ultimately cope. This falls in line with a more recent assertion from Helgoe (2002) that for the addiction-related grief process to be initiated, clients must first recognize there is something to be grieved. More specifically, the recognition that change brings loss and that one's reactions to loss can be labeled "grief." Counselors have an important role in validating the existence of grief, and in helping clients identify the emotions connected to losing their addictive pattern as well as other addiction-related losses.

In 1979 Skolnick wrote about the connection between unresolved grief and substance abuse. The argument was that substance abuse often correlates with losses in early childhood and that through grieving those losses more fully, the need for substance use would reduce or resolve. Attachment theory (Bowlby, 1977) also emphasized the importance of early attachments; the need for safety and security dominates and attaching to something that meets these needs has survival value. That's an interesting thought in the context of addiction. Gabor Maté is a more recent proponent of this connection between early life experience and addiction (2010).

Primary and secondary losses were thought to factor into this unresolved grief. As a refresher: a primary loss might be the loss of a parent or parental relationship and a secondary loss might be tied to the addictive pattern itself, such as loss of self-esteem or self-respect. Skolnick believed that children who were not able to cope well with large emotional pain might turn to substances as a way to regulate. If nothing changed in their life, that pattern was likely to continue into adolescence and adulthood. Basically, if the grief wasn't resolved or completed, the pain would stick around and continue to wreak emotional havoc (and sustain the addictive pattern).

People who turn to addictive patterns to manage such havoc get stuck in their grief; the substance (and accompanying behaviors) essentially block the grief process (Maté; Skolnick). The chemical reinforcement of the use or behavior becomes the solution, or at least a band-aid for the pain. The full impact of the loss is therefore never truly felt, only a dulled down version is. Helgoe (2002) also believed that substance use and other addictive patterns suppressed emotional pain; one could acknowledge a loss occurred but were blocked from the full impact of it. This incomplete emotional processing leads to the pain continuing and interrupts true healing. The term *"impaired mourning"* was used to describe this state (Skolnick, p. 286). Ultimately, for someone to address their addiction, they first needed to address their unresolved grief (Fields, 1992; Goldberg, 1980; Helgoe, 2002; Skolnick, 1979).

Researchers were also noting the relationship between addiction and grief in the 1980s and early to mid-1990s. Goldberg (1980) strongly believed that losing alcohol or another substance for the individual was so significant that this loss should take priority in treatment and be addressed first. Denny and Lee (1984) found that many of their clients had never processed their grief prior to treatment. They found that grief-specific groups (in the context of addiction treatment) helped bring unresolved feelings to the surface and allowed them to be processed in a setting with supportive relationships. They argued that this support was essential to combat the associated guilt and shame that was present for many. Fields (1992) later agreed with them and added that for some, shame is a feeling leftover from a traumatic loss in childhood. Fields also argued that treatment often fails and results in relapse, not because someone has failed to hit the so-called rock bottom, but because they have yet to accept and grieve their addiction.

Friedman (1984) believed that counselors should give outright permission to grieve, as well as education and support through the process. Martin and Lee (1989) also saw value in helping clients identify losses, examine coping strategies (including substance use) in response to loss, and taking time to grieve and mourn. The following chapters will continue this timeline and examine addiction-related grief through the lens of established grief, loss, mourning, and bereavement models.

References

Bowlby, J. (1977). The making and breaking of affectional bonds: II. Some principles of psychotherapy. *British Journal of Psychiatry, 130,* 421–431.

Denny, G. M., & Lee, L. J. (1984). Grief work with substance abusers. *Journal of Substance Abuse Treatment, 1,* 249–254.

Fields, R. (1992). *Drugs and alcohol in perspective.* Bellevue, Washington: Wm. C. Brown Publishers.

Friedman, M. A. (1984). Grief reactions: Implications for treatment of alcoholic clients. *Alcoholism Treatment Quarterly, 1,* 55–69.

Goldberg, M. (1980). *Loss and grief: Major dynamics in the treatment of alcoholism.* Presentation at the NASW 12th Annual All-day Alcoholism Institute at Fordham University (May 20). New York, NY: Haworth Press.

Helgoe, R. S. (2002). *Hierarchy of recovery: From abstinence to self-actualization.* Center City, MN: Hazelden.

Hirschberg, G. G., Lewis, L., & Vaughan, P. (1976). *Rehabilitation: A manual for the care of the disabled and elderly* (2nd ed.). New York, NY: J. B. Lippincott Company.

Martin, S., & Lee, L. J. (1989). Grief work with substance abusers. *Journal for Specialists in Group Work, 14*, 46–52.

Mate, G. (2010). *In the realm of hungry ghosts: Close encounters with addiction.* Berkeley, CA: North Atlantic Books.

Skolnick, V. (1979). The addictions as pathological mourning: An attempt at restitution of early losses. *American Journal of Psychotherapy, 33*(2), 281–290.

Sue, D. W. (2001). Multidimensional facets of cultural competence. *The Counseling Psychologist, 29*(6), 790–821.

4   Loss-Grief Addiction Model

In the mid-1990s, Beechem, Prewitt, and Scholar (1996) developed an assessment to help clinicians better identify unresolved losses in substance using populations entitled the Loss-Grief Addiction Model. Beechem et al. (1996) wanted to identify unresolved grief issues in people using substances. They predicated the need for an assessment on earlier research centered on unresolved grief in this population.

The loss-grief inventory was a 24-item measure that categorized losses as, pre-addiction losses (e.g., losses occurring before the addiction to a substance), losses associated with addiction (e.g., losses resulting from either drinking and/or drugging), and losses associated with entering treatment (e.g., losses experienced due to entering treatment programs) (Beecham et al., 1996, p. 192). Each item listed a type of loss and asked respondents to note whether this type of loss was applicable to their life. If so, they would then check a box to note two things:

a   Which category of loss it belonged to. Namely pre-addiction, loss associated with addiction, or loss associated with entering treatment. All three boxes could be checked if applicable.
b   The extent to which they were currently feeling the loss (on a five-point scale).

The 24 items were as follows (pp. 192–197):

1   Loss of freedom of choice(s)
2   Loss of support (e.g., friends, relatives, church, social services)
3   Loss of ability to remember details (e.g., blackouts)
4   Loss of a driver's license (DUI)
5   Loss of a goal or dream
6   Loss of security due to sexual, physical, or emotional abuse
7   Loss of a social life
8   Loss of financial stability
9   Loss of self-respect (negative feelings towards self)
10   Loss of someone special through death
11   Loss of a marriage through divorce or separation

12   Loss of children through divorce or separation
13   Loss of good health
14   Loss of self-trust
15   Loss of trust in others
16   Loss of security due to self-inflicted abuse
17   Loss of a romantic relationship
18   Loss of a social relationship
19   Loss of marital stability
20   Loss of self-confidence
21   Loss of confidence in others
22   Loss of time (e.g., wasted time)
23   Loss of respect for others
24   Loss of respect from others

Three additional items were listed so other losses could be added and specified.

During the initial development, Beecham et al. found that participants were predominantly impacted by losses associated with addiction. More specifically, participants noted losses related to freedom, choices, social life, self-respect, goals or dreams, respect from others, self-trust, financial stability, trust in others, health, self-confidence, time, and memory (i.e. blackouts). Pre-addiction losses related to the death of a loved one for many respondents. Other losses in this category included loss of self-respect and loss of confidence in others. Losses associated with entering treatment included loss of freedom and choice, loss of time, and loss of self-respect.

This inventory was intended as a starting point for conversation. Beecham et al. hoped to reinforce the point that loss and grief deserve a place at the table when working with addiction. Let's continue with that premise and look now to more recent approaches of grief and bereavement and how they may translate into the addictive and recovery context.

Reference

Beechem, M. H., Prewitt, J., & Scholar, J. (1996). Loss-grief addiction model. *Journal of Drug Education, 26*(2), 183–198.

5 Two-Track Model of Bereavement and Considering the Two-Track Model in the Context of Addiction and Recovery

This model of bereavement came out of frustrations with earlier models of grief and bereavement, particularly from the belief that they were incomplete or a bit fragmented (Rubin, 1999). More specifically, prior models generally seemed to look at one of the following to determine if someone was adapting to grief or not:

1 the degree and nature of the bond with someone who has died and considering that to be the most salient factor in grief (i.e. memories, feelings about them during life and now in death, unresolved issues, etc.) (Freud, 1917; Stroebe, Gergen, Gergen, & Stroebe, 1992) *or*
2 the level of functioning following a death (i.e. functioning at work? are other relationships being attended to? are other parts of life continuing?) (van der Kolk, McFarlane, & Weisath, 1996; Schut, DeKeijser, van den Bout, & Stroebe, 1996)

For option 1, the way to assess how someone was adapting to their grief was to focus on the relationship, degree of bonding, and now separation from the person who has died. For option 2, grief was viewed as a major stressor, and level of functioning was seen as a way to measure one's adaptation to that stress (Rubin, 1999; Rubin, Malkinsom, & Witzum, 2012).

To reconcile this seeming fragmentation, Rubin (1999) essentially combined the two approaches into the Two-Track Model of Bereavement.

Rubin's model advocates consideration of *two tracks*: track one centering on functioning and track two centering on the relationship with what you've lost. The idea here is that it can be helpful to assess both the positive and negative impacts of loss—look for the ways you've suffered and for the ways you've grown. This type of exploration helps individuals identify what needs are currently met and what growth or adaptation they are seeing. It can also help identify gaps where additional supports might be needed or beneficial (Rubin, 1999; Rubin et al., 2012). Below are some considerations for each track; notice the balance between strengths and challenges present in both.

Track One: Functioning

In assessing how someone is functioning after a loss, several things can be considered. Rubin et al. (2012) encouraged exploration of both strengths and difficulties in areas such as:

Anxiety = Assess the intensity level of anxious thoughts and feelings, how often they're occurring, any insight into triggers, and what's helpful in managing or calming them?

Familial Relationships = Assess the state of current relationships with family members in one's immediate and extended family and look for changes in these relationships, both positive and negative, since the loss.

Self-esteem = Are there any emerging feelings of helplessness or powerlessness, feelings of inadequacy, worthlessness, loneliness, or a shifting sense of self? Are there any emerging feelings of growth, competence, and/or resilience in the aftermath of the loss?

Depression = Discuss the intensity level of depressed thoughts and feelings, how often they're occurring, any insight into triggers, and what's helpful in managing or calming them?

Traumatic Responses = Inquire about the intensity level and length of traumatic symptomatology, assessing if responses are within or below diagnostic levels. Facilitating an appropriate diagnosis if clinically warranted.

Somatic Concerns = Assess how the body is functioning. Are there any health concerns? Is the person eating, sleeping, engaging in hygiene practices, etc.

Interpersonal Relationships = Check in on the state of current relationships with peers, coworkers, friends, neighbors, etc. and look for changes in these relationships, both positive and negative, since the loss.

Work = Are one's tasks and duties still being performed at work? Or are they lagging and failing to meet expectations in the wake of their loss?

Meaning Structure = Consider if the loss has produced changes, either large or small, in the way they view the world, their role in it, and/or their perception of spirituality or religion.

Investment in Life Tasks = This asks the question is someone living or merely surviving? Does the person still experience things like excitement and hope in life, or are they just scraping by? Is there any evident personal growth or has life become stagnant?

Track Two: Relationship

This track is centered on the relationship with the deceased, awareness of that relationship, changes to it, and adjustments to the new relational reality (Rubin, 1999; Rubin et al., 2012; Winokuer & Harris, 2012). As with track one, exploration of both strengths and difficulties are encouraged around areas of:

Reconnection = Assess how strong the desire for reconnection is. How intense is the desire to stay connected or regain what's been lost?

Emotional Closeness = Discuss how connected and emotionally close or bonded a person felt to what or who they lost. Consider and be observant about how they communicate that emotional connection and about their relationship more generally.

Conflict = Are there mixed feelings about the loss? Is the relationship being remembered as an unhealthy, conflictual, or problematic one?

Upsetting Impact on Self-System = Are there any emerging feelings of guilt, inadequacy, worthlessness, or a shifting sense of self?

Imagery and Memory = How much do they remember about the relationship? What exactly do they remember? Is it balanced remembering or more skewed to one side (positive or negative)?

Positive Perceptions/Affect = What *positive* perceptions, feelings, or moods are triggered when remembering? What exactly brings them about—what part of the memory or relationship specifically?

Negative Perceptions/Affect = What *negative* perceptions, feelings, or moods are triggered when remembering? What exactly brings them about—what part of the memory or relationship specifically?

The Loss Trajectory = Work to shift the expectation that grief is worked through in stages, and rather emphasize dimensions. Exploring different dimensions of the grief response, such as the ones listed here, is seen as beneficial and more inclusive of varying relational styles.

Preoccupation with the Loss = How much are they thinking about the loss? Is it dominating their time or is it fleeting in nature? What triggers the preoccupation and what helps tamp it down?

Memorialization and Transformation = Has the person found ways to keep the memory, or aspects of it, alive? Have they found ways to remain meaningfully connected to what's been lost?

Considering *the Two-Track Model* in the Context of Addiction and Recovery

Rubin's model is comprehensive in assessing the impact of a loss on functioning (track one) and the continued emotional attachment and relationship to what's been lost (track two) (Rubin, 1999; Rubin et al., 2012; Winokuer & Harris, 2012). This model provides a template for a thorough conversation and assessment about the impact of a loss in someone's life and psyche. Broadening such assessment of functioning and adjustment from only one type of loss—death—to other losses yields important information and, in many ways, mimics existing efforts to treat substance use and related disorders (i.e. whole person approach). For instance, when a person is working towards recovery, conversations often center around items from Rubin's track one (see below). The corresponding track one items are noted in parentheses:

- Withdrawal symptoms *(somatic concerns)*
- Affect *(anxiety and depression)*
- Shifting energy to other areas of life and finding meaning without the addictive pattern *(investment in life tasks)*
- Re-considering friendships associated with the addiction and working to build healthy supports *(familial and interpersonal relationships)*
  - The previous relationship with the deceased, or in our case substance, pattern, or behavior, can't serve as a replacement for current relationships (from this perspective at least), but only as an adjunct to them (Malkinson, Rubin, & Witztum, 2006). I understand this to mean that the old relationship can't be primary anymore—it can be a companion to new, current relationships, but we have to let go a bit and focus on the present rather than continue to be defined by the past.
- Working on self-concept and getting to know oneself in sobriety and recovery; strengths-based work *(self-esteem)*
- Working to meet life tasks and establish or reestablish employment or education *(work)*
- During the process of treatment and recovery, track two items become critical areas of assessment and conversation, particularly around the grieving process and relapse prevention. As above, the corresponding track two items are noted in parentheses:
- Determining how strong the cravings are and the desire to return to old patterns *(reconnection)*
- Talking about the emotional draw of addiction and how many people rely on addictive patterns or substances to regulate emotional states *(emotional closeness)*
  - I have had many clients recount addictive patterns like a love story; the substance or behavior provided much-needed relief from emotional turmoil or added joy where there was believed to be none; with reference to Rubin's point, observe how people communicate about emotional closeness and connection to their patterns/substances.
  - The way the bereaved, or again in our case, substance, pattern, or behavior was perceived in the past can't continue unchanged into the future—well it can, but at an emotional cost (Malkinson et al., 2006). If we believe one thing is the answer, we may not look for other options—we'll be restricted by our perceptions and pasts.
- Discussing the mixed feelings of leaving a substance or behavior behind; are memories filled with pain, relief, joy, or all of them? Essentially, how is the addictive pattern perceived after it's gone? *(conflict)*

- Considering the impact on the self and identity of an individual is also important when working on recovery; explore any guilt, shame, feelings of inadequacy, worthlessness, and overall identity changes during the recovery attempt. Doing any of these preempt or contribute to lapses or relapses along the way? *(upsetting impact on self-system)*
- Looking back and reviewing the addiction and sorting through memories with people can help piece together the full impact of their patterns and behaviors. Some people have rather complete memories, others fragmented. Some people remember more positive aspects of the addiction, others more negative. I have run groups dedicated to recall and perceptions of the "positives" and "negatives" of addictive behaviors; there's a lot to be said and explored here around both. *Cautionary note*: do not give in to the temptation to restrict discussion of memories to only the negative aspects of use. Allow people to remember in a balanced way—both positive and negative aspects. A realistic picture of what one is grieving about is necessary for many in order to move on to anything else. Sometimes we need to know what we're really letting go of in order to grab something new; allow the full memory in and let the client determine which aspects are most salient to their recovery efforts. *(imagery and memory)*
    - More specifically, have discussions around what positive feelings, perceptions, or moods are triggered by their memories of use/behaviors—what are they connected to? Substance? Pattern? Behaviors? Associated people? Relief of emotional pain? Introduction of positive emotional states? Other? *(positive perceptions/affect)*
    - Likewise, have discussions around what negative feelings, perceptions, or moods are triggered by their memories of use/behaviors— what are they connected to? Substance? Pattern? Behaviors? Associated people? Relief of emotional pain? Introduction of positive emotional states? Other? *(negative perceptions/affect)*
        - Examining both positive and negative perceptions/affects represents the identification of triggers—a hallmark of many addiction treatment approaches.
- Talking about recovery as an ongoing, lifelong process that has no simple answers, rather different dimensions to consider and attend to over time; sounds like grief doesn't it—something that changes over time but doesn't necessarily end completely *(the loss trajectory)*
- Assessing how much space cravings and triggers are taking up in someone's head and heart is an ongoing conversation in addictions work, as is the management of such symptoms *(preoccupation with the loss)*
- Finally, in what ways is the person still connected to their addiction/ pattern? Have they drawn lessons from it? Are they still hanging on to mementos or reminders—either tangible items (i.e. pipes, pills, purchased items they don't use, etc.) or relationships? Have they transferred their addictive patterns to another area of life? For instance, has

someone who previously relied on a substance to provide emotional relief/regulation now turned to people for that? Is the memorialization or transferring of patterns healthy (i.e. learning to ask for help and reaching out for support) or unhealthy (i.e. loss of self and/or dependence on others to decide for them)? *(memorialization and transformation)*

The overarching goal of Rubin's two-track model is to sustain meaning in life, maintain emotional well-being, and to find a balance between attachments to what's been lost and what remains (Rubin, 1999; Winokuer & Harris, 2012). Throughout the course of the treatment, clinicians can consider the degree of attention and understanding that there is around a client's track one and track two elements. Areas that have perhaps been left by the wayside can be attended to, and areas that have had a clear impact can continue to be understood and processed. This two-track, multidimensional model is inherently practical and comprehensive. In short, this is user-friendly and is quite helpful when assessing the impact and consequences of a significant loss.

References

Freud, S. (1917). *Mourning and melancholia, standard edition of the complete psychological works of Sigmund Freud.* London: Hogarth Press.

Malkinson, R., Rubin, S. S., & Witztum, E. (2006). Therapeutic issues and the relationship to the deceased: Working clinically with the two-track model of bereavement. *Death Studies, 30*(9), 797–815.

Rubin, S. S. (1999). The two-track model of bereavement: Overview, retrospect, and prospect. *Death Studies, 23*(8), 681–714.

Rubin, S. S., Malkinson, R., & Witzum, E. (2012). *Working with the bereaved: Multiple lenses on loss and mourning.* New York, NY: Routledge.

Schut, H. A. W., DeKeijser, J., van den Bout, J., & Stroebe, M. (1996). Post-traumatic stress symptoms in the first years of conjugal bereavement. *Anxiety Research, 4,* 225–234.

Stroebe, M., Gergen, M. M., Gergen, K. J., & Stroebe, W. (1992). Broken hearts or broken bonds. *American Psychologist, 47,* 1205–1212.

van der Kolk, B. A., McFarlane, A. C., & Weisaeth, L. (Eds.) (1996). *Traumatic stress: The effects of overwhelming experience on mind, body, and society.* New York, NY: Guilford.

Winokuer, H. R., & Harris, D. L. (2012). *Principles and practices of grief counseling.* New York, NY: Springer Publishing Company.

6 Continuing Bonds Theory and Considering Continuing Bonds in the Context of Addiction and Recovery

The Continuing Bonds Theory (Klass, Silverman, & Nickman, 1996) is closely related to aspects of Rubin's Two-Track Model. This theory emphasizes the continued connection people have with the deceased and the construction of a new relationship with that individual over time. The Continuing Bonds Theory is contrary to earlier ideas that in order to have a healthy adaptation to loss, one must cut ties and move on (aka leave behind what's lost and maintain life in its absence) (Winokuer & Harris, 2012); the leave the past in the past approach was highlighted in the "grief work hypothesis" and will be detailed later in the chapter.

Essentially, from this continuing bonds perspective, when someone dies, there is no linear process that leads you to the promised land of acceptance, closure, or moving on. Instead, there are adjustments and a process of redefining your relationship with the individual who's deceased to facilitate a continued bond with them. Basically, death does not sever the relationship, it changes it. The continued bond is not evidence of abnormal grief; rather it is viewed as a healthy and important part of grief. Klass et al. (1996) found that this continued relationship brought comfort for many people.

Several examples exist to highlight this idea. Think of someone talking to a deceased loved one and updating them on life or seeking counsel—these conversations could happen in a cemetery in front of a gravestone or just sitting on the couch at home; some other examples are, saying "goodnight" or "I love you" to someone who's passed, letting a balloon go with messages attached (*note*: this is terrible for the environment), continuing to text or call someone's old phone number, looking for signs of someone's continued presence (i.e. signs, smells, etc.), or getting a tattoo of a loved one's portrait, handwriting, or name; all these promote a continued remembering. The internet has added more technological options to this idea in recent years. Facebook, for instance, has an option to convert a deceased member's profile to a memorial page. When a person dies, the account is not automatically deleted, but remains as a forum for people to communicate and interact with the memory (Church, 2013; DeGroot, 2012, Kern, Forman, & Gil-Egui, 2013). Research has been done on this particular phenomenon and has highlighted the continuing bonds noted in this theory.

In 2016, Bouc, Han, and Pennington studied what living members discussed on memorial Facebook pages and analyzed how those messages changed over time. They completed a content analysis of over 2,500 posts on ten memorial pages (so that's ten deceased member pages). They identified three themes including: (1) Processing the death, (2) Remembering the deceased, and (3) Continuing the connection. Generally, people posted expressions of love and care (i.e. "I miss you," "I love you," etc.), emotional expressions, asked questions, made requests, posted memories and stories, updated them [the deceased] on life events since their passing, etc.

Posts centered on processing the death and remembering the person were highest right after the loss and then decreased with the passage of time. Posts related to the third theme though, continuing the connection, increased with the passage of time (Bouc et al., 2016). Moreover, the initial responses to loss were to focus on the loss itself and associated memories of the person and as time went on, continuing the connection, rather than focusing on what's been lost, took priority. Researchers viewed such posts as efforts to make sense of the loss and an attempt at meaning-making; that is, people are working out what the continued relationship, and their role in it, will look like now that the person is physically gone (Neimeyer, 2001; Pennington, 2013; Silverman & Klass, 1996).

Other researchers have cast some doubt on the presumed health of continued bonds and have questioned if continuing a bond is any healthier than letting go of one (Field, 2008; Field, Gao, & Paderna, 2005; Stroebe, Schut, & Boerner, 2010). The conclusion reached was that there's no straight answer pointing to one (continuing a bond) over the other (letting go of one); essentially different people will find different things healthy and effective. This reads as a cautionary note and reminder to me that what works for one, might not work for another so we should use caution in recommending all, or even most people, seek continuing bonds. Compare, for instance, a healthy relationship in life versus an abusive one; a continuing connection may be desirable in the former circumstance and less so in the latter. Consider the individual you are working with and the circumstances around their loss. For some people, this approach will be helpful and relatively smooth; for others it may be less so on both fronts.

Stroebe et al. (2010) used Attachment Theory (Bowlby, 1969, 1980) to add specificity to their position that the adaptiveness of continuing bonds will vary, using attachment styles to highlight potential differences. Adult attachment styles include: secure, insecure-dismissing/avoidant, insecure-preoccupied (aka ambivalent/anxious), and insecure-fearful (see appendix A for style descriptions). For individuals with a secure attachment style, they posited that a continued bond or attachment to the person who died would be both possible and useful in facilitating acceptance of the loss.

Individuals with a secure attachment tend to rely on others and value emotional connections; as such, Stroebe et al. (2010) reasoned that these people might turn to the deceased for guidance and find comfort in remembering what's been lost. Securely attached people would be able to eventually strike a balance between a continued bond and relocation of the loss; they would stay connected, continue to remember, and yet not be totally bound by that connection. Moreover, the individual would internalize the connection/bond, and be able to draw on that internal comfort or security, while acknowledging that it no longer exists in the outer physical world (Stroebe et al., 2010). Securely attached individuals might find success with the continuing bonds approach and would likely be capable of self-regulating the development and transformation of the bond after the loss; aka, they wouldn't need much outside help and in time could likely swing this transformation on their own (Boerner & Heckhausen, 2003; Stroebe et al., 2010).

For individuals with an insecure-dismissing/avoidance attachment style, continuing bonds may be less frequent and less effective in adapting to loss (Stroebe et al., 2010). The thought here is that a dismissive style would likely result in a person denying the need for continued connection. Beyond denial of need, independence and separation from thoughts, emotions, and memories of the deceased might be sought. As a result of this defensive reflex, an ongoing symbolic attachment to someone deceased might not be desired or tenable (Mikulincer, 2008; Mikulincer & Shaver, 2008; Stroebe et al., 2010). People with this style could be advised to confront their loss, work towards establishing a continued bond, and continuing to think about the meaning of the lost relationship. Researchers posited that this could be especially prudent since other people are generally viewed in a negative light with this attachment orientation; overall, finding meaning in the lost relationship might be a beneficial challenge to existing schemas and thought processes (Boerner & Heckhausen, 2003; Stroebe et al., 2010).

In comparison, the insecure-preoccupied attachment style might produce an opposite response dominated by clinginess, yearning, and fixation on the lost relationship. The continued relationship with the lost person might start to take priority over living relationships and an imbalance between reminiscing and current life may take hold (think obsessive worry and possibly regret) (Stroebe et al., 2010). Individuals with these patterns may benefit from loosening the grip a bit; an effort could be put toward rebuilding one's life in the absence of the relationship and focusing more on independence rather than strong ties to someone now gone. The intense-preoccupation orientation generally produces a view of others that is idealized and a view of the self that is undervalued or demeaned (Stroebe et al., 2010). Working to find more balance between perceived dependence on the other (and their idealized image) and increasing self-efficacy (i.e. one's sense of capability) might also prove useful and adaptive over time (Boerner & Heckhausen, 2003).

The intense-fearful style might produce confusion around a continuing bond above all else. People might gravitate and foster a continued bond for a period of time and then seemingly abandon it near entirely, preferring to move forward. The back and forth of connection and disconnection can produce feelings of being stuck as well as that of uncertainty around if, how, and whether it's worth moving forward with a continued bond (Stroebe et al., 2010). Such individuals will likely need help building coherence after a loss. Guidance around facing the loss and the meaning associated with it could precede the development of a continued bond (Boerner & Heckhausen, 2003). Start with an exploration of the meaning and impact of the loss, then gradually work toward relocation of the loss. People with this attachment orientation generally have negative views of both themselves and other people and as a result might struggle a bit more with this style of functioning than the other to integrate and relocate a lost relationship (Stroebe et al., 2010). Consider how difficult it might be for someone who doesn't think much of themselves to believe they are capable of new perspectives and thoughts, particularly in the wake of loss, and also questioning their power to do it (or ours to help). It's a tall order and both empathy and patience are essential.

Considering the Continuing Bonds Theory in the Context of Addiction and Recovery

Applying this theory to the recovery process can be quite useful. Essentially, this is another way to conceive of the balance between continued connection and relocation of the loss; it's a way of keeping the adaptive parts of a connection alive and gradually giving less attention to the parts that didn't serve them as well. Let's consider this approach applied to the former "addict" identity for those entering recovery. In this context, it's learning from the past, retaining connections and awareness, so that one is not doomed to repeat it. Individuals with a secure attachment style would likely be capable of recognizing the aspects of their former self that would be useful to carry forward (i.e. tenacity) as well as the aspects worth letting go of (i.e. dependence). Letting go of the past entirely—severing a bond or trying to forget a loss—doesn't always work or bring comfort (Klass et al., 1996).

Reminiscing on and retaining a connection to the former "addict" self may *promote* recovery rather than threaten it. Some people need reminders, either tangibly or internally, that represent where they've been so that they don't go back. Other people might benefit from the development of compassion and empathy for their formerly addicted selves. Work to increase awareness of strengths that existed during the addiction when there seemed to be none and appreciate their survival value (i.e. tenacity, grit, resilience), at the same time, help clients disown aspects that might lure them back toward addictive patterns or tendencies (i.e. unhealthy relationships, reliance on external means in order to cope, narrow thinking patterns, low self-efficacy or worth). Again, it's about balance—retaining the adaptive parts of the connection to the past and relocating aspects that no longer serve the current self. Over time, individuals may also internalize the lessons and draw comfort from their progress and transformation; people can feel proud of how far they've come (Stroebe et al., 2010). This is a hope I have for all clients—that in time their former struggles and the strengths demonstrated in surviving them will lay the foundation for a longstanding recovery.

Individuals in recovery with an insecure-dismissing/avoidant attachment style may struggle to find meaningful connections to the past (Stroebe et al., 2010). This struggle around what the past means to them may transfer to their recovery efforts, and the pitfalls may not be as noticeable or manageable. More specifically, increasing social supports and learning to rely on others to some degree may be especially tricky. Denial of need, tendency to go it alone, and detachment from one's thoughts, emotions, and a preference for leaving the past in the past might impede recovery. They may simply not see the use in discussing or piecing out the past in terms of strengths/weaknesses. Building a strong therapeutic alliance—basically proving that you are worth their time and engagement—will be important. Remember always that avoidance is *protective*. Work not to demand confrontation of the past, but to gently encourage it. Such gentle encouragement of what's been lost before, during, and following addiction could prove useful in time, but it may be a slower process compared to other attachment styles.

Aim to find aspects of their former self that are worth hanging onto. I often say in class that the building blocks for recovery are often found in the addiction itself, but we often fail to recognize them due to the surrounding pain and/or destruction that's at the surface. Think of those people that find lost pets or a meaningful memento in the rubble of a tornado-ravaged home. Many times, it's been days or weeks until those things are located, and many fear or believe there's nothing alive or salvageable because of the immense destruction that's seen from the surface. With damaged homes, *and with people*, it takes persistence, hope, and digging through the remains until you locate what you've been searching for.

As with securely attached individuals, dismissing/avoidant individuals might benefit from the development of compassion and empathy for their former selves as well as awareness of strengths that existed inside the addictive patterns. Survival is often skill-based. Help clients realize the skills they used to survive and to continue the connection with those aspects of self: perseverance, ability to endure pain, grit, dedication, tenacity, resilience, creativity—they are all present in an addiction, but in that context, they're applied in ways that serve the compulsions rather than health. Recovery will mean applying these skills to healthier contexts, we don't necessarily need to start from scratch.

Here's another metaphor to illustrate this point: think of a house that's been deemed uninhabitable. The main structure may need to completely come down—it's unhealthy, unlikely to withstand a major event and remain standing, and is potentially filled with items that no longer serve the living. Tearing down everything above ground might reveal a sturdy, or sturdy enough, foundation. With some repair, a new house can be built on top of it—the entire foundation does not necessarily need to come out—it needs shoring up. People moving from addiction to recovery are similar in my mind. The current state of being (addiction) is no longer tenable or healthy and major changes are needed inside and out. But the foundation may be okay—the person, their actual identity might just be covered or clouded by the addiction. Reduce the ill-health above, and you might reveal a strong foundation that needs tending to, not total demolition or reconstruction. This point and metaphor seem especially relevant to me when thinking about dismissing/avoidant individuals who might have trouble finding meaning in lost relationships and generally hold a negative view of others. Challenging them to think about negative aspects of the past (and past relationships) and how they can possibly be transformed—either in thought or in the actual world—might challenge long-standing maladaptive thinking patterns and begin to move them slowly toward health and recovery (Stroebe et al., 2010).

In contrast, individuals with an insecure-preoccupied attachment style may struggle to let go of the past (Stroebe et al., 2010). This might translate to the continuation of addiction-based relationships even when the clients themselves have worked hard to progress into recovery. It might also mean hesitancy or difficulty letting go of the past identity and all that came with it. Making such a life change—moving from addiction to recovery—is filled with loss (as discussed in Chapter 2); these individuals may feel that impact more than other clients. Clients with this attachment style may also find difficulty in striking a balance between holding on and letting go. In other words, they may struggle to retain the adaptive elements (the good, useful stuff) and relocate or let go of maladaptive patterns and relationships (the not so good, less useful stuff). As Stroebe et al. (2010) pointed out with death, these individuals may struggle with regrets and rumination about past experiences or relationships; the same may prove true in recovery. The same strategy for death-related grief could apply here: help individuals loosen the connection to the past and be more forward-thinking. Consider the present and where they are headed now in the absence of the addiction, relationships, and patterns. Finally, as this attachment style tends to hold idealized views of the other (in this application, the substance, pattern, or relationships) and self-degrading views of the self, working on building and strengthening the self-concept, levels of self-efficacy and esteem, and fostering independence may be indicated.

Clients with insecure-fearful attachment styles might also experience the push and pull of recovery; they may make great progress then retreat to old behavior patterns. I have had many clients over the years express a fear of success and/or an aversion to "moving on." These fears have been expressed in several ways including:

> "What would it mean if I did change—would it actually be better or just different? Then what if I fail out of it—what would that make me then? Hopeless? The failure I already fear I am? I go back and forth on that a lot."

> "What if I'm not really capable of living any other way? It might hurt worse to try and find out that I can't do it. I almost don't want to risk it."

> "Everyone that cares about me or that I actually spend time with uses. What good is recovery or sobriety if I'm alone? I don't want to move on because my life is back there [in the addictive environment]?"

> "I want to hang on to the past, because I met some good people. Really f—cked up behaviors, but good people. but I'm also scared that if I do hang on, it'll suck me back in. I don't know if I'm strong enough to say no. It might be better if I just wipe it from my brain and pretend that I'm just starting over completely. I'm just not sure I can make it happen. I don't know."

Questioning the usefulness of a continuing bond or connection with aspects of one's addiction may arise—either from the client, loved ones, or other providers, frankly. I love Boerner and Heckhausen's suggestion (around death-related grief) that discussion around facing the loss and the meaning associated with it could help sort some of those questions out (i.e. what impact would it have to continue a connection? To not have one? What would be gained or lost on either side of that coin?) (2003). It doesn't mean that all clients will want to end up fostering a continued connection to parts of the past, but it will encourage exploration of what's been lost and what it means that it's now gone.

The work of integrating past parts of life and identity might take more patience with this attachment style, and yet it seems that our efforts, and the client's, would be well-placed. Remember that this particular style tends to hold negative beliefs about self and others and may question anyone's capability (including their own) to facilitate change (Stroebe et al., 2010). Don't fall into the hopelessness pit with such clients. Empathize with their fears, explore their roots, and help people find ways to relocate (redefine and integrate) aspects of loss and retain others that may prove meaningful over time.

In 1999, Stroebe and Schut proposed a model of bereavement called *The Dual Process Model* (DPM). In 2010, Stroebe et al. looked toward theoretical integration of the DPM with aspects of the Continuing Bonds Theory and found meaningful overlap and complements. The Dual Process Model will be presented in the next chapter along with considerations around the integration of attachment principles and the role of continuing bonds in the Dual Process approach.

References

Boerner, K., & Heckhausen, J. (2003). To have and have not: Adaptive bereavement by transforming mental ties to the deceased. *Death Studies, 27,* 199–226.

Bouc, A., Han, S. H., & Pennington, N. (2016). "Why are they commenting on his page?": Using Facebook profile pages to continue connections with the deceased. *Computers in Human Behavior, 62,* 635–643.

Bowlby, J. (1969). *Attachment and loss: Vol. 1: Attachment.* London, Hogarth, New York: Basic Books.

Bowlby, J. (1980). *Attachment and loss: Vol. 3. Loss: Sadness and depression.* New York: Basic Books.

Church, S. H. (2013). Digitizing gravescapes: Digital memorializing on Facebook. *The Information Society, 29,* 184–189.

DeGroot, J. (2012). Maintaining relational continuity with the deceased on Facebook. *Omega, 65,* 195–212.

Field, N. (2008). Whether to relinquish or maintain a bond with the deceased. In M. Stroebe, R. O. Hansson, H. Schut, & W. Stroebe (Eds.), *Handbook of bereavement research and practice: Advances in theory and intervention* (pp. 113–132). Washington, DC: American Psychological Association Press.

Field, N., Gao, B., & Paderna, L. (2005). Continuing bonds in bereavement: An attachment theory based perspective. *Death Studies, 29,* 1–23.

Kern, R., Forman, A. E., & Gil-Egui, G. (2013). R.I.P.: Remain in perpetuity. Facebook memorial pages. *Telematics and Informatics, 30*(1), 2–10.

Klass, D., Silverman, P. R., & Nickman, S. L. (Eds.). (1996). *Continuing bonds: New understandings of grief.* Washington, DC: Taylor & Francis.

Mikulincer, M. (2008). An attachment perspective on disordered grief reactions and the process of grief resolution. *Grief Matters: The Australian Journal of Grief and Bereavement, 11,* 34–37.

Mikulincer, M., & Shaver, P. (2008). An attachment theory perspective on bereavement. In M. Stroebe, R. O. Hansson, H. Schut, & W. Stroebe (Eds.), *Handbook of bereavement research and practice: Advances in theory and intervention* (pp. 87–112). Washington, DC: American Psychological Association Press.

Neimeyer, R. A. (2001). *Meaning reconstruction and the experience of loss.* Washington, DC: American Psychological Association.

Pennington, N. (2013). You don't de-friend the dead: An analysis of grief communication by college students through Facebook profiles, *Death Studies, 37,* 617–635.

Silverman, P. R., & Klass, D. (1996). What's the Problem? In D. Klass, P. R. Silverman, & S. L. Nickman, (Eds.). *Continuing bonds: New understandings of grief* (pp. 3–23). Washington, DC: Taylor & Francis.

Stroebe, M. S., & Schut, H. (1999). The dual process model of coping with bereavement: Rationale and description. *Death Studies, 23*(3), 197–224.

Stroebe, M. S., Schut, H., & Boerner, K. (2010). Continuing bonds in adaptation to bereavement: Toward theoretical integration. *Clinical Psychology Review, 30,* 259–268.

Winokuer, H. R. & Harris, D. L. (2012). *Principles and practices of grief counseling.* New York, NY: Springer Publishing Company.

7 Dual Process Model of Coping with Bereavement and Considering the Dual Process Model in the Context of Addiction and Recovery

The emergence of the DPM in 1999 challenged a notion that underlies grief and bereavement models employing the so-called "grief work hypothesis" mentioned earlier (Stroebe & Schut, 1999). Through this lens, 'grief work' was understood as a...

> cognitive process of confronting a loss of going over the events before and at the time of death, of focusing on memories and working toward detachment from the deceased. It requires an active, ongoing, effortful attempt to come to terms with loss. Fundamental to current conceptions is the view that one needs to bring the reality of loss into one's awareness as much as possible and that suppression is a pathological phenomenon.
>
> (Stroebe, 1992, pp. 19–20)

From this perspective, "grief work" reads like an ultimatum—*'confront your emotions or suffer the consequences.'*

This idea was seen early on from Freud (1917) in "Mourning and Melancholia"; he argued that the grief process is both withdrawal of energy and detachment from what's been lost. He thought that if people freed up the energy tied up in the loss, they could reinvest it into new relationships. A process of recall and review of memories was advised and working through the pain was essential to achieve detachment. Stroebe and Schut were quite clear in their belief that this "grief work hypothesis" was inadequate, rigid, and ineffective. Essentially, they rejected the idea that one must face the totality of their pain and circumstances head-on, for if they don't, they won't heal, and the grief work will be incomplete. They believed this "confront your emotions and work through the pain" paradigm was too inflexible and limited. They argued instead that acknowledging a loss on one hand, and yet railing against the reality of it on the other is normal. Further, they normalize and de-pathologized denial (I'm particularly appreciative of this point). From this view then, it's normal to have an urge to confront a loss or emotion *and* an urge to avoid a loss or emotion—both are viewed as coping skills (Stroebe & Schut, 1999; Stroebe, Schut, & Stroebe, 2005).

Building on this idea that grief is more dynamic than perhaps other models accounted for, Stroebe and Schut made the points that grief and coping don't happen in isolation. There is an entire social context to be considered and grief will include *both* intrapersonal and interpersonal elements. For instance, one may struggle with identity, deep sadness, and fear (intrapersonal), but how their social world responds to their intrapersonal struggles also matters (interpersonal). For example, if one expresses sadness and is told that *"your life is so much better now, what's to be sad about? Just smile,"* one could feel invalidated, unsupported, misunderstood, and conflicted. Such feelings could complicate or prolong the grief process and the person may be left feeling that they are grieving "wrong." Another example is a loved one believing someone is "not grieving enough" or in "the right way." Differing definitions of what grief *should* be and what it *should* look like can cause relational conflict; comments like, *"shouldn't you have moved on by now? The past is in the past."* may inflame conflict or feelings of isolation. In essence, the interactions we have with others matter and can impact the grief process and one's ability to adapt in the wake of loss (Stroebe & Schut, 1999; Stroebe et al., 2005).

Another stated shortfall of these grief work models was the perceived lack of specificity about what exactly was lost, and what changes followed such a loss (Stroebe & Schut). Further, they felt that the complexity of loss was ignored; more precisely, the secondary losses and associated stressors weren't accounted for. The example of losing a partner and needing to shift routines and duties illustrates their point. The primary loss is significant, but it's not everything. Basically, they believed that if you left out the *impact* of a loss—the meaning, the changes, the adjustments needed—you were missing important parts of the grief equation.

Stroebe and Schut also noted a distinct medical model focus running throughout many approaches. Basically, they noticed that many models strove for reduced physical and psychological symptoms as a positive outcome of grief work. They instead argued that perhaps we need to think more practically and broadly. For instance, cementing memories of what's been lost and reconstructing meaning is critical for some, and changing roles and identities is central for some others. Continued relationships, restoration of family functions (i.e. people filling in the gaps left by the loss), and embracing the pain may also factor in. Another point that's appreciated by this author is their caution that if we pathologize grief and see it as a problem to solve, we risk pathologizing negative emotions and working to rid ourselves of them as soon as possible. A counterpoint is that through suffering can come meaning, and we should instead strive for balance between positive and negative emotions, even in the aftermath of great loss.

The final area of concern for Stroebe and Schut was the lack of universal application of the grief work hypothesis. They suggested that many models do not take into account gender considerations, particularly gender socialization. Specifically, that the preferred masculine response to emotion, especially sadness, may be to ignore or contain it, rather than directly and openly confront/feel it. They questioned whether or not we had a gender-neutral grief hypothesis, or one that was skewed toward the more traditionally socialized female (i.e. emotional). Another concern around universal application was cultural specificity. They argued that the grief work hypothesis was culture-bound. That means that it didn't account for the different, yet healthy, ways people grieve in non-Western cultures. For example, some cultures skip the confrontation of emotion, while others engage in rituals (i.e. mutilating one's body) as expressions of grief (Stroebe & Schut, 1998, 1999).

In response to these shortcomings, Stroebe and Schut (1999), with support later from Stroebe et al. (2005), presented their DPM of coping with bereavement. The DPM is an alternative to the linear, task-based grief "work" models and understands the oscillation (the back and forth) of grief as realistic, healthy, and adaptive (Stroebe & Schut, 1999; Stroebe et al., 2005). It views bereavement and loss as an event(s) with multiple stressors and angles to be considered. Some things are changeable, and others are not. This model advocates for changing the things you can (i.e. routines, relationships, etc.) and adjusting to and deriving meaning from those you can't (i.e. loss of safety, uncertainty, fear, the past). Interestingly, they add that underlying all of it—the changes in routines, shifting responsibilities, fear, sadness, etc. is the emotion of grief. So even when we and/or clients focus on solving the "problems" the loss has created, we are still engaging in emotion-focused work; please don't fail to appreciate that.

The real beauty of this model is the flexibility and applicability to a wide range of people, losses, and cultures. This model is flexible in the *how* and *when* of the grief process. It sets the expectation that people will likely move back and forth between focusing on the loss and trying to adapt to it. More specifically, people may have periods where they actively avoid their grief and others where they are taking steps to adjust. Another high point of this model is the acknowledgment that denial and avoidance are normal and healthy. We all need a break from our pain at times and this model embraces that.

Their DPM works to simplify ideas around grief and bereavement. Rather than only focusing on the grief over what's been lost, this approach considers the stress of changing routines, shifting responsibilities, and feelings of isolation and/or loneliness (all secondary losses). Two types of stressors are identified: *loss-oriented activities and stressors* and *restoration-oriented activities and stressors*.

Loss-oriented activities and stressors are related to primary losses. Some common experiences include crying, yearning, or wanting something back that you can't have because it's either permanently gone or inaccessible to you. Additionally, sadness, denial, anger, and dwelling on the circumstances of the loss are included here—think rumination and hyper focusing on it. This loss-orientation can range from positive, pleasurable memories to painful recollections and yearning. It's not uncommon for people to avoid restoration activities when focused on the loss-oriented stressors. Some might label this avoidance as denial or a so-called "failure to confront reality or move on." It *is* denial and avoidance and *it's totally healthy.*

Sometimes people focus more on their pain and emotions around the loss than on how to adapt to their new circumstances. I recall one client who was recently incarcerated. He was entirely focused on the loss of freedom and his new housing for about two weeks. Following that period, his focus shifted to the lost time with his daughters and how to maintain a relationship while locked up, inability to provide financially for his family, and fears about his employability once released. He started out with a loss-orientation (noticing and mourning the loss of his freedom, a primary loss). Then over time, he shifted to a restoration-orientation, focused on the impact and implications of that primary loss (secondary losses).

Restoration-oriented activities and stressors are associated with secondary losses. As mentioned in Chapter 2, secondary losses come in the wake of a primary loss. Restoration-oriented activities noted in this model include adaptation to new circumstances or roles and/or lifestyle, managing changing or disrupted routines, establishing new ways of connecting with family and friends, and cultivating a new way of life in the midst of all this adjustment (Stroebe & Schut, 1999). Essentially with restoration, circumstances have changed, and individuals are working to change with them. It's about rebuilding in the aftermath of loss and working to restore or establish stability and routine.

In the above example, the client who was incarcerated started to write regular letters to his daughters to try and maintain a relationship. He got on the list for employment in the prison and enrolled in GED classes to improve his resume post-release. These restoration-oriented activities worked to compensate and account for the secondary losses. Consider another example: if I lose my job (primary loss), I also lose my income, my identity as a counseling professor (at least temporarily), my daily routine, my health insurance, my coworkers, etc. (secondary losses). Restoration-oriented activities would focus on maintaining or regaining financial stability, updating my vita and applying for positions, establishing a new daily routine, finding coverage for health insurance, working to maintain relationships with former coworkers or establishing new relationships outside the workplace, and gaining new insight into how I define myself. For instance, I would put energy into valuing my roles as a mother, friend, and wife while transitioning to a new professional identity or job.

Of significant note, while the DPM model specifically addresses death, I encourage you to broaden it to *loss*. The simple, yet nuanced, structure of loss-oriented and restoration-oriented activities and stressors can be quite helpful when discussing the transition from addiction to recovery. Notice also that this model values continuing a connection with what's been lost amidst the adaptation and restoration efforts for those who are interested in such a connection (Stroebe & Schut, 1999; Stroebe et al., 2010). This is reminiscent of the Continuing Bonds Theory in some ways and will also connect to ideas from upcoming theories. The oscillation between loss-oriented and restoration-oriented realms allows for people to grieve in smaller doses and as a result, creates a space for continuing a connection or bond with what's been lost. Essentially, the DPM doesn't overwhelm people with their grief. It advocates taking grief as it comes and not piling it all on at once, leaving time for reminiscing and connecting to those memories.

Attachment Principles Applied to the DPM

As previously mentioned, attachment principles can also add another layer when anticipating grief reactions in the dual process framework. Be sure to notice the opportunities for integrating continuing bonds within the DPM (I'll note them too).

Clients with secure attachment styles might move back and forth between the loss and restoration orientations with relative ease. Securely attached people would likely find meaning in both the positive and negative aspects of their experience (i.e. missing the past and also realizing they are now healthier or carrying less pain) (Stroebe et al., 2010). Adaptive thoughts would be more plentiful—that is they would have healthier, than unhealthy thoughts. Stroebe et al. (2010) believed that the grief process would be rather smooth and normal, yet still noted intense pain and sadness might be present. Over time, continuing bonds would be forged, and the loss relocated; that is, the loss would occupy a new, defined space in the person's life rather than consuming it. This echoes the attachment principles applied to the continuing bonds theory. The positive and negative remembering would produce a relatively balanced recollection of what's been lost; individuals could then let go of what no longer serves them and retain the connections or memories that continue to nourish their life. The relatively smooth grief and relocation process of securely attached individuals contrasts with the skewed nature of the insecure-dismissing/avoidant style.

The insecure-dismissing/avoidant style would likely tip the scales toward a focus on restoration-oriented activities, relegating the loss and associated stressors to the wayside (Stroebe et al., 2010). There would be no oscillation and in time individuals might ignore their loss-oriented stressors altogether. As previously noted within the Continuing Bonds Theory, there would likely be no continued connection sought and outright rejection of the meaning the lost-object, person, or relationship held in their life. Remember that with restoration-oriented activities, circumstances have changed, and individuals are working to change with them. This rebuilding in the aftermath of loss, though preferential for insecure-dismissing/avoidant individuals, will be tough. It's like trying to move on from something without acknowledging it actually mattered. It brings to mind the image of a crater left by a massive meteor strike. Instead of reflecting on the significance of the event that just occurred, the literal hole before them, they might instead focus on removing debris, filling in the hole, and moving on. When help arrives to assist with the physical and emotional labor of such a task, one turns it away preferring to work alone. The idea that what's done is done and forging a path forward may be the predominant focus of such individuals; little reflection on the past or loss itself is to be expected (Stroebe et al., 2010).

Interestingly, the opposite would likely be true for the insecure-preoccupied attachment style. The focus would mostly sit with the loss itself, the secondary losses, and the ongoing pain (Stroebe et al., 2010). In the dual process framework, this would translate to a person stuck in the loss-orientation. As with the insecure-dismissing/avoidant individuals, there would be no oscillation between loss and restoration. The individual would have trouble imagining or putting into practice activities aimed at adaptation/restoration and would essentially appear cemented to their loss—unable to move forward (Stroebe et al., 2010). This rumination is significant; Nolen-Hoeksema (2001) found that rumination as a means of coping with loss leads to persistent grief.

As previously discussed, thinking about recovery, people with this attachment style might have trouble ending relationships that are no longer healthy. Letting go of previous identities and roles may be challenging, which could also impede the development of new roles. Thinking of the meteor metaphor, this style of attachment would likely result in someone staring at the crater, ruminating about the debris and meteor itself, the damage it caused, mourning what used to occupy the space and unable to imagine what could fill the gap in the future. The damage and pain would feel irreparable and permanent.

Individuals with the insecure-fearful attachment style might be oscillating between loss and restoration orientations frequently—moving back and forth in a disorganized way. Within the same day they may be focused on the loss and pain, then on moving forward and leaving all that behind, then back to the loss and pain again. The oscillation may be hard to track and can feel scattered. Negative meaning and emotions would be derived more often than positive meaning and emotions. Confusion would predominate resulting in the person not knowing whether to let go of, hold on to, or move on from the bond/connection (Stroebe et al., 2010).

Considering *the DPM* in the Context of Addiction and Recovery

Losing the ability to engage in use or addictive behaviors can prompt a number of loss-oriented activities and stressors such as distress, denial, withdrawal, craving, panic, fear, and/or relief. Some people hyper focus on the absence of the substance and have trouble looking forward toward the next step. Some may cope via outright avoidance of recovery activities. It is not uncommon for some people to feel stuck in early recovery and teeter between moving forward toward recovery or back toward old patterns (ambivalence). Remember this oscillation between taking a step forward and then taking one back is viewed as healthy and adaptive. As a provider, I agree. It's normal for people to feel doubt when approaching or working toward a major life change. These times are an opportunity to examine the hesitations, fears, and ambivalence that the loss(es) have spurred and to adapt treatment to meet those needs.

Persistent thoughts of the loss and the circumstances surrounding it may also dominate the mind for a period of time. I have found this to be particularly true for clients whose lives have been consolidated around their use or pattern; that is their friends, daily activities, joy, and pain has all become connected to their use and/or behaviors. This approach considers the multiple angles of loss and the inclusion of secondary losses is evidence of that. One moving from addiction toward recovery is not just losing something or someone; they are losing reality as they've known it to be for some time.

The secondary losses around losing a substance, behavior, or pattern can be numerous and quite significant. The world-at-large can minimize or be ill-informed about the difficulties that come with losing a substance or pattern and often portrays recovery as a matter of will power and persistence. Rather it is often a combination of persistence plus identity reconstruction, meaning-making, relationship repair, resume building, attachment-seeking (and finding), and learning how to emotionally regulate, among other things.

Consider some of the secondary losses in play with SUDs or addictive patterns. If the substance or pattern goes, one may also lose their source of emotional or physical comfort, escape or distraction, social connections, possible "addict" identity, possible income if dealing, established routines, sense of normalcy, and more. Restoration-oriented activities and stressors may include social isolation and loneliness, learning to manage emotions that were previously managed via drugs or unhealthy behaviors, learning to make or reestablish social connections with new or different people (possibly family reunification), finding financial stability and employment when relevant, and working to figure out who they are without the addiction (identity).

Consider other addiction-related losses and the secondary losses that follow. For instance, substance use may lead to miscarriage. The stress and grief that can come with such a loss might spur others such as questioning the sense of self and responsibility, relationship strain, medical complications, medical bills, etc. Experiencing a death related to addiction (i.e. overdose, car accident, suicide, homicide) can bring an array of secondary losses including loss of routine, loss of a confidant, friend, or partner. Social isolation and loneliness may factor in as well.

Losses connected to addiction and the grief that follows, viewed through the DPM, reminds people—clients and practitioners alike—that grief is a push and it's a pull. It can feel like an emotional tug of war between the past and the future. The simple, yet nuanced nature of this approach is applicable to a number of losses. It's a realistic model of bereavement that is not bound by concrete, linear expectations of what grief will look like and on which timetable it will occur. The process of both acknowledging and processing various losses allows for consideration of what is changeable and what is not. This model emphasizes changing what you can and accepting or adjusting to what you cannot; treatment and recovery philosophies often operate under the same premise. Finally, this model advocates an important point: adjusting and adapting to change is work, and it is emotional work. The emotional labor that underlies problem-solving deserves both recognition and appreciation.

References

Freud, S. (1917). *Mourning and melancholia, standard edition of the complete psychological works of Sigmund Freud.* London: Hogarth Press.

Nolen-Hoeksema, S. (2001). Ruminative coping and adjustment to bereavement. In M. Stroebe, R. O. Hansson, W. Stroebe, & H. A. W. Schut (Eds.), *Handbook of bereavement research: Consequences, coping and care* (pp. 545–562). Washington, DC: American Psychological Association Press.

Stroebe, M. (1992). Coping with bereavement: A review of the grief work hypothesis. *Omega, 26,* 19–42.

Stroebe, M. S., & Schut, H. (1999). The dual process model of coping with bereavement: Rationale and description. *Death Studies, 23*(3), 197–224.

Stroebe, M. S., & Schut, H. A. W. (1998). Culture and grief. *Bereavement Care, 17,* 7–10.

Stroebe, M. S., Schut, H., & Boerner, K. (2010). Continuing bonds in adaptation to bereavement: Toward theoretical integration. *Clinical Psychology Review, 30,* 259–268.

Stroebe, W., Schut, H., & Stroebe, M. S. (2005). Grief work, disclosure, and counselling: Do they help the bereaved? *Clinical Psychology Review, 25,* 395–414.

8 Mental Representations Theory and Considering Mental Representations in the Context of Addiction and Recovery

Boerner and Heckhausen (2003) appreciated earlier models, like the DPM and Continuing Bonds Theory, but felt they did not adequately describe *how* people form and maintain continuing connections to the deceased. The Mental Representations Theory (Boerner & Heckhausen) strives to understand how people construct *mental representations* of people who've died and how those representations change over time. *Mental representations* are memories of the lost individual that can be recalled from explicit memory (aka memories we have access to); that'd be memories based on events, images, and interactions that involve the lost individual, for example: "that painting reminds me of my sister" or "I remember when Mike used to do this exact thing and it never worked out for him" (Boerner & Heckhausen, 2003; Knox, 1999).

Representations are unique in that they can be tied to specific memories or events, rather than a larger message taken away from a relationship. The larger message or values are known as *internalization of representations* (i.e. "I'm a giving person because of my husband" or "I'm more patient because of my past"). Internalizations can't be tied to a specific memory or event, but these internalized messages can shape attachment style, personality, value systems, and expectations (Boerner & Heckhausen, 2003; Bowlby, 1980). The internalized messages and values may also influence the type of connection/continuing bond one forms and maintains with someone now lost, or whether a continuing connection is sought at all. Consider the internalization "he always made me feel small"—an individual might not desire a continued connection to that message and feeling.

Continuing connections then are based on two types of mental representations: *preexisting* and *newly constructed*. Some of these representations will be drawn from experiences with the person when they were alive—remembering something they said or particular preferences or behaviors (preexisting representations). Others are an extension of those memories after they are gone; imagining what someone might say or do, for instance (newly constructed) (Boerner & Heckausen, 2003). Mental representations give a sense of the relationship. Some people might turn to the deceased for advice or to update them on current life; according to researchers, these behaviors would suggest a supportive, positive relationship existed when they were alive. Others may work to continue someone's legacy with regard to work or projects; this might suggest that a more professional, collaborative relationship existed in life. Still others who experienced both types of relationships—personal and professional—are likely to have both areas show up in their representations (Boerner & Heckausen, 2003; Klass, 2001).

Interestingly, newly constructed representations are most likely when the living person had a limited relationship with the deceased—think of a parent dying from cancer while a child is young. Or a parent who loses a child to overdose and finds out that their child has been using heroin for the past year and a half without their knowledge. Newly constructed representations may also show up around parts of a lost person's life that the living individual didn't have much connection or access to (i.e. work life, behaviors or hobbies/behaviors not talked about) (Attig, 2001; 2000; Boerner & Heckhausen, 2003; Neimeyer, 2001; Neimeyer & Sands, 2011). In these circumstances, the living may search other people's memories about who their loved one was in life more generally or in specific contexts to build a narrative of who they were and who they'll remember them to be. Journals or diaries might be sought, or other relics that would illuminate who someone was (Attig, 2001). It's like trying to complete a puzzle, but you're searching other people's boxes for the pieces you need since you're not sure what the finished puzzle will look like just yet. It's a picture that forms over time as pieces are fit together.

Within the mental representation's theory, the authors are working to describe how people adapt to loss and the mechanisms that come into play during that adaptation. One theory that's drawn on to inform their approach is the *Life-Span Theory of Control* (Heckhausen & Shulz, 1995). This life-span theory talks about two types of control that influence how people adjust to loss: *primary* and *secondary control*. Heckhausen and Shulz (1995) defined primary control *"as bringing the environment into line with one's wishes"* and secondary control "as bringing oneself in line with the environment" (p. 285).

Primary control refers to behaviors that are aimed outward toward the external environment. Think of how we tweak our circumstances to get what we want, and/or engage in behaviors that will get us where we want to go. That's primary control. After a significant loss, people can begin to wonder about how much control they actually have in life. For instance, many of us like to believe we're generally safe, but are we actually? This question reflects uncertainty about levels of primary control; perhaps we don't have as much say about our worlds as we would like. This realization can result in feelings of fear, apathy, low mood, and helplessness or hopelessness (Boerner & Heckhausen, 2003). Secondary control can be thought of as sort of an emotional cleanup crew when primary control is lost or reduced.

Secondary control is more on the internal end (inside of us). It is meant to minimize the pain of losing primary control, to keep whatever remains, and to expand our options in primary control to gain, or regain, more power over our environment (Boerner & Heckhausen; Heckhausen & Shulz). Let me translate that: secondary control is about maintaining a grip on primary control; we use our internal resources (i.e. coping skills, motivation, cognitive processes, emotional regulation) so the last little bit of control doesn't slip away. Secondary control strategies can also show up as activities people choose to engage in or draw meaning from. Two examples include reading a good book or listening to other's positions on how to live or find meaning in this life (Heckhausen & Shulz). If someone is seeking out new information or new perspectives in response to a loss of primary control, this would be considered a secondary control strategy. Secondary control becomes especially relevant when dealing with a loss that is irreversible and permanent. The external world has changed in a significant way (loss of primary control) and our secondary control strategies come online as that internal damage control in response to loss. Both types of control, primary and secondary, are meant to help us achieve new goals and handle loss.

Primary control—working to control our external environment—is seen as adaptive and healthy as long as we actually *do* have some control or influence over situations. However, people have to find a way to internally adjust even when the external environment is not going to come around to what they want it to be (i.e. sustaining a permanent loss that can't be undone). When this is the case and we have a permanent loss, a person needs to let go of things that cannot be. For instance, the desire to bring someone back from the dead, or wishing a different decision was made, or that the past had played out differently. Boerner and Heckhausen (2003) call these types of desires "futile goals" (p. 215). There is a need to let go of the things that are no longer realistic because the external circumstances and environment have changed and one's insides must adjust to that new reality.

Internally, motivation and emotions need to be protected from the impact of that external loss (Boerner & Heckhausen, 2003). Essentially, we don't want to crumble internally because our external environment has. Holding one's insides together is one goal of secondary control. So, when a person is faced with an irreversible loss, one that results in a loss of control, secondary control strategies come into play. One example is *goal disengagement* (i.e. letting go of what we were hoping for or are used to because it's no longer possible). Think of a person going with their normal routine of trying to call or engage with someone they're used to connect with. However, when that person or relationship has been lost and that connection is no longer possible in the same way, frustration can result. The environment has changed, and the change wasn't necessarily wanted. Secondary control comes online and is thought of as compensatory; creating new mental representations can fill a gap that can no longer be filled by a person, relationship, or thing that is now gone. It's like recorking a bottle. The original cork is long gone, the liquid was spilling out, and this new cork plugs the gap and acknowledges the new reality of what's in the bottle. Some liquid has been lost, but the new cork helps secure what remains. Secondary control helps manage the internal state and helps people adapt to new external realities.

Secondary control also deals with something called *selectivity* (Boerner & Heckhausen). There are endless options in life of what people could do, and at some point, people have to narrow down the direction they will head in. Selectivity relates to which direction and goals people decide to pursue. For instance, in the wake of a loss, if someone wants to regain a grip on their external world, their primary control, they might focus on more restoration-oriented activities that aim to reestablish stability (remember this idea is from the DPM). Disengagement from the lost person or relationship or paying less attention to the loss-oriented stressors and activities (also from DPM), might allow this restorative focus to take shape. When I said earlier that one purpose of secondary control is to expand our options in primary control—this is what I meant. Focusing on a selected path—in this case to regain stability through restoration-oriented activities—is possible because secondary control helps us to divide our attention (Boerner & Heckhausen; Heckhausen & Shulz). In this example, focus on what you can control first, and disengage from what you can't.

Goal disengagement can be a helpful strategy in other ways too. Letting go of what one's been used to (i.e. the actual presence of someone or something) and instead beginning to engage with the memory or legacy (Boerner & Heckhausen, 2003; Heckhausen, 1999; Wrosch, Shulz, & Heckhausen, 2002). Moving the relationship from external to internal; reflecting back on the memories, imagining how things would have gone down, talking to someone in the "beyond" or having conversations with the universe so to speak, drawing on the positives or negatives of a relationship will enable people to draw meaning from them. Using one's power to control how the memory of someone or something is shaped inside themselves. Secondary control allows an individual to determine how a memory is going to play out and stick around internally.

Implications for recovery will be discussed in the following section and will be followed by a more in-depth presentation of the Life-Span Theory of Control; there are some points in this approach that have yet to be mentioned which connect directly to recovery and associated loss responses.

Considering *the Mental Representations Theory and Life-Span Theory of Control* in the Context of Addiction and Recovery

There are several implications for recovery and treatment here; let's start at the top. First, clients can begin by recognizing the irreversible and permanent losses they have incurred. Referring back to the description of primary and secondary losses in Chapter 2, broaden your approach. Remember that a primary loss spurs the loss of other things. The substance or behavioral pattern may be the primary loss, but secondary losses such as loss of pain management, loss of control, relationships, familiarity, security, housing, employment, respect, and self-esteem may be more significant in terms of day-to-day functioning and in the grand scheme of things.

Acknowledgment of how those losses have changed their routines and perceptions in the world, both externally in their environment and internally as to who they are, matter. Take time to think about, discuss, and appreciate how life will now be different in the wake of the loss(es) and with the beginning of recovery. Boredom and downtime might come into play in a new way that's uncomfortable rather than desired. Loneliness might be a factor if many friends and acquaintances are still stuck in addictive patterns or have been alienated. One may struggle with who they are in the absence of an addiction or behavioral pattern or doubt their ability to cope in other ways, etc. Helping people create new mental representations of who they were—the addicted self—and how to relocate that identity will be important. This is a process of redefining one's self.

Engaging in the process of selectivity means that clients will narrow down their focus or direction (my mind immediately goes to treatment planning and goal selection). The direction that seems the most doable and desirable will of course vary from client to client. Some may prefer to go down the path of total abstinence and others may prefer a harm-reduction approach. Some clients may select healing relationships with others as priority number one and some other clients may want to focus more on self-healing and personal development early on.

Whichever direction clients head in, some level of disengagement with old relationships and/or patterns is expected in order to gain more control over their environment in the long-term. Remember that primary control and the desire for it is healthy as long as it's actually possible. When clients reevaluate their past patterns and connections, they may find they had less control in reality than they thought they did. For example, if a client believed that during active addiction their behaviors didn't really impact others, they may be surprised to find that family and friends had a vastly different experience.

Disengaging from the substance and addictive pattern, retaining the motivation to pursue a different path, and the self-efficacy to try new behaviors are reflective of secondary control.

New understandings or mental representations of the past (i.e. "I wasn't as pulled together as I thought" or "I damaged more than just myself") can aid in this disengagement—the letting go of something from the past in order to allow for something new. The emphasis on regaining some control back over their inside/internal self, and over who they are going in the present also draws on secondary control. Reflecting on the preexisting mental representations that clients hold about their addiction and about themselves can inform the conversations; look back at both the addiction and the addicted self (identity) and see what was there and what the client now thinks about both. Accessing memories of behaviors, attitudes, experiences, interactions, feeling states, and a general sense of who they were while addicted can highlight what aspects of the former self and life they are holding onto (preexisting representations). Having clients imagine what that past self might say or do in response to a trigger or situation can spur discussion about other options that may now exist in the present.

Essentially, we are working to help clients rely more on the relationship with the present self than the past self; a continuing connection with newly constructed elements that acknowledge the new reality and promote empowerment. When faced with discomfort (which can come in many forms), many people turn back to old relationships for advice or guidance. Typically, this guidance is sought from relationships that were valued or were familiar and constant. In my clinical mind, this includes relationships with others *and* with self. If those past relationships were positive and healthy, positive and healthy outcomes are likely. However, if the relationships were unhealthy, reliance on those memories and ways of being may be less useful.

With recovery, one aim is to help clients recognize this—that some preexisting mental representations—the memories one relies on to guide current behavior, might be helpful, but they might be harmful too. For example, remembering that heroin took away the pain and numbed the physical and emotional ache is a risky one to rely on. Noticing instead that using was a form of coping and survival, an adaptive, albeit unhealthy, response to pain might produce different options in the present.

Focusing on the healthy qualities versus the unhealthy ones can shift the options that are currently available. This brings up selectivity again. If clients select the road of mourning what's been lost *only* and fail to select what's been retained or gained through addiction, different paths may emerge. Compare two possible assumptions about the former behavior (i.e. heroin use):

1 That it was about finding a quick end to the pain.
  or
2 That it was about finding an end to the pain that's likely to ensure survival, to work.

The former feels more temporary and fleeting than the latter. The former also presents only one option as a method of effective pain relief (i.e. heroin). The latter frames it more as an attempt at survival; clients can focus on learning different survival techniques instead of being restricted to one choice.

As stated earlier, these ideas are about using one's power to control how the memory of someone or something is shaped inside themselves.

Secondary control allows an individual to determine how a memory is going to play out and stick around internally. Clients can move into recovery feeling shameful about past behaviors and memories or they can learn to draw meaning from their past, change the relationship with their former self (think grace and self-forgiveness), and use it to inform their future.

One question to consider is who is likely to have some trouble making these transformations or mental shifts that center on secondary control? Boerner and Heckhausen (2003) and Heckhausen (1999) thought that people who routinely seek out primary control—those who prefer and want to control their circumstances and worlds—may struggle. Some ways of addressing this include the client and counselor looking for ways to increase primary control over their environment. Helping clients to avoid the "futile goals" of changing the past will be the priority for some. Focusing on realistic changes in the present that one has control over is the aim here. Put very simply, look for things that are changeable. For instance, how one copes with pain (emotional and physical), learning how to connect and reconnect with healthy, supportive people, learning or using assertiveness skills, employment status or beefing up a resume through educational or volunteer opportunities, taking parenting classes, attending to health and dental care, mending old relational wounds (or attempting to), etc.

The process of forming a continued connection or a newly constructed representation is often filled with searching other people's memories about who the loved one was in life generally or in more specific contexts. Think of how neat the application to recovery could be here. Clients could talk to people who knew them before and during their addiction; they could also search their own memory banks or look at old photos, journals, diaries, etc. Clients could inquire about how they were perceived before the behaviors began and what is remembered about their pre-addiction self—personality, preferences, dreams or goals they wanted to pursue that perhaps took a sideline when the addiction took over. Likewise, they could search others' memories about how they changed during the addiction and how the perceptions shifted. These perspectives may enlighten clients and two points/discoveries come to mind:

1   That they had changed with the addiction and which were changes most salient to those around them (or to themselves).
2   That they had changed from *something*. That is, they moved away from a version of themselves that was likely healthier by a degree or more and now have a chance to swing the pendulum back in that direction.

Perception is key. In my experience, many of us forget the positives of the past when struggle is in play and even when we try to look back, it's blurred by what's happened in the interim. Searching memories (ours or others) in order to construct a representation of who one was and who one could be somewhat like again, can be powerful. It's one form of hope—that another reality was once true. It also gives power over the memory (this is secondary control)—focusing more on the negatives in the past versus balancing them with the positives or lessons learned. We don't have to ignore the past or forget who we were in order to become someone new.

Valuing the legacy of addiction and the pre-addiction self is worth considering. Attig (2000) noted that a generalized view of who someone was can be the basis of a continuing connection. Finding ways to help clients connect to their pasts that draw out a sense of survival and strength versus shame and doubt is important. Who will they remember their addicted self to be, a victim or a survivor? A bad person, or a good one who was working hard but had few options? A person chained to the past, or someone who has a future? Narratives are powerful. Learning to wield power over our present and pasts (specifically our perceptions of both) is the central focus here.

The Life-Span Theory of Control (Heckhausen and Shulz (1995)) and Boerner and Heckhausen's (2003) interpretation of it stir up some interesting ideas around all of this. Some have been mentioned already but some additional points can be considered. Heckhausen and Shulz, in reference to bereavement, understood the transformation of the relationship with that lost person or relationship as a process of simultaneous deconstruction and construction. People deconstruct representations that rely on that former/lost person's presence (Boerner & Heckhausen). This ties back to the ideas of "futile goals" and disengagement—the letting go of what's no longer possible.

As people repeatedly find that what they want (i.e. the past to come alive again) is not going to happen, frustration and distress result. As a result of such feelings, people begin to deconstruct those representations—to let go of the idea that what once was will be again—and instead move toward realistic ways of maintaining a connection to the past/person/relationship (Boerner & Heckhausen). The feelings of frustration and distress foster change rather than stagnation. This idea that when discomfort becomes big enough people shift and make movement often comes up when change of any kind is being talked about, and that's true for addiction and recovery as well (i.e. rock bottom).

It's also noted that people and relationships don't often lose value after they die or end; many people continue to venerate the lost person and/or relationship (Heckhausen & Shulz; Wortman & Silver, 2001). Bonanno, Papa, Lalande, Zhang, and Noll (2005) later added though that for some people, when the grief becomes untenable, minimization of the person or relationship may occur. Basically, if people find their pain is too big, they tamp down on the significance of that person or relationship, so the impact of the loss seems smaller. This is known as *devaluation* and it's meant to reduce emotional pain.

Devaluation can be one of two things:

1 A complete reevaluation of the lost relationship more generally.
   or
2 A more precise reevaluation focused on certain parts that are no longer available (i.e. in-person contact or the availability or health of something) and then working to fill those gaps.

Consider how some clients will devalue the role the substance, relationship, or behavioral pattern had in their lives in order to minimize how big of a loss it is (i.e. "I didn't need it anyway," "I only used it a few times a day," "I'll be fine. It's fine."). Devaluation is a coping skill in response to the loss of primary control (external control); please recognize it as one that's sometimes rooted in grief and loss. Also recognize that not everyone will cope this way. Some clients will continue to idealize the substance, relationship, or behavioral pattern (i.e. "I need it badly; It was everything to me"; "I miss it so much," "It worked for me like nothing else has").

Boerner and Heckhausen believed that devaluation wasn't as likely if the bond was perceived to be a positive one in life. They thought that devaluation would lead more toward disengagement from connection rather than a balanced transformation of holding on and letting go; if the bond was perceived as more negative in life, devaluation was expected. Basically, we need to know how our clients perceived their addiction or behavioral patterns—were they more helpful or harmful (in their minds, not ours). For clients who tend to devalue the substance, relationship, or behavioral pattern and minimize its impact, take this as a cue that they may be working to disengage more quickly from it. They may be working hard to regain control over their lives by dumping something they saw as taking control away. Help them slow their pace and find balance.

Striking a balance between holding on and letting go is more likely to happen if people *reevaluate* connections rather than devalue them. Looking for the positive and negative points of the connection may be helpful for clients who do not engage in devaluation *and* for those that do—considering how the substance, relationship, or behavioral pattern served them and how it/they perhaps didn't. Reevaluating and reconsidering the impact of the loss and figuring out how to adjust and move forward retaining the more meaningful parts is a goal here.

A reminder that this reevaluation and transformation process may not be feasible for everyone. Most notably, if people live or engage in environments (including counseling!) where sharing or talking about memories isn't welcomed or acceptable, the recall of preexisting representations or the construction of new ones is less likely (Boerner & Heckhausen; Heckhausen & Shulz). The earlier point that people who have a strong preference for primary, or external control might struggle with the transformation or construction of new representations applies here as well. The reason being that mental representations engage secondary (internal) control strategies which acknowledge the loss of primary control. This acknowledgment may be harder for some than others.

Another way of disengaging is known as *substitution*. The idea that someone subs in for another person or relationship to replace what was lost in someone or something else. My mind immediately goes to the idea of substance or behavior-jumping—for example, someone stops using opiates and begins using cocaine or starts working compulsively. Relationship-jumping also happens—one relationship ends, and some people enter into another soon after to fill the holes left by the previous break-up. This behavior pattern might come up most commonly when people are finding it hard to let go of those things that require the physical presence of someone or something else (Heckhausen & Shulz). Gaps are filled or replacements are sought to reduce the discomfort; they're just not sure they can live with the absence.

Consider the application of these concepts to an addictive context; a substance or behavioral pattern could be viewed as a form of substitution. If someone has lost a connection with a person through death, break-up, incarceration, etc. and finds that the holes filled by this person (i.e. companionship, relieving boredom, serving as a person to vent to and discharge emotion, etc.) are now empty, the substance or pattern may sub in to close those gaps and minimize the impact of the loss. Here's another example: someone experiences trauma and has their sense of safety stripped away. Using a substance to either distract from that feeling of fear or to increase comfort when around people can be viewed as substitution—they are using something else to fill in for something they seem to have lost.

Substitution is another attempt to increase primary control—reducing the impact of the loss and finding a way to survive it through control over the environment. Consider also that the substitution might be around the relationship component; I have had several clients in my time describe their substance or pattern (gambling comes to mind most prominently) as a love affair or lover. Substitution might also factor in when someone is working to end use or behavioral patterns. Relationships, other substances, and/or different behaviors might sub in to meet the needs once met by the substance or problematic behavior. In treatment, we often encourage substitution of a healthier behavior in place of the addictive one (ex. when you're bored—journal, when you feel triggered—meditate, when you feel alone—reach out, etc.).

Boerner and Heckhausen (2003) made an important point around substitution: having alternatives that approximate what's been lost is likely to make the adjustment/substitution process smoother. This is somewhat obvious, yet so important. If we try to meet needs through substitution, the thing being substituted has to be close enough to the original to work well. A silly, yet apt example I give in class around this idea involves macaroni and cheese (hang with me—I really do have a point). I love brand name boxed macaroni and cheese—love it. If I am no longer able to buy or eat my preferred brand due to cost, availability, health concerns, others' preferences in my home, etc., substitution is an option. I can try either a different brand of mac and cheese, make it myself at home, or try a healthier alternative of vegan mac and cheese. But here's the crucial piece: if none of these hit the spot and satisfy the craving I'm seeking to satisfy; I'll likely go back to the original or really, really want to. I need to find the closest thing to the original to make the transition away from brand name boxed mac and cheese smoother.

If someone dies and provided emotional support and encouragement to another, that person now has to find someone or something else that meets their emotional needs in most of those same ways for a smoother adjustment. If a person gives up methamphetamine, they need to find someone or something else that meets their emotional needs in most of those same ways for a smoother adjustment.

It boils down to this: if you suggest any coping skills or other behaviors that are meant to take the place of something like meth, or a beloved person, or even macaroni and cheese, they better be good and meet the same needs. This means that we need to know the needs the original thing or person satisfied so we can help identify suitable substitutes. Please remember to explore these areas with your client. Explore the function/purpose of their behaviors, what they were meant to accomplish, and how well they worked.

Also keep in mind that this substitution can occur in real life with an actual person or thing (substitution) and it can also occur in the mind through a mental representation (indirect substitution) (Boerner & Heckhausen, 2003). So, if no close approximation (substitute) in life can be found, indirect substitution may come into play and be quite useful. This idea takes us back in research time. Hobfoll (1989) argued that when direct replacement of resources after loss isn't possible, people will engage in this *indirect substitution*. Basically, it's a plan B.

When people try and fail repeatedly to reengage in a relationship that is no longer possible, one way to continue is to "resurrect the lost person in terms of mentally represented legacy components" (Boerner & Heckhausen, p. 219; Heckhausen & Shulz). Some examples include, "what would this person have done or said?" or "how would they have responded or reacted?" Essentially, one relies on the memory to create a mental representation of the person that *can* remain in their life; their legacy lives on inside the person. This way, one can focus on building and elaborating on those mental representations to continue the connection, rather than futile attempts to reconnect with something now gone. The indirect substitution makes moving forward manageable; one can engage with a legacy even when the person or relationship is lost or no longer present.

Ultimately, substitution can be one of two things:

1 An internal coping mechanism for the lost relationship (i.e. legacy components or reliance on memories) as it allows people to continue meeting needs in the absence of something.
   or
2 A more literal replacement, where a new person or thing takes the place of what was lost.

The former relies more on our internal understandings and memories than on what exists in the world at present. The latter recognizes that some relationships or patterns can be swapped in terms of need fulfillment.

These ideas have implications for someone grieving the loss of an addictive pattern as well. One can still engage with the desires of the "addict" identity and question what they would have done in those times (for better and for worse) and get a sense of old thought and behavioral patterns. Old relationships that were, perhaps, not the healthiest can still be valued for what they were and also recognized as things to let go of. Again, we don't have to ignore the past or forget who we were in order to become someone new.

Reflecting on the legacy of the addiction can yield important information on needs and wants, what works, what doesn't, and areas for growth. When people work to let go of the "addict" identity and look to the legacy of the addiction, they may be able to draw meaning (i.e. "that relationship or pattern was/is not sustainable or healthy for me"), guidance or direction (i.e. "I can find other ways to meet my needs and accept that the loss of this substance or pattern is permanent"), or comfort (i.e. "looking back, I survived and I wasn't all bad, even if the behaviors were").

An emphasis on transformation also came up in Fleming and Robinson's (1991) more cognitive model of bereavement. They saw grief as transitional and the transition from hurting to healing centered on the search for meaning in the experience of loss. Legacy components also factored in. Basically, they believed that maintaining a connection to the lost person's legacy eased the pain and facilitated a smoother grieving process (not unlike more recent theories presented thus far). Something I really like about their approach though are the learning opportunities. They advocated that people question what they had learned from the lost person/object and to explore how that relationship or experience shaped who they are. The lovely bit, in my opinion, is their belief that the legacy of a person or experience is carried *in us*. That the ways we grew or transformed through knowing or engaging with them/it before the loss can be the continuing connection; our present selves which have been shaped by the past—that's the connection. We are living testaments to what has been and why it mattered.

For me, these thought exercises could add tremendous value to sessions for some clients. Exploring what they learned about themselves and their world because of their addiction and behaviors could yield important information about self (i.e. they are capable of surviving more than they believe or give credit for, some people care about them no matter what and others may not, finding they're adaptable, tenacious, brave, and/or fearful and lacking options, etc.). Considering how the experiences of addiction also shaped who they currently are (i.e. want more for themselves than that life, working toward change, increased reflection on the impact behaviors had on the self or on others, grit, hope, etc.) could also be fruitful.

This is about helping our clients embrace that they have been shaped by the past in both positive and negative ways and learning to value their survival and current self as legacy components. Acknowledging and sitting with the idea that their history and experiences mattered and were impactful, presents an opportunity for further growth. If they have been shaped by the past, and can learn from it, they now have more control over their future and how that legacy (i.e. themselves) continues or changes. Again, many of these ideas are echoed in other, more recent theories we've discussed, but that's part of the point. *Learning from the hurt, and growing from the pain, and finding value where there seems only despair.* For me, and many others, those are key elements to recovery and healing. You'll also see these ideas echoed when we explore the connection between addiction, grief, and trauma in a later chapter.

Before moving on, I want to note my appreciation for researchers (Boerner & Heckhausen; Fleming & Robinson; Heckhausen & Shulz; Stroebe & Schut) who acknowledged that adapting to loss and shifting levels of control is really hard. Letting go of something that was important and prominent in your life and trying to construct a new internal way of relating to that person or thing is tough. It's hard and it's also possible.

References

Attig, T. (2000). *The heart of grief: Death and the search for lasting love.* New York: Oxford University Press.

Attig, T. (2001). Relearning the world: Making and finding meanings. In R. A. Neimeyer (Ed.), *Meaning reconstruction and the experience of loss* (pp. 33–53). Washington, DC: American Psychological Association.

Boerner, K., & Heckhausen, J. (2003). To have and have not: Adaptive bereavement by transforming mental ties to the deceased. *Death Studies, 27,* 199–226.

Bonanno, G. A., Papa, A., Lalande, K., Zhang, N., & Noll, J. G. (2005). Grief processing and deliberate grief avoidance: A prospective comparison of bereaved spouses and parents in the United States and the People's Republic of China. *Journal of Consultation in Clinical Psychology, 73,* 86–98.

Bowlby, J. (1980). *Attachment and loss: Vol. 3. Loss: Sadness and depression.* New York: Basic Books.

Fleming, S. J., & Robinson, P. J. (1991). The application of cognitive therapy to the bereaved. In T. M. Vallis, J. L. Howes, & P. C. Miller (Eds.), *The challenge of cognitive therapy: Applications to nontraditional populations* (pp. 135–158). New York: Plenum.

Heckhausen, J. (1999). *Developmental regulation in adulthood: Age-normative and socio-structural constraints as adaptive challenges.* New York: Cambridge University Press.

Heckhausen, J., & Schulz, R. (1995). A life-span theory of control. *Psychological Review, 102,* 284–304.

Hobfoll, S. E. (1989). Conversation of resources: A new attempt at conceptualizing stress. *American Psychologist, 44,* 513–524.

Klass, D. (2001). The inner representation of the dead child in the psychic and social narratives of bereaved parents. In R. A. Neimeyer (Ed.), *Meaning reconstruction & the experience of loss* (p. 77794). Washington, DC: American Psychological Association.

Knox, J. (1999). The relevance of attachment theory to a contemporary Jungian view of the internal world: Internal working models, implicit memory and internal objects. *Journal of Analytical Psychology, 44,* 511–530.

Neimeyer, R. A. (2001). *Meaning reconstruction and the experience of loss.* Washington, DC: American Psychological Association.

Neimeyer, R. A., & Sands, D. C. (2011). Meaning reconstruction in bereavement: From principles to practice. In R. A. Neimeyer, D. L. Harris, & H. R. Winokuer (Eds.), *Grief and bereavement in contemporary society: Bridging research and practice* (pp. 9–22). New York: Routledge.

Wortman, C. B., & Silver, R. C. (2001). The myths of coping with loss revisited. In M. Stroebe, R. O. Hansson, W. Stroebe, & H. Schut (Eds.), *Handbook of bereavement: Consequences, coping, and care* (pp. 405–429). New York: Cambridge University Press.

Wrosch, C., Schulz, R., & Heckhausen, J. (2002). Health stresses and depressive symptomatology in the elderly: The importance of health engagement control strategies. *Health Psychology, 21,* 340–348.

9 Four Tasks of Mourning and Considering the Four Tasks in the Context of Addiction and Recovery

Worden (2009) defined mourning as the adaptation to loss and believed that four tasks were involved. He believed that for someone to regain a sense of equilibrium, the four tasks had to be completed.

Task I: To Accept the Reality of the Loss

This task is about acknowledgment and acceptance. It focuses on coming to terms with what's been lost and sitting with the idea that it won't or cannot return. The world can sometimes give what appear to be glimpses of the lost person or object that can make this trickier than it may seem initially (think of a person who looks like someone now dead or a familiar scent or image that keeps popping up). The randomness of the world, one's hopes, and one's pain can get in the way of accepting that someone or something is gone forever. This task accounts for that and emphasizes the importance of acknowledging and remembering that the loss is permanent. Therefore, denying the occurrence of the loss or the permanence of it would be seen as an indicator this task still needs work (Worden, 1991, 2001, 2009). Denial can come in many forms according to this model, but typically revolves around three areas:

1 *The facts of the loss/ the details of what happened*
   - Can range from minor denial (i.e. laying out clothes each day for someone dead) to delusions about the state of the world (i.e. moving about life as if nothing has truly changed and occupies a different state of reality—for example, "They aren't dead, they're just on vacation! They'll be back soon. I know it.")
2 *The meaning attached to the loss*
   - Individuals might minimize the impact of the loss (i.e. "I'm better off without him/it") or remove items soon after to avoid reminders of the loss. Worden characterizes this latter instance as protection through the absence of things. If there's nothing to look at, perhaps one won't dwell on it, or feel about it, or wish for its return.

- Another variation of this type of denial is termed "selective forgetting" (Worden, 2009, p. 41). Basically, after a loss, people can block all or most memories of someone or something. Over time they can work to regain access to their memories, but it seems to be a play on the earlier form of denial through absence—if there's nothing to remember, perhaps then remembering won't cause pain. It's a means of protection.

3   *The permanence/irreversibility of the loss*

- For some people, the permanence of loss is very scary, sad, lonely, and unbelievable, etc. As a result, some people might reject that reality and work to convince themselves that it really isn't true—that someone or something will return at some point and it was all a misunderstanding somehow. From this model, part of the therapeutic work would be to accept that it is permanent, and a reunion will not happen, even if desired (ex. "Stop telling me they're dead. They'll be back soon, and you'll regret saying that," or "I'll see them in my dreams," or even going to a psychic to make contact with the departed).

  - ★One additional note here. Worden, on page 41 notes that "the chronic hope for such a reunion is not normal." I disagree slightly; I take issue with the word "normal." I would agree that chronic hope for a reunion is not necessarily healthy—meaning it can keep us from the present and detract from current relationships and life. But healthy and normal are not always the same thing. For the sake of clear interpretation and allowing for individual expression of grief, I felt it important to make this note.

Worden emphasized that the completion of the task involved both an intellectual acceptance of the loss as well as an emotional one. He cautioned counselors to be alert and not mistake intellectual acceptance—that is, cognitive recognition of loss—as total acceptance. The emotional processing is equally important, and both are necessary from this perspective/model. Worden also believed that taking part in rituals following a death or loss (funerals or other means) helped to solidify and validate the new reality and advocated for participation in such events.

Task II: To Process the Pain of Grief

This model again emphasizes a complete processing of pain—intellectual, emotional, and literal physical pain when present. The consequence of leaving these areas untouched are physical symptoms (think psychosomatic) or behavioral changes. Parkes's (1972) conclusion that unless people go through and experience the pain of grief, the grief work will remain incomplete, and grief will continue long-term. Worden (2009) leans on this idea as support for the existence of this task. In short, if one suppresses their pain, they won't heal. Varying levels of pain are acknowledged depending on the relationship to what's been lost. Again, we'll explore Worden's mediators of mourning in a bit, but this boils down to two simple points:

1   If there was a deep attachment or connection with what's been lost, pain is expected. The exact level of pain will depend, but it will be present.
2   If there was no attachment or significant connection, pain may not be present. For some people, loss (and death in particular from this perspective) may not induce pain or suffering of any kind. Bonanno (2004) agreed with this and noted that it depended on one's attachment style. More specifically, for individuals characterized as avoidant-dismissing, lack of pain may be the predominant response (see appendix A for a refresher on attachment styles).

The completion of this task can be impaired by the world's response to pain. Worden spoke about subtle messages spurred by the discomfort others feel when in the presence of another's pain. For example, someone responding to one's grief with statements like: "It's time to move on"; "You're thinking too much about it"; "You're feeling sorry for yourself at this point. It is what it is"; "They (deceased) wouldn't want you to be this sad or feel this way. Smile and focus on the positive memories or on what's left"; "You'll have another chance. Don't let this make you lose hope"; "You're young—there's still time to try again." All are likely intended to be helpful, but they typically aren't. The main reason for their ineffectiveness is that they only attend to the giver's discomfort versus the receiver's grief (the bereaved). Such statements dismiss the need to feel the pain and encourage the bereaved to move away from the pain, rather than closer to it. This can translate to emotional and cognitive avoidance (don't feel, don't think about it) and outright denial of pain (Worden).

Avoidance can also be emotion-specific; that is, some people will only focus on the positive memories or elements and ignore the pain-filled ones (i.e. "they're in a better place"). Individuals might not report sadness either. Loneliness, guilt, anger, or others may take center stage. Alcohol, drugs, and/or compulsive behaviors (i.e. shopping, eating, gambling, working, exercising, etc.) may come into play as distractions from the pain or as a means of managing the intensity of it. Others may literally move away from the pain and change their geographic location or place of residence. According to Worden, all forms of avoidance and denial of pain will ultimately result in prolonged grief. The goal of this task is to help people feel this pain so that it doesn't stick around in problematic ways long-term. Worden and Bowlby (1980, 2009 respectively) both agreed that suppressed pain will emerge at some point—typically in some form of depression. A quote from author John Green (2012) seems to sum up task II rather well: "That's the thing about pain" … "It demands to be felt" (p. 63). Task II is meant to encourage, allow, and help that process along.

Task III: To Adjust to the World without the Deceased

Worden asserted that there are three primary areas that need to be attended to in the wake of loss: external adjustments, internal adjustments, and spiritual adjustments. Let's take each separately to understand their proposed impact and course:

External Adjustments

This is largely speaking to practicality and daily life. When we experience a loss, our world can sometimes shift with that loss. External adjustments address how it has shifted—how the loss (he notes death specifically) impacts everyday functioning in the world (Worden, 2009). Depending on the scale of the loss, the impact will vary. For instance, losing a distant relative may require no external adjustments. Losing someone closer to home like a partner or child may require many. I can only imagine what losing my child would mean day-to-day. My entire daily routine would change; it would be far simpler and self-focused. I would not wake anyone else up or prepare breakfast for anyone but me. I would not worry about baths or laundry for him, nor would I rush out the door on busy days to get to daycare on time. Planning our time together after daycare would no longer be needed and I wouldn't need to shop for favorite foods or clothing sizes as he grew. Bedtime in the evenings would be self-paced and lonelier. My consistent, reliable source of giggles and smiles would be gone and my favorite snuggler wouldn't be tiny anymore. My schedule and responsibilities would be lighter, but my heart would be indescribably heavy.

Worden gave another example about the loss of a spouse. The remaining partner might face an empty house, maintenance of that house, financial changes, parenting solo (if children are present), and spending more time alone. External adjustments may take time as it becomes gradually apparent which roles need to be filled. Responsibilities, once shared, may now fall squarely on one person's shoulders. Worden noted two ways to help clients adjust when tackling this type of adjustment. First, redefining the loss so that some positives are seen (i.e. you're capable of handling more than you believed; you had a wonderful love for a period of time). Second, making sense of the loss and finding benefit in it shift the focus toward meaning-making (Worden, 2009). Neimeyer (1999), Neimeyer and Sands (2011), and Attig (1996, 2000, 2001) were also proponents of meaning-making following loss.

Internal Adjustments

While external adjustments center on the impact the loss has had on the practical world of the client, internal adjustments look at the impact the loss has had on the self. Shifting identities may be in play. For example, shifting from spouse to widow/widower, parent to parent of a deceased child, employed to unemployed, "addict" to a person in recovery, married/partnered to single, etc. More than that though, these internal adjustments also reference changes to sense of self: shifts in self-esteem or efficacy, one's self-definition, sense of value or worth, and purpose in life, etc.

If someone defined themselves as a parent and that definition centered on the caretaking of that child, the loss may represent a loss of self or purpose. The child no longer needs caretaking, so who is the parent without that role fulfillment? For a person who has lost a spouse or partner, who will make the decisions around _____ now? He/she/they (lost person) used to do that. For an individual working toward recovery, how will they handle emotions or pain now? Are they capable of living without it (drug or behavioral pattern)? This task would address such questions. In doing so, internal shifts would gradually occur, and a new definition of self would emerge in time.

Attachment style and its impact on one's bereavement process came up in Worden's model as well. Recall the earlier conversations about attachment around the Continuing Bonds Theory and Stroebe, Schut, and Boerner's (2010) belief that attachment style impacted one's grieving process. While the thoughts of Stroebe et al. on attachment are far more elaborate, Worden noted that if someone that the survivor had a secure attachment to is lost, that really matters. In particular, "if the deceased person was making up for serious developmental deficits in the mourner" (Worden, 2009, p. 48).

Consider someone who has a history of terrible, unstable, or abusive relationships. Ultimately though they form a relationship with someone who offers the things they were missing and needing (i.e. stability, kindness, acceptance, love). The healing that the relationship offered would increase the stakes in terms of loss. Put simply, if this secure, reliable, healing figure were to die, it would represent more than the loss of the person—the healing (or chance to heal) might perceptively die too. To help them heal and adjust, both losses would need to be acknowledged, discussed, and transformed. So, ultimately, internal adjustments involve the acknowledgment of and attention to the internal impacts of a loss. Adjusting to the new reality by redefining one's identity is the overarching goal (Worden).

Spiritual Adjustments

This element of adjustment deals with one's perceptions of the world. When there is a significant loss, the sense of the world sometimes changes, and foundational beliefs can suddenly become questionable. Some examples include losing direction, questioning safety, losing the meaning of life, and conclusions about deservingness of life (Worden). The benevolence or goodness of the world, the world making sense and having order to it, and the worthiness of self and others are specifically noted by Worden. He believed that these assumptions could be challenged or changed by loss and that those shifts in beliefs were significant. Some questions/statements reflective of this type of adjustment might sound something like:

"Why them? They didn't deserve to die."
"Why would God allow this to happen?"
"My home was supposed to be a place of safety."
"I live in a good area; things like this aren't supposed to happen here."
"Is there really a God if he/she/they let this happen?"
"Is anyone safe? Am I safe?"
"What's left for me now?"

All of these questions reflect a search for meaning. People that voice concerns like this are searching actively for answers (Worden). Part of counseling is helping them find answers that help them move to a different place in their grief and find a greater sense of control. Sometimes, there truly is no answer and the aim then shifts to helping clients learn to live without one and relinquishing control altogether.

To sum up task III, let's consider how we might know if someone is failing to meet it. Worden believed that people were stagnant or failing to meet task III when they promoted their own helplessness, failed to develop new coping skills or rely on old ones, withdrew from the world, and failed to meet their responsibilities day-to-day. On the other hand, he also believed that most people find ways to adapt to these areas (eventually) and progress toward a different outcome. The overall goals include acknowledgment of changed circumstances (external adjustments), new understandings and identity elements (internal adjustments), and a new or renewed sense of the world (spiritual adjustments) (Bowlby, 1980; Worden, 2009).

Task IV: To Find an Enduring Connection with the Deceased in the Midst of Embarking on a New Life

Over time Worden has evolved his thinking on task IV. In the previous two editions of his book (1991, 2001), he promoted the idea that it was necessary to detach from the dead in order to reinvest one's energy into other relationships. Currently, he aligns more with the Continuing Bonds Theory (Klass et al., 1996). If you recall, the main point of that approach is to find ways to maintain a connection after death/loss rather than let go and move on. The bond is meant to facilitate a continuing relationship/remembering and promote continued growth in the person. Worden agreed that helping clients to form a continuing bond was useful and healthy. He advocated for memorializing what's been lost and relocating that loss into one's life (Attig, 1996, 2001; Field, Gal-Oz, & Bonanno, 2003).

Remember that the concept of relocation is all about fitting the memories into life; a life that continues to be lived in the presence of the memories. In sum, grief + memories + other things (i.e. work, hobbies, relationships, sleep, etc.) = relocation. If a client is in this place, it might sound something like:

> I'll always love him and miss him. I'll never forget. But I'll also keep moving forward and living my life. I can be happy and hang onto the memories at the same time.

For someone struggling with the completion of task IV, they might sound something like:

> I can't let go. I still love him and can't go on without him. I don't know how, and I'm scared I might never figure it out. How do you keep living when your life seems lonely?

The former individual has recognized that the memories can coexist with other things. The latter individual is still stuck and fully immersed in their pain; they aren't able to see outside of it yet. Working with this latter person on task IV would center on finding ways to retain the connection to the love and memories.

Exploring options of memorialization (i.e. pictures, familiar items, talking to them, etc.) so that the lost person still has presence in the survivor's life would be helpful. Additionally, helping the client to search for meaning in the continued connection that promotes living rather than stagnation. Life must continue in the absence, otherwise the death would have killed them both. Worden noted that task IV is hard and deservingly so; completing this task will take time and attention.

Wrapping up these four tasks of mourning, there's one final note. Worden stated that when approaching grief and mourning through his four tasks, providers should retain a flexible viewpoint. Tasks are not fixed stages and can be partially completed, left and revisited, and be worked on simultaneously. Grief is a dynamic ongoing process that is not fixed. As previously mentioned, several factors are believed to influence the intensity and process of mourning. In the next chapter, the *mediators of mourning* will be explored in more depth.

Considering *the Four Tasks* in the Context of Recovery

If we consider the four tasks through the lens of addiction and recovery, several things come to mind. Let's start at the top.

Task I: To Accept the Reality of the Loss

Coming to terms with what's been lost and sitting with the idea that some things won't or cannot return is central to this first task. For instance, a substance or maladaptive behavior pattern may no longer be compatible with life. For health to enter and be sustained in someone's life, some things will need to be edited out and remain absent permanently. In other cases, it really is about recovery, about finding something again and reclaiming it. I think of the more abstract losses like loss of self-respect, self-compassion, and identity here. The addiction has spurred the loss of such things in many cases and for some the first step is to acknowledge that they have been shaped internally by their external behaviors.

Also recall that this task is about acknowledgment and acceptance that a loss has occurred. This feels somewhat reminiscent of the first step in Alcoholics Anonymous (AA, 2019): "We admitted we were powerless over alcohol—that our lives had become unmanageable" (p. 1). Narcotics Anonymous (NA, 2019) has a similar first step: "We admitted that we were powerless over our addiction, that our lives had become unmanageable" (p. 1). Taken together, the main idea is to acknowledge and accept that something has changed as a result of one's addiction, and that change has been significantly impacting one's life.

Whether or not you ascribe to AA or NA, the idea that in order to help someone heal, we must first define what they're trying to heal from, is valid. Helping someone to define and accept the losses around addiction is a useful starting point; you can consider it a loss-inventory of sorts. Earlier in the chapter, I wrote about Beecham et al.'s (1996) loss-grief inventory that categorizes losses as, pre-addiction losses, losses associated with addiction, and losses associated with entering treatment. There was also a section that allowed for "other losses" to account for any they missed. Measures like the loss-grief inventory might be useful in helping clients to consider all the losses that have occurred around their addiction—literally building a list that can be later processed in counseling (or on one's own) loss by loss.

I would also advocate for a conversation, rather than a pencil-paper type assessment, to determine the impact of one's addiction and the losses it's connected to. Talk to clients about their primary losses and consider the blast radius of those losses (i.e. secondary losses). Was their addiction (in their view) in response to a loss(es) as a means of coping? If so, how are they feeling about losing their primary coping skills? That'd be a hard reality to accept for many of us—that what we do to help ourselves can no longer be the way we cope. Conversely, did the addiction (in their view) seemingly cause the losses? If so, regret, guilt, and/or shame may be present. The idea that any one of those feeling states would prompt someone to deny, hesitate, or ignore the reality of their situation makes sense. Explore the process of accepting a reality that likely sucks. Don't simply ask for a simple acknowledgment that the addiction is no longer tenable (or worse, mandate it). Dive into the process of acceptance and what's being internalized as "reality."

As Worden noted with death-related grief, the randomness of the world, one's hopes, and one's pain can get in the way of accepting a loss. One signal that this task needs more time, attention, reflection, and processing is when clients struggle to accept that their addiction has resulted in significant losses (for them or others), or that the loss of the addiction itself is now prudent for survival. Some might label that as "denial." I would instead advocate for labeling that "hesitancy." People are often hesitant to accept things they don't want to be true. Worden agreed. One detail I disagree with Worden on is the emphasis on denial. The four types he noted within task I included:

1   The facts of the loss/ the details of what happened
    • Some clients may dispute that a problem with use or behaviors exists. Others may question how bad their problem really is and wonder why others are so worked up or concerned. And some clients may be adamant that no one but themselves were hurt by their behavior. Others may provide compelling evidence that another reality is true. Be cautious around labeling here. Trying to convince someone that they are in denial about the hurts they've caused will produce defensiveness (and justifiably so). Most people in the world don't want to admit that they have hurt others, sometimes deeply—it's a psychological threat to one's self-concept. Tread lightly here and consider what you or someone else might be asking the client to accept or acknowledge: that their behaviors have injured others even when they have not intended them to, that sometimes people question their intent or believe they don't care about anyone else (i.e. "addicts are selfish"), and that in order to heal those hurts, huge change is required. Gently navigate these conversations and help people realize that they can be good people with behavioral patterns that cause pain. Bad behavior doesn't equal a bad person.
2   The meaning attached to the loss
    • Client's might minimize the impact of the loss of their addiction or start of recovery (i.e. "I'm better off without heroin anyway; I'll be fine!" or "I can do this on my own; I don't even think it'll be that hard.") or remove items soon after to avoid reminders of what used to be alive in one's life (i.e. cleaning house and removing any reminders or addiction-associated items or people). Worden characterized this latter instance as protection through the absence of things. If there's not something to look at, perhaps one won't dwell on it or feel about it or wish for it to return. This protective strategy might be useful for some as long as there is still

the intellectual and emotional acceptance that a loss has occurred. The comparison point would be someone ridding their life of all signs that they had a history and moving forward pretending that the time of life, pain, or pattern never existed. As noted earlier, a simple verbal acknowledgment that something is now over or gone is not enough to satisfy task I. A cognitive *and* emotional acceptance is what's needed to begin healing (Worden).

- Recall that another variation of this type of denial is termed "selective forgetting" (Worden, 2009, p. 41). After a loss, people can block all or most memories of someone or something. It's a means of protection (Worden). This brings trauma to my mind. In the next chapter, we'll explore the connections between trauma and addiction more fully but start thinking about this now. Is it "selective forgetting" or the suppression of traumatic memory? That answer will depend on the client, circumstances, and more, but it's worth considering. As Worden asserted, over time people can work to regain access to their memories, and I would agree. However, if it's trauma that's behind the memory loss or cloudiness, a different course of treatment will be recommended. If it truly is a play on the earlier form of denial through absence (i.e. if there's nothing to remember, perhaps then remembering won't cause pain), discussions around the protective nature of forgetting and processing the meaning of the loss may be appropriate and adequate.

3   The permanence/irreversibility of the loss
- For some people, the permanence of loss is very scary, sad, lonely, and unbelievable, etc. As a result, some people might reject that reality and work to convince themselves that it really isn't true— in this context, this might lead to beliefs that they can learn to moderate and control their use/behavior (i.e. "I'll only drink socially."; "I'll just use once and that's it."; "I can control it now and I can choose to do it or choose not to."). Focus your efforts on helping clients to begin defining their life in other ways, rather than with addictive behaviors as central components or coping skills. Work to find what makes them who they are: what they value, enjoy, believe in, their resilience (healthy coping skills are often found here), and their challenges. Begin to construct a self-image that does not depend on the presence of a substance or addictive behavioral pattern. Essentially, make the permanence of the loss less scary.
- My disagreement with Worden's idea that chronic hope for a reunion isn't "normal" still stands here. From this model, part of the therapeutic work is to accept that the loss is permanent, and a reunion will not happen, even if desired. But it's okay if it IS desired. Completely letting go of something and setting a rock-solid

expectation that it will never be missed or longed for is not realistic in my opinion. Discuss what they will miss about the addiction **and** what they will gain in its absence. While hyper focusing on what's missed can detract from the present, a balanced remembering of the "good"/functional parts of an addiction along with the "bad"/painful parts can be useful in helping people grieve.

I have one final recommendation for task I. Consider avoiding labels that also assign blame (I would argue that "denial" does). I believe that the vast majority of clients are not truly in denial, they just don't agree with another's assessment of what's real for them. When processing through task I areas, consider responding with curiosity about their hesitations instead:

> "What's scary about considering the loss that's come with use/behaviors?"
> "What does it feel like knowing you might never be able to rely on these patterns again?"
> "How capable do you believe you are in the absence of all this? (i.e. addiction, substance, behaviors, etc.)"
> "Help me understand your hesitation to accept that maybe this part of your life needs to end now."
> "How confident are you that this loss (i.e. leaving addictive behaviors behind) is permanent? Do you worry about lapse or relapse? How much? Let's talk about it. Fear can be a powerful motivator of what some call 'denial'. I think you're hesitating to accept that this needs to go for reasons that matter. Tell me about them. What makes it hard to let go?"
> "What's it like having to accept or at least acknowledge a reality you don't want to be true? That's got to be something.... hard, annoying, sad … something."

Worden's cautionary statement that counselors must not mistake intellectual acceptance—that is, cognitive recognition of loss—as total acceptance is quite apt in the addiction's context. For the sake of efficacy (or other reasons altogether) providers sometimes get the verbal recognition from clients that something needs to be changed or lost with regard to addictive behaviors and then move on. Don't shortchange yourself or your clients on these deeper conversations around meaning and true (emotional + cognitive) acceptance.

Finally, Worden's idea that rituals can help solidify the permanence of a loss can also apply to addictions work. I recall a former graduate student's story of walking outside her facility with her client and sifting through rocks next to a creek. The client selected two rocks and talked about what they wanted to leave behind at the treatment center upon discharge (the past represented by one rock) and what they wanted to take with them (represented by the other). Following the conversation, the client threw the "past" rock in the creek and put the "keep" rock in her pocket. She stated that she was glad to know that when she was ready to invite the past back into her life more fully, she knew where to find it. The ritual helped her separate her life into metaphorical segments and she felt a greater sense of control over her past and its intrusion on the present.

Task II: To Process the Pain of Grief

The main bits of this task include the processing of pain and allowing for grief after someone or something important has been lost. The loss of an addictive pattern or substance certainly qualifies as significant. Worden believed that if people suppressed or ignored their pain, they wouldn't heal and would remain stuck. Remember Worden's two ideas around the level of connection/attachment? It's ok if you don't—there's been a lot of info coming at you! Here's a recap: if there was a deep sense of connection or attachment, pain is expected. If there was no attachment or significant attachment, pain may not be present, and people may adjust more readily than anticipated. For some people, walking away from an addiction and all it entailed cognitively, emotionally, physiologically, and behaviorally will be tremendously difficult and pain-filled. For others, it may feel or appear easier and come with less suffering.

The first point here is that we want to be open to the client's experience and interpretation of their change process. For some people, their lives will have coalesced around the addiction/patterns, meaning life has become small and the addiction takes up most of it. Some clients become consumed by their patterns and the idea of extricating themselves from that life feels impossible in some ways. Consider the time, energy, financial resources, emotional resources, friendships, or other relationships, etc. that go into sustaining many addictions. If there's a big investment, there's the potential for a big loss as well. In losing the pattern or substance, one will also lose their routine, their source of energy or pain relief, source of coping, joy, or distraction (among other things) and any relationships connected to this pattern will likely change in significant ways.

In task I, the goal is to help clients to acknowledge and accept that losses have occurred. Here in task II, it's more about helping them realize the impact of those losses and inviting the resulting emotions in, whatever they may be. I think of this task as the beginning of new coping skills—instead of deflecting, ignoring, minimizing, or outright rejecting emotions, we help clients to welcome them. Encourage clients to invite them in to be talked about and as the counselor, validate them. Also, help the client to validate what they feel and their reasons for feeling whatever they do. Process the meaning behind the losses and their personal reactions/feelings. Feelings might be centered on pain around loss, but as Worden noted, they might also be centered on other things like relief, joy at the loss, excitement for the future, regret, hopelessness, fear, anger, loneliness, loss of control/power, guilt, shame, etc. Be open to whatever the client feels.

Another important aspect to consider in the addictive context is Worden's note that the world (aka people) can interfere with the client's ability to process their loss-related emotions. With regard to death, he talked about how the world can push people to move on sooner than they are ready for. This can sound like:

> "It's time to move on."
> "It's been a year. You have to stop living in the past."
> "You're overthinking this."
> "You're making this harder on yourself than you need to."
> "You're just feeling sorry for yourself at this point."

It's obvious (I hope!) that the stigma around addiction and people working toward recovery is pervasive. *Consider how the world sometimes gets in the way of recovery by pushing people toward it.* Here are some examples of messages I've heard personally, or that clients have reported to me. Keep in mind, these mostly came from trusted sources (i.e. former counselors) or loved ones:

> "You've destroyed your life and you have no one to blame but your-
> self. Stop blaming the world and do better."
> "You can do this. Don't look back, just look forward. You can do
> this."
> "You're capable of so much more."
> "Recovery is your only option at this point."
> "If you go back to that life, I'm leaving."
> "This has to happen. I can't keep watching you decline."
> "Why don't you want to help yourself? Are you happy?"
> "Stop playing the victim. You did this to yourself."

I know full well that damage to others can result from someone's addiction and I don't want to minimize that pain. And yet consider how any one of these statements might land. While they are likely intended to motivate, encourage, or mandate someone to enter recovery, they will likely induce shame, guilt, anger, sadness, and fear for many people. They might keep someone from recovery rather than get them closer to it. Most of these examples, at their face, ignore the pain that comes with leaving the addiction or patterns behind and focus instead on what must or will come next.

When thinking about death-related grief, Worden believed that these types of statements translated to emotional and cognitive avoidance (don't feel, don't think about it) and outright denial of pain. In addition to avoidance and dismissal of emotions, he noted that some people will distract from their pain. One distraction in particular is especially salient here—alcohol, drugs, and/or compulsive behaviors. These ideas fit within the addictive context as well and his cautionary statement is valid. Some efforts at support and encouragement, like the ones listed above, could steer clients back toward use and prolong the unhealth they were intending to reduce. So, what to do and what to say instead? Here are some alternate options that might land differently and help toward the completion of task II:

> "I know you're trying, and I know there's things that are keeping you where you are. Let's talk about them."
> "Talk to me about your life. Are you happy?"
> "Tell me about what you're missing. What do you wish you had more of? Do you think it's possible to actually find it any other way (aside from the addictive pattern or use)?"
> "You deserve a life that is easier to live. I know letting go, even the idea of it, might be scary, feel unrealistic, or seem out of reach. I want to help if I can."
> "Let's talk about all the things and people you'd be leaving behind if you gave recovery a shot."
> "What are you scared to lose?" or "What do you want to hang on to?"
> "What's it been like to walk away from _____?"
> "What do you miss?"
> "What are you sad about no longer having? How big does the sad get?"

These are aimed at exploration and discussion of the pain, loss, and other associated feelings. They consider the client's perspective rather than mandating what they should focus on or feel. As a counselor/helper, *pay attention to your message, not just your intent.* They both have to align in order to help someone process their pain/emotions. If they don't, you'll send messages you don't intend to, and clients will takeaway something you probably don't want them to (i.e. a sense of shame vs. a sense of support). Remember, the goal of task II is to help people feel their emotions, so they don't stick around in problematic ways long-term. Keep your eye on the ultimate goal—long-term, sustained recovery. And remember, that you can't shame someone into health.

Task III: To Adjust to the World without the Deceased

Task III can be taken as a stand-alone if you find that you don't prefer Worden's model overall. Adjusting to the world without a substance or addictive pattern is relevant to recovery and will take up the bulk of the treatment conversations. In short, when it comes to addiction and recovery, task III conversations are worth your (and your clients') time.

Let's start by considering the *external adjustments* related to ending an addiction. Practically, when an addictive pattern is changed or stopped, a lot could change. Again, one's daily routine could be entirely different. Consider a former client who was considering an attempt at ending heroin use. Here's the gist of what she said:

> I plan my day around my use. I go to sleep knowing that when I wake up, I'll be ok. I typically have my morning dose already—I keep it in my bedside table. I wake up, cook it, use (inject it), then have my coffee and make breakfast. It's my wake-up routine and it's been that way for about 2 years now. It's not even exciting anymore, it's just habit. Getting out of the automatic nature of that is going to be tough because there's not even much thought that goes into it anymore. It's just what I do. That's my stability. Knowing I won't be sick and just integrating that guarantee into my morning. I have a mid-morning or lunch routine that is pretty similar. I prepare my food and I prepare my syringe. Most breaks and mealtimes have that component to it, so it'll be weird when they don't.

External adjustments which are reflected here include the change to routine, particularly the automatic nature of it (i.e. "It's just what I do."). Mealtimes and breaks would adjust and take on a different structure and preparation; keep in mind her "guarantee" of avoiding withdrawal was dependent on those structures. Her thought patterns around her days and what they entailed would shift, and she'd have more money and time on her hands if she did stop using.

As with death-related loss, providers can work to redefine the loss to highlight some positives. For example, pointing out the financial and time gains to the client would highlight potential benefits of the routine. Working to alter the automatic nature of her behaviors might result in more mindful interactions more broadly and more engagement with the little things in life; essentially, she might gain more insight into her habits and herself through the change process.

Also note that she was capable of not only establishing a set routine but maintaining it for two years. If that doesn't scream hope, I don't know what does. She's proven herself capable of sustained behaviors—recovery would swap out the behavior, yes, but the structure and ability to consistently do something is within her grasp. In short, she's not starting from scratch. Additionally, if her primary motivation for the heroin-related aspect of her routine was avoidance of withdrawal, there are medical options for managing symptoms that might be problematic during the transition off heroin (e.g. suboxone). Her routine would change, but she wouldn't necessarily be punished for it physically via withdrawal. Moreover, external adjustments are a definite consideration when working with someone attempting or thinking about recovery.

The *internal adjustments* related to an attempt or consideration of recovery might be numerous; it really depends on the client. Recall that this type of adjustment relates to the impact of the loss on the self. Adjusting to the new reality (in this case cessation of use or recovery) by redefining one's identity is the overarching goal here. Discussions could center on shifting identities, levels of self-esteem or efficacy, hope, one's self-concept, locus of control, sense of value or worth, purpose in life, etc.

Engaging clients in conversations around the addiction's influence on their self-definition/self-concept and overall identity will be useful. Some questions/invitations that reflect this intent include:

> "When you think about who you are as someone with an addiction, what images or labels come to mind?"
>
> "How worthy do you feel as a person?"
>
> "Do you think you deserve a different way of life?"
>
> "Do you think you're capable of living another way?"
>
> "How do you think about yourself or what do you say to yourself when you're alone?"
>
> "Do you define yourself as an 'addict' or as a person with an addiction? I'm wondering if you believe that in order to change, you have to become an entirely different person vs. change the parts connected to the addiction but keep the core of who you are."
>
> "Who are you without _____ (substance or behavior)?"
>
> "Tell me about yourself before the addiction really took hold and compare it to who you are now."
>
> "Do you have hope that you can keep the good parts of yourself and remove or change the bad patterns and/or behaviors you've got going on? What gives you that hope? How much of it [hope] comes from inside yourself vs. how much of it relies on the input of others?"
>
> "How much of yourself have you lost to your addiction?"
>
> "Describe the person you see yourself becoming once you figure out recovery. How's that person compare to when addiction is present? What's similar? What's different?"
>
> "How much does your past define you? How much power does it have in your life? What needs to happen to shift that balance of power?"

Thinking about exploring levels of self-esteem and self-efficacy specifically, questions/ invitations reflecting that intent include:

> "How much do you rely on your substance or pattern to help you manage your insides?"

> "How capable of coping with life do you feel when it's absent?"
>
> "Talk to me about the things you like about yourself."
>
> "Tell me what you value about who you are (with the addiction). Talk to me about your goodness."
>
> "Do you think you can get by without _____ (substance or behavior)? If so, tell me what skills or characteristics you have that you'll lean on in its absence. If not, talk to me about what you think you're missing that _____ (substance or behavior) provides."
>
> "How successful do you think you can be on our own, without the addiction?"
>
> "How much faith do you have in your ability to meet your goals?"
>
> "How much faith do you have in yourself?"

Please note that these examples are not exhaustive and are meant to get you thinking about how to literally start these conversations with clients. Worden believed that exploring and understanding the internal adjustments would gradually lead to greater insight and ultimately a new definition of self. That's a worthy goal for clients working toward recovery as well.

Finally, Worden noted that the impact of a loss might be greater if someone (or something in the addictive context) is lost that the survivor relied on to make up for developmental deficits such as abuse, lack of self-concept, low self-esteem, etc. For some clients, the substance or pattern will represent an attempt at coping with past hurts. Please don't underestimate what we're asking of clients when recovery is on the table. It's not simply the absence of a substance or pattern; sometimes it's the renewed presence of something (i.e. fear, insecurity, inadequacy, feeling out of control, pain, etc.). Internally adjusting to those elements—learning to survive and even thrive in their presence—will be important for recovery efforts and overall mental well-being.

Spiritual adjustments will focus on one's perceptions of the world; remember that this is much broader than religion it's how people make sense of the world; sometimes an event or series of them (i.e. addiction) can shake one's foundational beliefs. I have encountered clients who have tried to enter recovery, struggled, and then questioned their faith due to the perceived lack of support/redemption (in those cases, a faith rooted in religion). Other clients have struggled with the judgment of others. For example, someone once said to a client, "If you die, you'll have earned that. I don't even think I'll be sad since I've cried all my tears for you. I have none left." To make matters worse, it was the brother of my client who said that to him. That statement and the perceived derision in his brother's voice when he said it spurred questions of whether or not the world would be better off without him [client], if he deserved to live, and ultimately his overall sense of connection and meaning in the world.

Ultimately, Worden believed spiritual adjustments boiled down to meaning-making. Clients struggling with questions of worthiness, such as whether they are a burden or not, if they actively contribute or detract from the world, if they belong, are deserving of another chance etc. are trying to adjust spiritually to the death of their former self/life/addiction. As with death-related grief, part of counseling is helping them find answers that help them move to a different place in their grief. Sometimes, that shift results from finding answers to such questions. Other times, it's about learning to live without an answer or creating an answer that will satisfy the internal world of the client, even if the rest of the world still disagrees. For the client mentioned above, he ultimately cut ties with his brother and created a new definition of family that no longer relied on his brother's presence or love. Essentially, he redefined a meaningful world as one that included "family by choice" rather than "family by blood."

Examples of questions/invitations that reflect an exploration of spiritual adjustments include:

> "How has your addiction changed the way you see yourself in the world?"
> "Have your experiences changed the amount of hope you have?"
> "Do you tend to believe that the world is a safe place? Is it safe for you?"
> "How has your faith supported you during all of this (for clients who ascribe to a faith)?"
> "Do you see the world any differently now? Do you want to?"
> "Think about how you've been treated by others through your addiction (for better and for worse). Have any of those experiences influenced how you view people?"

Before we move on to task IV, recall that the overall goals of task III include acknowledgment of changed circumstances (external adjustments), new understandings and identity elements (internal adjustments), and a new or renewed sense of the world (spiritual adjustments). Worden believed that struggles with task III (any bit of it) were evidenced by stagnation, continued helplessness, repeated failure to develop or use new coping skills, reliance on old means of coping, social withdrawal, and failure to meet daily responsibilities. *Evidence in these areas does not equal failure, only struggle.* That means that as counselors, we need to readjust ourselves and refocus our energy to helping clients sort out and make these adjustments. That is our job. It's never our job to punish or shame someone for lack of progress. Worden held out hope that over time, people could find a way to adapt to loss and progress toward a new outcome and way of being. I would ask that you also hold out hope for your clients. Help them sort these adjustments out and keep sorting until they make headway.

Task IV: To Find an Enduring Connection in the Midst of Embarking on a New Life

As I noted earlier in the chapter, Worden's thinking has evolved over time to align with more recent understandings of grief and the need and/or ability to maintain an ongoing connection with something that's been lost. The old way of thinking promotes the idea that one must detach from what's been lost to reinvest in new relationships. The more recent understandings and models tell us that it can be important to maintain connections to the past and draw meaning from their ongoing presence in our lives.

Unfortunately, in relation to addiction and recovery, it seems that some people and systems remain rooted in the past. I'm talking about opinions, some treatment philosophies, and every now and again treatment providers who encourage clients to 'let go' of their addictive patterns (behavioral, emotional, and cognitions) and to leave them in the past. The unfortunate nature of that, in my opinion, is that when we relegate something to the past, we can lose sight of its impact on the present; we can lose the value those experiences brought and *still* bring. One main impetus of writing this book is this idea—that the world often shoves people toward recovery without full consideration or integration of their pasts. As noted, the intent of a continuing bond (Klass et al., 1996) is to facilitate a continuing relationship or remembering of a relationship or time in one's life in order to help that person grow. Think of the implications for recovery there; there are many and they are exciting!

Let's consider that idea of relocation again in this context. Remember that the concept of relocation is all about fitting the memories into life; a life that continues to be lived in the presence of those memories. So, in this case the equation would look like: grief + memories of an addiction (any component) + other things (i.e. work, sobriety, new relationships, renewed relationships, focus on physical and mental health, hobbies, relationships, sleep, etc.) = relocation.

Statements that might reflect relocation of an addiction/patterns or components of either may sound like:

> "I might always want to go back [to using]. It was a time that was challenging, but familiar and that can be tempting. *But* looking at my life now, I have so much more than just challenges. I have people, and some who I believe care—not all, but some. I am more checked in to the world and I care about some other people too. I have a job again and money and I feel pride for that. That's new, but I'm getting used to not hating myself. Life is coming back."
>
> "I do my best to forget what life was like then, but I'm not so sure that's always a good thing. Remembering keeps me on my toes and reminds me how far I've come and how far I'd fall if I went

back that direction. I need to appreciate what I had and how I survived, but I also need to learn and use new ways of surviving. Sometimes looking back helps me move forward."

"Not all of it was bad. A lot was, but not all of it. I want to find the good parts and keep them. It's not as scary to do something new when you don't have to start from total scratch. My addiction nearly killed me a few times. But figuring out how I survived and some of the qualities I have that can help me now [in recovery] is important for me. I was ready to throw myself away and now it's more of a salvage mission."

"The past hurts, but it's not a bad hurt all the time. When I get to see my granddaughter and think of how much time I lost with her, that kind of hurt feels good. Does that make sense? It's like a smack in the head telling me to look around and see where I am now."

On the other hand, for someone struggling with relocation (and the completion of task IV), statements might sound something like:

"I can't let go [of substance/patterns] just yet. I don't know any other way to live and until I figure that out, why would I walk away. It's scary."

"Who am I if I'm not a junkie?"

"The past doesn't exactly feel like it's in the past yet. It's like it's staring me right in the face."

"It seems like the only people who every gave two sh*ts about me were my using buddies. They cared if I lived or died. That might sound pathetic, but it's true. I haven't found that kind of loyalty in anyone else yet. So, what would it mean about me if I just dumped them?"

"I'm not sure of what's next and I'm not a fan of that much uncertainty. I know how to live with heroin. What if I don't know how to live without it?"

"I miss knowing that the pain could go away. I miss that guarantee."

"I remember feeling powerful and like people respected me because of how much I knew [about injection use]. Now I just feel like a nobody."

Notice that the statements reflecting relocation note a present life, not just a past addiction. The memories coexist with other things and reflect a new understanding. The statements reflecting difficulty with relocation are filled with unanswered questions, uncertainty, fear, and pain/longing. The former set of statements reflects more progress in recovery, the latter reflects an earlier stage.

Strategies to help clients relocate their loss, as discussed earlier in the chapter, have their place here too. Exploring options for the memorialization of one's past can be helpful reminders of where one has been, so they don't return. Holding onto pictures of the "using" self, keeping and occasionally reading journals reflecting challenges and bright spots from the past, holding a metaphorical or real funeral for the "using" self or writing an obituary for the "addict," reminiscing with loved ones who are supportive of recovery about the old version of someone or old behaviors; be sure to note the strengths and weaknesses reflected in that version of the self.

Counselors can also help the client and/or families search for meaning in the continued connection to the past. Sometimes it seems that people think that the past will haunt us if we keep it around. But what if we invite it in? Interact with it rather than pretend it isn't there. Find a connection to the past that promotes life in the present and the future. As the saying goes, "Those who cannot remember the past are condemned to repeat it" (Santayana, Wokeck, Coleman, & Gouinlock, 2011, p. 1). Invite memories in and give them a place at the table. Acknowledge them and find meaning. Help the client to define and determine how much space to give them and which are worth holding on to and remembering and which are worth letting go of.

Finally, remember that sobriety doesn't equal recovery; that's just one piece of the bigger puzzle. Please refer to the full definition of recovery in chapter two which encompasses the ten principles of recovery if you need a refresher.

References

Alcoholics Anonymous. (2019). *The twelve steps of alcoholics anonymous.* Retrieved on March 19, 2019 from https://www.aa.org/assets/en_US/smf-121_en.pdf

Attig, T. (1996). *How we grieve: Relearning the world.* New York: Oxford University Press.

Attig, T. (2000). *The heart of grief: Death and the search for lasting love.* New York: Oxford University Press.

Attig, T. (2001). Relearning the world: Making and finding meanings. In R. A. Neimeyer (Ed.), *Meaning reconstruction and the experience of loss* (pp. 33–53). Washington, DC: American Psychological Association.

Beechem, M. H., Prewitt, J., & Scholar, J. (1996). Loss-grief addiction model. *Journal of Drug Education, 26*(2), 183–198.

Boerner, K., & Heckhausen, J. (2003). To have and have not: Adaptive bereavement by transforming mental ties to the deceased. *Death Studies, 27,* 199–226.

Bonanno, G. A. (2004). Loss, trauma, and human resilience. *American Psychologist, 59,* 20–28.

Bowlby, J. (1980). *Attachment and loss: Vol. 3. Loss: Sadness and depression.* New York, NY: Basic Books.

Field, N. P., Gal-Oz, E., & Bonanno, G. A. (2003). Continuing bonds and adjustment at 5 years after the death of a spouse. *Journal of Consulting & Clinical Psychology, 71,* 110–117.

Green, J. (2012). *The fault in our stars.* New York, NY: Penguin Group.

Klass, D., Silverman, P. R., & Nickman, S. L. (Eds.). (1996). *Continuing bonds: New understandings of grief.* Washington, DC: Taylor & Francis.

Koehler, K. (2010). Sibling bereavement in childhood. In C. A. Corr & D. E. Balk (Eds.), *Children's encounters with death, bereavement, and coping* (pp. 195–218). New York, NY: Springer.

Narcotics Anonymous. (2019). *How it works.* Retrieved on March 19, 2019 from https://na.org/admin/include/spaw2/uploads/pdf/litfiles/us_english/misc/ How%20it%20 Works.pdf

Neimeyer, R. A. (1999). Narrative strategies in grief therapy. *Journal of Constructive Psychology, 12,* 65–85.

Neimeyer, R. A. (2001). *Meaning reconstruction and the experience of loss.* Washington, DC: American Psychological Association.

Neimeyer, R. A., & Sands, D. C. (2011). Meaning reconstruction in bereavement: From principles to practice. In R. A. Neimeyer, D. L. Harris, & H. R. Winokuer (Eds.), *Grief and bereavement in contemporary society: Bridging research and practice* (pp. 9–22). New York: Routledge.

Parkes, C. M. (1972). *Bereavement: Studies of grief in adult life.* California: International Universities Press.

Santayana, G., Wokeck, M. S., Coleman, M. A., & Gouinlock, J. (2011). *The life of reason, or, the phases of human progress* (Critical ed., The Works of George Santayana; Volume 2, Book 1). Cambridge, MA: The MIT Press.

Stroebe, M. S., Schut, H., & Boerner, K. (2010). Continuing bonds in adaptation to bereavement: Toward theoretical integration. *Clinical Psychology Review, 30,* 259–268.

Winnicott, D. (1953). Transitional objects and transitional phenomena. *International Journal of Psychoanalysis, 34,* 89–97.

Worden, J. W. (1991). *Grief counseling and grief therapy: A handbook for the mental health practitioner* (2nd ed.). New York, NY: Springer.

Worden, J. W. (2001). *Grief counseling and grief therapy: A handbook for the mental health practitioner* (3rd ed.). New York, NY: Springer.

Worden, J. W. (2009). *Grief counseling and grief therapy: A handbook for the mental health practitioner* (4th ed.). New York, NY: Springer.

10 Mediators of Mourning and Considering the Mediators of Mourning in the Context of Addiction and Recovery

Mediators of Mourning

As noted already, grief is dynamic and will change depending on the person and the circumstances. In understanding someone's grief process then, we need to consider the context. Grief may be excruciating (i.e. losing something you wanted to keep) and it may also be relieving and welcoming (i.e. losing something you wanted to lose).

Worden (2009) identified seven factors that could impact the mourning and grief process of the client. Basically, these areas can influence the level of grief. They were intended as a complement to the four tasks and can help explain why some people might struggle in some tasks more than others. They can also explain why some sail through the tasks with seeming ease. The seven mediators of mourning included,

Who was the Person Who Died

This is pretty much what it sounds like at first glance. Was the person who died your partner or spouse? Were they strangers? A close relative versus a distant one? Your child or someone else's child? Your sibling? Coworker? Were they elderly and long-lived or young with life mostly ahead of them? Depending on who the person was, the loss will be felt differently. Beyond the relational classification, it's important to consider and explore who were they to the survivor. Were they a primary support and role model or more of a nuisance or a demeaning figure? Were they somewhere in the middle of either of these; someone present in their life, but not of significant impact? Something else entirely? The hopes, expectations, interactions, and relationship quality with the deceased will vary from survivor to survivor, even when the same loss is experienced. For instance, if my son died, my husband and I would grieve very differently for him. How he contributes to our external lives are similar, but our internal understandings of him and what it means to be his mom or dad are surely quite individual. In sum, when considering this mediator, be sure to look at the demographics of who the person was—mom, dad, friend, coworker, stranger, etc. and also at the meanings attached to that relationship—what did this person bring to the survivor's life, and who they were in their own personal world. Both factors matter and will likely influence the intensity of grief responses (Worden).

The Nature of the Attachment

This mediator elaborates on the attachment to the person who has died and in some ways is similar to mediator one. To better understand the personal experience of grief, information should be sought from the client in the following areas (Worden).

The Strength of the Attachment

According to Worden, the stronger the love and attachment, the stronger the grief. It's an intuitive idea. I'd invite you to consider that love is only one aspect of attachment and is quite subjective. For instance, what one person considers loving, another might consider abusive (e.g. wanting to know one's whereabouts or being involved in every decision). Be sure to access the client's understanding of the relationship and the love that existed, or didn't. Be open to both and gather information on what the client believed the attachment to be, rather than what it may seem to you.

The Security of the Attachment

Think reliance. How much did the client/survivor rely on the deceased person to complete or fulfil them? If the level of reliance was high, the grief will presumably be high. If the person believes that they can survive without this person, even if they don't want to, the grief may feel more manageable. In the end, if the security and safety of the survivor depended on the deceased's presence, the intensity of grief will magnify.

The Ambivalence in the Relationship

This element speaks to the balance of positive and negative feelings toward the person who died. If the memories and feelings are more positive than negative, the grief reaction is viewed as more manageable. I read this as the presence of less guilt. There's pain still, but less guilt around how the relationship could have been different in life. Worden does not state this, but it seems that the same would be true for high negatives. If someone experiences low ambivalence (i.e. they know exactly how they felt about a person), grief may be more manageable. They only have to reconcile one set of feelings. According to Worden, if there's more of a balance between negative and positive feelings and memories, the grief reaction can be "difficult" (Worden, 2009, p. 58). He argued that with high ambivalence (equal amounts of positives and negatives), "a tremendous amount of guilt, often expressed as 'Did I do enough for him?' along with intense anger at being left alone" will be present (Worden, 2009, p. 59). I am curious about this conclusion and wish Worden had provided sourcing for this conclusion. Remembering that grief will impact each person differently, and that's true for ambivalence as well.

Conflicts with the Deceased

This also is pretty much what it sounds like. If there were conflicts in the history of the relationship, or close to the time of the death, grief reactions may reflect a sense of unfinished business. Considering the varied conflicts that exist in the world, these might range from a fight over who was supposed to do the dishes all the way to sexual or physical abuse. Sudden death can complicate this more, as there might literally have been no time to attempt healing or reconciliation. When an abuser dies, some might feel relief and gratitude that they are no longer present in the world. Others may feel slighted and robbed of their chance to face their abuser, have questions answered, and more. In sum, the history, degree, and nature of the conflicts matter.

Dependent Relationships

Earlier we noted that greater attachment can sometimes equal greater grief. Same idea here. The more one depended on the deceased, the more they will grieve the loss. High levels of dependence can impair the external, internal, and spiritual adjustments encapsulated in task III. It's harder to learn to live without someone if you depended on them for nearly everything from food preparation to emotional support.

How the Person Died

As with mediator two, there are multiple considerations around how the person died including, type of death, proximity, suddenness or unexpectedness, violent/traumatic deaths, multiple losses, preventable deaths, ambiguous deaths, and stigmatized deaths. We'll take them one by one:

Type of Death

Worden uses the acronym NASH to indicate four types of deaths: *n*atural, *a*ccidental, *s*uicidal, *h*omicidal. Depending on which category of death is applicable, grief responses may vary. For instance, if a friend dies by suicide versus a car accident, different emotions and/or questions may arise. If a child dies in a mass shooting versus from an illness, different emotions and/or questions may arise. Think this through and examine the impact of the means of death with your clients. Depending on their understanding of the world and expectations of safety and human behavior etc. they are likely to process different deaths, differently.

Proximity

The first aspect of this dimension is the location of the death. Was it close to home or far away? Depending on the answer, you may see fluctuations in levels of vulnerability and/or acceptance. If something happens out of sight, out of your day-to-day reality, it can be harder to accept as true; it simply feels distant and can be easily (or more easily) denied. Worden noted that this sense of denial or unreal-ness can contribute to problems in completing task I which centers on that acceptance. Having a death close to home, literally, can also cause difficulties for some people. Some may feel guilty about the level of care provided. Others may note that the home feels different after a death has occurred in it; this may be due to an association built between death and what used to be a safe space. Point is, it can be hard if it's close to home and if it's far away; the type and level of difficulty will vary from person to person.

Suddenness or Unexpectedness

A sudden or unexpected death can be differently painful from an expected death. Worden noted, however, that in relation to natural deaths, the longer a person had to prepare for that death, the smoother the adjustment. Personal variance is again an important consideration here though. I have had some clients who nearly sink as they wait for a death to arrive. I recall one client who knew her unborn daughter/fetus was not viable once out of the womb. The six to seven months of advanced notice and preparation did not buffer her adjustment at all, in her opinion. She reported more significant distress once her daughter was born, and I recall her essentially saying "I saw what and who I'd be missing out on. It was more painful than I ever imagined it was going to be in the months prior."

Violent/Traumatic Deaths

Worden noted that this particular dimension could impact the completion of task III elements. With regard to internal adjustments, one's self-efficacy could be threatened and lingering questions around "could this have been prevented?" can consume one. Spiritual adjustments may also be challenging in the wake of this type of death, primarily due to lack of safety. The world can feel less settled and predictable. Additionally, complications can arise if people feel, or are told straight up that they shouldn't talk about the death. Sometimes the world isn't comfortable about listening to traumatic stories or recollections; clients may be actively discouraged from speaking up if the material is deemed disturbing to others or if the provider/listener doesn't know how to respond and reflects that through unhelpful body language. Either way, implicit or explicit, some people are told to keep it down with their pain and stories. If individuals are not able to process their pain, task II will remain incomplete and impair the overall grief process (according to this model).

Multiple Losses

Put simply, if people lose a lot all at once or lose a lot in a short period of time, the grief can become so big that it overwhelms one's resources to deal with it. According to this framework, this overwhelming would impact the completion of task II (processing the pain). Consider losing your entire family in a car accident or having three friends die within the span of a year. When multiple losses are experienced, Worden recommends taking them one by one. Processing each loss, the meaning attached to it, and gradually finding ways to grieve for each as time goes on.

Preventable Deaths

When survivors consider a death preventable, it can impair or stall the grief process. Pending lawsuits in some cases (ex. wrongful death suits) may also prolong the adjustment period and overall grief process. When a death is, or is perceived as, preventable, Worden anticipated guilt and blame to surface. Questions like "who's fault was it?" "What could have prevented it? Why wasn't it done? Should I have done something?" and, even, "Why did they do this to themselves? How selfish!" may arise.

Ambiguous Deaths

This mediator hearkens back to a concept defined in Chapter 2, ambiguous loss. If you recall, this kind of loss can result in either *physical absence* or *psychological absence* (Ali, 2010; Boss, Roos, & Harris, 2011). Being *physically absent* is when a person is physically absent but psychologically present. For instance, in the case of a missing person, there's no definitive way to know if they are alive or dead. As a result, loved ones are left in emotional limbo, uncertain of what to feel and unsure of when (and if) the emotional turmoil will resolve. Examples include military deployments with no contact, missing in action classifications, accidents where no bodies are recovered, runaway cases, abductions, and other unexplained disappearances. *Psychological absence* refers to when a person is physically present but psychologically absent. Essentially, the body of a person is with you, but the personality you once knew is no longer there. Remember that examples here can include health conditions like dementia or Alzheimer's, traumatic brain injuries, autism, depression, schizophrenia, PTSD, addiction, and more (Boss et al.). The not knowing and lack of closure can complicate grief and acceptance of the death and the ambiguous elements sometimes attached to it will be primary topics of conversation in counseling (Worden).

Stigmatized Deaths

This mediator is also reminiscent of a concept defined in Chapter 2, disenfranchised grief. Remember that grief is disenfranchised when the loss is not acknowledged or valued by society (DiBase, 2012). The stigma around the person, type of death, or means of death can lead to determinations of 'worth' by society. That is, some losses are not seen as legitimate or worthy of our sadness or grief. The categories of loss that may result in this type of grief include (Doka, 1989, 2002):

- *Loss is undervalued or seen as less worthy of grief* (ex. loss of pets, miscarriage and/or infertility, the loss of a substance or behavior pattern, etc.)
- *Stigmatized relationships* (ex. loss of an abusive or "unhealthy" partner or relationship, same-sex relationships ending or a partner dying, deportation, etc.)
- *When the method of death is stigmatized* (ex. suicide, homicide, overdose, drunk driving, abortion, etc.)
- *The individual experiencing grief isn't recognized as deserving* (e.g. coworkers, acquaintances, ex-partners, grieving the death of a stranger, etc.)
- *How someone grieves is seen as unacceptable* (e.g. not crying or emoting "enough" or at all, isolating vs. reaching out, etc.)

Worden noted that one significant complication with disenfranchised grief is that there tends to be a lack of support for the mourner. This could slow down the movement in and through tasks II, III, and IV. Please refer back to Chapter 2 for a more detailed definition of disenfranchised grief.

Historical Antecedents

As is true for most areas of counseling, client histories can be valuable to our current understanding of someone. That's true here as well, according to Worden. Past grief experiences and adjustments can shed light into how one might grieve in the present. For some clients, there may be a backlog of hurts. That is, they have not partially or fully grieved previous losses and that may slow down or complicate the adaptation to more recent grief. Individuals with depression may also experience a recurrent depressive episode during their grieving period (Worden; Zisook, Paulus, Shuchter, & Judd, 1997). Family responses to grief can also impact one's individual response; obtaining a family history in terms of how, and if, members have grieved may prove useful. Moreover, to help in the present, we may want to know about the past.

Personality Variables

Several personality variables are included in Worden's model (2009) and they are largely based off Bowlby (1980). They include age and gender, coping style, attachment style, cognitive style, ego strength (self-esteem and self-efficacy), and the assumptive world (beliefs and values). Let's take each of these, one by one.

Age and Gender

Socialization is the major player here around gender. Women are sometimes thought to be more emotional, but that's not reflecting an internal difference in women; it is more likely an assumption made by a society that allows women to demonstrate emotions more freely than men (Worden). On the intervention side, men sometimes find affect-stimulating (aka emotions) interventions more helpful, with women finding greater benefit from interventions centered on problem-solving (Stroebe, Stroebe, Abakoumkin, & Schut, 1996; Worden). That will certainly not be the case for all clients, but it's an interesting consideration.

Worden does not actually speak of age in much detail when presenting the mediators of mourning, other than noting that men in their 50s were the most effective copers when considering the death of a spouse. I'll add that we want to consider age more fully. In particular, our world tends to shortchange children on their ability to grieve deeply. Children lead complex emotional lives and are capable of understanding death and loss when presented in a concrete, developmentally appropriate manner (i.e. the body stopped working vs. they're sleeping; National Child Traumatic Stress Network, 2012). Past studies showed that for young children just learning language, grief is often expressed through behavior and body movement (Bugge, Darbyshire, Rokholt, Haugstvedt, & Helseth, 2014). Somatic expressions may also pop up including headaches, stomach or gastrointestinal issues, muscle tension, changes in appetite, sleep disturbances, and an overall sense of fatigue (Sood, Razdan, Weller, & Weller, 2006). In terms of cognitions, children may report feeling isolated, alone, different, fearful that others may soon die, and/or worry about separation from remaining adults or loved ones (Bugge et al., 2014; Dowdney, 2000; Koehler, 2010). Behavioral and emotional regression are not uncommon. More than anything, the family environment, particularly the adults' ability to cope with grief following a death is most important in buffering a young person's grief response/adjustment (Bugge et al., 2014; Melhem, Moritz, Walker, Shear, & Brent, 2007; Prigerson, 2008).

Coping Style

Three types of coping functions are noted by Worden.

1   Problem-Solving Coping = Essentially some people are better than others at solving problems. Some people use and reuse ineffective strategies or abandon ship/give up when the one strategy they're banking on doesn't work. These responses/efforts would reflect a skills deficit according to Worden and teaching problem-solving via a cognitive behavioral therapy intervention would be the recommendation from his perspective.

2   Active Emotional Coping = Considered by Worden to be the most effective strategy for managing both problems and stress. One major component of this type of coping is to reframe or redefine the negatives in a situation. Also known as finding the silver lining. The ability to find the good in the bad is valued here. Worden asserted that in order for one to experience "growth through grief" (p. 65), redefinition must be utilized effectively. Humor is also valued as a means of coping as is venting. The former is viewed as a form of distancing; the latter as a means of discharging emotions. Worden noted that there should be a balanced venting where both positive and negatives are shared. Active emotional coping also involves accepting support from others and is thought to enhance both self-esteem and self-efficacy (Worden).

3   Avoidant Emotional Coping = Considered by Worden to be the least effective strategy for managing both problems and stress in response to loss. This assessment was based on their short-term nature; they only work in the immediate time frame and do little for long-term solutions. Avoidant coping is characterized by distraction, blaming (self and others), denial, and social withdrawal.

Worden cited three studies to support his theory. Worden (1996) concluded that the best outcomes resulted from active emotional coping, particularly through redefinition (aka reframing). Schnider, Elhai, and Gray (2007) noted a connection between active coping and positive outcomes following a traumatic loss. In that same study, authors found that avoidant coping was linked to the development of PTSD and complicated grief. Finally, Folkman (2001) asserted that strategies like redefinition and cognitive avoidance (aka not thinking about it) were more stable and fixed in people (think harder to change or modify). Skills like problem-solving and the ability to use social support were more flexible and able to be taught. Worden agreed with these conclusions and that's evidenced by his stated support (2009, p. 66) and the inclusion of these coping styles in his model.

Attachment Style

Worden focused on attachment style in a similar fashion to previously discussed researchers; most notably Stroebe, Schut, and Boerner (2010). Recall that Stroebe et al. applied attachment theory to the continuing bonds theory (Klass, Silverman, & Nickman, 1996). I will say though, Stroebe et al. provided a more expansive description of attachment style and its impact on the formation of continuing bonds compared to Worden. Refer back to that earlier discussion if you need a refresher.

Individuals with a secure attachment style experience the pain of loss but are able to manage and process that pain and ultimately establish a continuing bond (should one be sought) (Klass et al.; Stroebe et al., Worden). Worden added that with secure attachment, the pain experienced immediately after a loss does not overwhelm one's ability to complete task I (accepting the reality of the loss).

Considering insecure attachment styles, however, yielded differing responses to grief. The sensitive nature of individuals with anxious/preoccupied attachment styles speaks to deficits in independent emotional regulation. Worden noted that people with this style tend to meet their self-esteem needs through others; meaning "If they think I'm worthy, I'm worthy. If they don't, I'm not." Therefore, if a significant person who aided in emotional- and self-regulation dies, the anxious/preoccupied person might really struggle. High levels of distress might be seen and when prolonged, might lead to complicated grief. The person who helped to help manage stress, emotions, and self-worth is now absent; the survivor may appear to flounder and may ruminate heavily on the loss (Worden). High levels of pain may lead to avoidance in order to manage the emotional fallout and rein it in.

Basically, one may stop engaging with the pain or reminders of the pain (and therefore the lost person or object). Helplessness is one hallmark of low self-efficacy here; one believes they are not capable in the absence of the loved one. An attempt to latch on to another regulatory figure (aka someone to help them cope or manage emotions) is not uncommon. Worden believed that treatment should focus on letting go of the need for physical proximity to the lost person and instead focus on an internalization of the relationship; a more psychological presence/connection. This mirrors the idea of relocation discussed earlier in the chapter (Boerner & Heckhausen, 2003; Stroebe et al., 2010).

The anxious/ambivalent attachment style often results in relationships that have both love and hate present in equal measure (Worden). Others are not relied on or seen as dependable. Such relationships are often rife with conflict. The anger is thought to be protective against underlying anxiety (Worden). Consider the idea that "If I shout loud enough, I won't have to talk about how scared I am"—that's kind of the idea here. Another manifestation of this style in grief might look like aggrandizing the deceased. This simply means making them seem way more important, loving, significant, smart, or strong, etc. than they actually were in life. Worden believed that this response was yet another way to guard against the underlying fears—focus on the positive so much that you're distracted from the negative. Therapy would be focused on balance; remembering both the positive and negative qualities and experiences (Worden). The main task is around anger and integrating it with the love—again, striking a balance between the two emotional forces.

The avoidant/dismissing attachment style results in the dismissal of others; persistent self-reliance is the hallmark here. In response to a loss, there may be little evident impact (Worden). The attachment was low, and therefore the distress at its severance is also low. Worden teeter tottered on the idea of whether or not people with this style would eventually feel the impact of the grief, either in a delayed response or in a somatic form (the body being impacted). Other researchers were similarly unsure; Fraley and Bonnano (2004) did not believe that a delayed response of either kind would come, whereas Stroebe, Schut, and Stroebe (2006) thought that a somatic reaction was likely at some point. Stroebe et al. presumed that a need to let go existed outside of conscious awareness and the body would engage in that at some point. Either way, Worden noted that individuals with this style might struggle to complete task III (adjusting to the world without the deceased) due to difficulty in acknowledging the meaning and impact of the loss.

Finally, people with the avoidant/fearful attachment style would struggle the most in adapting to loss (Worden). This style would exhibit a preference for "tentative attachments" (2009, p. 70). Basically, these people have been burned by relationships in the past, and while they want them badly, they are scared of being burned again. When a death occurs, it can spike fear and result in depressive symptoms. Symptoms are again thought to be protective against anger (Worden). Social withdrawal acts as a further means of protection. Worden rested on Winnicott's 1953 conclusion that when healthy attachments are broken, grief results, but when less healthy attachments are broken through death, anger and guilt result. For people that often highly depend on others (an aspect of some personality disorders) or those who more generally have trouble forming relationships, attachment considerations might be especially helpful when considering grief responses (Worden).

Cognitive Style

This boils down to whether or not a client skews positive or negative in how they view the world—glass half full kind of person? Or glass half empty kind of person? Worden noted that a positive cognitive style was associated with lower levels of depression in one of his previous studies (Worden, 1996) and added that other researchers have reached similar conclusions related to anxiety, grief, and depression (Boelen & van den Bout, 2002). This is fairly intuitive, especially in the context of depression. People with depression are not filled with hope, positivity, or a balanced view of life. Cognitive distortions are often the hallmarks of depression (if one is looking through a cognitive behavioral lens, that is) (Rnic, Dozois, & Martin, 2016).

Rumination is also specifically noted by Worden. He believed that if a person ruminated (i.e. turned thoughts around again and again in their heads with little direction or relief) around death and loss, they would experience unrelenting grief. This prolonged grief response would impede progress with task II (processing the pain of grief) and may ultimately lead to depression (Nolen-Hoeksema, 2001; Worden). The goal of sitting with the pain was presumed to be the same in ruminators versus non-ruminators: find meaning and carry forward with life. The ruminators were less likely to find it though. Why would someone engage in this cognitive style when there was no seeming end or benefit? Worden hypothesized that some people might ruminate as a way of holding on to something they're hesitant to let go of. That could be the person's presence in their life, memories, or other ties to the deceased. Treatment would center on building more effective continuing connections (task IV), problem-solving skills, and increasing use of social supports.

Ego Strength: Self-Esteem and Self-Efficacy

This mediator of mourning speaks to the attitudes people hold about their self-worth and self-efficacy. Worden noted that death can sometimes impact how one sees themselves and the perceived ability to impact their world. When doubt creeps in, this can make task III (To adjust to the world without the deceased) more challenging, particularly around the internal adjustment (Worden). Recall that those internal adjustments focus on the impact the loss has had on the self.

Consider who's been lost and what the relationship entailed. If the deceased was the counterargument to negative self-talk or if the survivor associated that individual with their positive circumstances, feelings, or self-perceptions, the internal adjustments may be more complicated. If the survivor did not rely on that person to counter negative beliefs about self or supply self-confidence, then the adjustment to their absence may not be compounded by those reemerging self-doubts.

In terms of one's sense of self-efficacy, Worden connected it to the locus of control. Essentially, if a person believes they have some control over their world, grief and transitioning through task III (To adjust to the world without the deceased) is likely to be rather smooth (though not necessarily easy). Additionally, Worden asserted that people with higher levels of efficacy were better able to find meaning in the loss and had an easier time forming new identities in the wake of the loss. Compare that to someone who feels that they lack control and do not have the power to influence their own life (low-efficacy). Such individuals may struggle with adjusting to loss and the absence of a loved one (Worden).

Assumptive World: Beliefs and Values

The final factor for mediator five focuses on what Worden called one's Assumptive World. In simple terms, an assumptive world is one's assumptions about how good/benevolent and meaningful the world is (Worden). This mediator would encompass someone questioning a higher power's plan in response to a significant loss. If one believes in a God of any kind, that would apply here. Losing one's assumptive world, then, means that a negative life event has challenged one's assumptions about the world (Attig, 2001; Neimeyer, 2001; Neimeyer & Sands, 2011; Winokuer & Harris, 2012). The world no longer makes sense and the puzzle pieces of what one believed to be true can't be fit together any longer. It can feel like emotional, confusing, chaos. Consider how this might sound:

> "Why me? I've prayed every day and now this. Why?!"
> "Why would God allow this to happen?"
> "I'm not sure if I believe in the same way I did before. This has really tested my faith. I just don't know anymore. What do I do with that?"

Take the religious element out entirely, and other questions might arise for someone, such as:

> "I used to think that the world was good and safe, and now I feel like a fool."
> "If this can happen to them, it could happen to anyone."
> "How could someone do that? Why would someone do that to another person?" (this particular sentiment was in reference to a school shooting)
> "I want to believe the best in people, but I'm not sure I trust in the same way anymore."
> "I didn't see this coming and I don't know how to make sense of it."
> (this was in reference to a partner dying in a car accident)

Worden believed that when a death or loss challenges one's assumptive world, task III can again suffer, this time most prominently in spiritual adjustments. Predictability, stability, safety, order, the goodness of people and the world at large, and when applicable, the trust in a higher power, can be called into question when a death is unexpected, gruesome, cruel, and/or perceptively underserved. With regard to the religious element, at least one study has shown that people who are able to view significant losses as part of a God's larger plan display lower levels of distress after a partner dies compared to those who do not see it this way (Worden; Wortman, & Silver, 2001).

Social Mediators

In short, social support matters. While that may seem like an obvious point, sometimes the world only remembers that in the short-term. The so-called "honeymoon effect" can affect mourners and can be significant. If you've never heard this term, it's referencing the sometimes intense social support offered in the immediate aftermath of a loss—the food, funeral attendance, well wishes, cards, flowers, sympathetic looks, phone calls or texts, emails, sometimes financial donations or support. Over time though, that can fade and the bereaved can begin to feel unseen or forgotten; as well, some take the receding support as either an overt or covert signal that he/she/they should be moving on from their grief.

While Worden stresses that social support is important, and wait for it … supportive, he also notes that it's not the answer to one's pain. I greatly appreciate this point and agree wholeheartedly. You can be tremendously supported and still hurt like hell. Having said that, Stroebe et al. (2005) reviewed literature around this idea and found that more social support was associated with lower rates of depression (Stroebe et al., 2005; Worden). Three social mediators in particular were proposed and advocated by Worden:

1 Support satisfaction

This speaks to a few things. One of which is the perception of social support—one has to actually notice and believe it's present. Second is one's satisfaction with the offered support. This brings to mind efforts to help, which are often backed by very good intentions, and yet still fail to help or even come across as well-meaning. Social support satisfaction is primarily influenced by two things: how much time is spent with others and how much the supports are accessed (Worden). That makes sense on the face of it—if a person is engaging with others fairly regularly and using the resources offered when they need to, they are likely to feel supported.

2 Social role involvements

The more roles a person occupies in life, the better the adjustment to death (Worden). Roles can be many and varied including friend, parent, partner, employee, volunteer, pet parent, etc. To me, this again makes sense—the more social involvement and the more interaction one has in their life, the more likely they are to be supported or at least be offered support.

3 Religious resources and ethnic expectations

To understand this piece of social support, it's important to know your client. Learn about their culture and which aspects of it they find meaningful around death. Some clients will surely have cultural or religious/spiritual rituals they associate with death and find comfort in. Others may adhere to the cultural identity but want to divorce themselves from some rituals they personally find less than comforting. This can present challenges for some when others in their lives expect their participation, belief, or attendance. In sum, know thy client and ask. Ask what they do in response to death and if they're alone in doing it. Ask what helps others around them and if they also find it helpful. Ask what the family, religious (if applies), and/or cultural expectations are and their thoughts and feelings around them. Rely on your client to inform you and work to not enter that conversation with preconceived notions based on demographics or assumed cultural identity.

Ultimately, remember that social support (from friends, family, acquaintances, strangers, and even pets) is important, but it's a buffer. I think of it as bumpers on a bowling lane. It helps the grief along but doesn't guarantee a strike or a win. It's something that simply reduces your chances of ending up in the gutter.

Concurrent Stresses

If you think back to Chapter 2 (if you've even read it!), the term 'secondary loss' might sound familiar. If not, know that secondary losses come in the wake of a primary loss. So, if I lose my job (primary loss), I also lose my income, my identity as a counseling professor (at least temporarily), my daily routine, my health insurance, my coworkers, etc. All of these are secondary to the primary loss; put very simply, they come second. Again, it's worth noting that sometimes the secondary losses are as, or more, impactful than the primary loss. Order does not equal importance. Worden talked about this same concept around concurrent stress. Essentially, if a person has multiple secondary losses that follow a death, the adjustment is expected to be more difficult. Worden specifically noted that rates of depression may increase when an individual has multiple secondary losses. Be on the lookout for it and don't forget that the initial loss is just that, the initial loss. Remember to assess the secondary losses and corresponding impacts on someone's life and well-being.

Overall, the seven mediators of mourning provided an important context for appreciating the variable nature of grief; it's different depending on the person and the loss. Issues such as the strength and nature of the attachment to the deceased, the survivor's attachment style and the degree of conflict and ambivalence with the deceased are important considerations. Additionally, death-related factors, such as physical proximity, levels of violence or trauma, or a death where a body is not recovered, all can pose significant challenges for the survivor's adjustment.

Worden made a point to note that there existed a tendency to oversimply grief and mediating factors. Again, remember to look beyond the initial loss and consider the whole world of your client and how it will shift in response to that loss. All of the information needed to determine the impact of a loss comes from the client. Talk to them and explore the meanings attached to the person in life and to their absence.

Finally, as you may gather at this point, this model subscribes to the grief-work hypothesis mentioned earlier in the chapter. Essentially, unless one confronts the full measure of pain, there will be negative long-term consequences (Stroebe, 1992). I make note only to remind you that multiple understandings of grief and mourning exist. Consider each and consider your client. All researchers to this point have agreed that there is no one correct way to grieve. I would add that there is no one totally correct way to think about grief either. Explore the options and move forward with what makes sense to your brain and heart and, more importantly, to that of your clients.

Considering *the Mediators of Mourning* in the Context of Addiction and Recovery

Placing the mediators of mourning into the context of addiction and recovery yields important considerations. Remember that Worden's point with the mediators of mourning was to note that depending on one's circumstances, grief processes will change. Essentially, what makes up one's life and what surrounds one's loss will influence the impact of a loss. This is an important reminder for counselors to search for context.

Mediator 1: *Who was the Person who Died*

This first mediator could be looked at from a couple of angles when thinking about addiction. First, if an individual does experience a death of someone that's linked to the addiction, for example, someone who died from an overdose, cirrhosis, drunk driving, drug-induced heart attack or stroke, etc.; there's a real connection that the world can see between the addictive circumstances and the death. The second angle relates not to a person, but to the drug or behavior itself. In either case, we'll want to consider how significant the person/thing/pattern was to the individual who's lost it. Was it/they a reliable, consistent part of their life or a more distant connection they engaged with occasionally? Was it/they a primary means of support in time of joy or distress? Was it/they loved, or valued, or loathed? Was it/they somewhere in the middle of both of those; someone or something present in their life, but not of significant impact? Was it/they a new addition to the individual's life or a longstanding one? What does this loss represent to the survivor—a minor inconvenience, a painful though manageable loss, or a devastating absence? Depending on these factors, the impact of the loss will vary as Worden noted with death-related bereavement.

The substance or pattern, frequency of use/engagement, psychological dependence, and desire to maintain a behavior will vary from client to client. Similarly, one's hopes for recovery, expectations about life without a substance or pattern, level of self-efficacy in the absence of the addiction, and more will also vary even when the same substance or pattern is addressed. Don't be presumptuous that one person's struggles with methamphetamine, for instance, will carry the same meaning as another's.

Look beyond the identified loss (in this example meth) and look to the place it held in the client's life. Perceptions, connection, dependence (psychologically and physically), emotional response, and reaction will differ when recovery is considered, attempted, or achieved and that's the point. Talk to your clients about what this absence does or will mean to them. In sum, look at the demographics (i.e. what/who was lost) and the meanings attached to the relationship. Resist the temptation to oversimplify recovery; it's much more than abstinence.

Mediator 2: The Nature of the Attachment

This mediator really gets at the personal connection the client had with what was lost. Several things can be considered including the strength and security of the attachment, ambivalence, conflicts, and level of dependency in the relationship.

The Strength of the Attachment

Recall that according to Worden, the stronger the love and attachment, the stronger the grief. In this context, also be sure to ask about and discuss the clients understanding of their relationship with their substance or behavioral pattern. Did they feel it was loving? Did they find that the substance or pattern was there for them in ways that people have failed to be? Was the attachment strong due to consistency, stability, and reliable emotional regulation? If so, it will likely be harder to pull away from. It's like walking away from an acquaintance versus a lover or partner. There's simply more invested in one relationship and so it's a bigger blow when it goes away. Be open to both and gather information on what the client believed the attachment to be, rather than what it may seem to you, and don't undervalue the love that a person can have for a pattern or substance.

I invite you to consider other aspects of attachment as well (aside from love) and it makes even more sense why someone might struggle to grieve or let go of an addiction. Attachment principles in particular come to mind. More specifically, Bowlby (1982) talked about the ideas of safe haven, proximity maintenance, secure base, and separation distress.

Throughout this mediator, each seems to make an appearance. Around the strength of the attachment, *safe haven* fits. A safe haven is who or what you can turn to when you're feeling threatened, distressed, scared, or in danger. The comfort is sought, and it's provided. One classic example is a child whose toy has been taken away and calls out for his/her/their mother. The mother responds and soothes the distress with a hug. In this example, the mother can be relied on for support and comfort. Think about that idea but substitute a substance or behavior (i.e. shopping) for the mom. If the substance or behavior can be relied on to provide comfort and relief from threats, danger, distress, or fear, people can come to seek it out again and again, especially, if they do not have interpersonal relationships that provide the same type of support. It's the idea of substitute attachment; a substance or pattern has filled in the gaps of subpar relationships.

The Security of the Attachment

Security and reliance are a hair apart here. How much does the client rely on the substance, behavioral pattern, or identity of "addict" to complete or fulfil them? If the level of reliance was high, the grief will presumably be high. If the person believes that they can survive without the substance or pattern, even if they don't want to, the grief may feel more manageable. In the end, if the security and safety of the individual in recovery also depends on the substance's or behavioral pattern's presence, the intensity of grief will likely magnify. Worden believed that to be true with death-related grief; I believe it to be true in the context of addiction and recovery as well, particularly when the idea of a *secure base* (Bowlby) is considered. Think of a secure base as a safe starting point/foundation from which one can venture out and explore their surroundings and retreat to if it goes south.

Remember that safety can be subjective, for instance, people who drink to reduce social anxiety; the safety lies in the guarantee that they can blame the alcohol if they were to act like an idiot or not recall what they did; both options are buffers for embarrassment, rejection, and shame. Another example might be someone who finds that their substance or behavioral pattern is the only thing consistently there for them; they can trust its presence and effectiveness in managing emotions. They try new things and experiment in the world (perhaps with recovery efforts) but return to it when stressed and in need of reassurance.

The Ambivalence in the Relationship

This element speaks to the balance (or imbalance) of positive and negative feelings toward what was lost. If we again consider attachment, *proximity maintenance* feels familiar (Bowlby). This is the idea of who or what you want to keep close as you explore the world. I can think of several clients in early recovery who were holding tight to a low level of use (i.e. frequency) as they explored early recovery ideas. There's a balance here of wanting to move away from something and also wanting to keep it close.

Worden thought that in the wake of a loss or impending loss the grief reaction might be more manageable if the memories, associations, and feelings are more positive than negative. This **may** differ for people moving from addiction to recovery. For instance, if no significant distress or hurts are, in the client's mind, connected to the substance, behavior, or addiction, they may see no need to move away from the relationship and may struggle with low ambivalence (i.e. they want to remain as they are and see little need for change).

On the other hand, if one knows they hated their life when addicted and want to let go of the substance or behavioral pattern because of that, they may find the transition from addiction to recovery more manageable (low ambivalence; they're ready to change and see a need for it)—in short, there may be less to mourn and they only have to reconcile to one set of feelings.

Then you'll have the clients who fall more in the middle ground. People that have a mix of both positive and negative memories, feelings, and associations may struggle (according to Worden's initial theory). The reason why is because there's more to sort out and this can result in high levels of ambivalence. They may not be sure if the substance or behavioral pattern is something that really needs to be lost and they may go back and forth on that point. It's a busier process in that one has to decide if they want to and see a need to modify behavior and life. If so, they must also grieve what they're leaving behind, and reckon with an unknown future. If not, they must accept the present and the consequences that come with it and reckon with an unknown future.

Finally, *separation distress* (Bowlby) is when someone experiences distress when separated from a caregiver. Again, if we envision a substance or pattern as a caregiver (i.e. reliable, soothing, accessible), this becomes reminiscent of forced abstinence (i.e. can't find any to buy or are otherwise unable to engage in the behavior) or withdrawal (psychological in particular). I have had many clients who are fearful of how they'll feel physically and psychologically in the absence of their substance or pattern. Some have also expressed fears around how desperate they may become if they cannot locate a dose or engage in their behaviors/pattern in the preferred time frame. The latter is more a fear of what that desperation might lead to, like stealing, prostitution, or other situations in which morals are compromised to accomplish a task.

Conflicts with the Deceased

This aspect of the mediator could relate to the loss of relationships during the course of recovery. Suddenly entering treatment, for example, might also mean a quick exit from one's social circle or routine; some clients may experience guilt or sadness. Others may see it as an abandonment of friends who are still caught up in the addictive world. Another circumstance that may yield such feelings is getting arrested and locked up; it's that idea again of having unfinished business and it can be heavy. A more appropriate name for this mediator in the addictive-recovery context might be *conflicts related to the lost person, object, or pattern*.

Death may of course factor in here as well. When individuals die from an overdose or other addiction-related causes unexpectedly, guilt, sadness, fear, shame, etc. may be present for survivors. Questions may be left unanswered and with no opportunity for true resolution, some people can flounder while others may grow. As with any death, depending on who that person was, positive emotions like joy or relief may follow. I can recall one former client who was pimped out to random men by her significant other as a means of paying for their heroin. He exercised his power over her and she felt she had no power to stop it. The significant other died in a car accident about two years into their relationship and the client felt free. She decided she was ready to take her power back and wanted to learn how to regain control; his death spurred her entry into treatment. The death itself was not drug or recovery-related, but the impact of it sure was. As Worden noted, the history, degree, and nature of the conflicts matter. Explore conflicts with clients and consider the following questions/invitations to begin those conversations:

> "Is there any unfinished business you have related to your addiction? Anything you feel you've left behind that worries you?"
>
> "Talk to me about this transition. Even when we make changes that we want, it can still be hard to walk away, and we can feel conflicted."
>
> "Do you feel a pull from anything in your past (recent past counts too)? Any unresolved things you wish could be resolved? What's it like (or mean) that some things might remain unresolved forever?"
>
> "What can I (as your counselor) do to help you resolve any of these conflicts? What do you need from me?"
>
> "Help me understand what it's like to live with unanswered questions."
>
> "What's it like to walk away and move toward a different place in life? Sometimes that's hard and other times it's less so. What's it been like for you?"

Dependent Relationships

Remember that greater attachment can sometimes amount to greater grief. The degree to which a client was dependent on their substance or behavioral pattern, the harder the break might be and the greater the grief response as well. Consider someone who has relied on cocaine to manage moods, energy levels, and psychological comfort—giving that up will be difficult. It boils down to the ideas of primary and secondary losses—the cocaine might be the primary loss, but the loss of dependable emotional regulation and comfort are secondary (and significant!).

Consider further examples: for a person with chronic physical pain that's been managed through pain pills (illicitly), giving up the pills may mean the introduction of pain, fear, discomfort, and uncertainty. For an individual engaging in unhealthy relationship patterns as a means of coping with the fear of inadequacy or being alone, losing that relationship might bring feelings of inadequacy, fear, loneliness, self-doubt, panic, and/or a general feeling of emptiness. Losing the ability to gamble may bring boredom, loss of control (or the illusion of it), loss of excitement or power, loneliness, sadness, or fear (if one was counting on recouping previous losses).

The point is that the impact of the loss matters. In this mediator, the focus is on the level of dependency. If one can no longer rely on what has been relied on to meet important needs, the transition and grief can be great. Worden believed that high levels of dependence impaired the external, internal, and spiritual adjustments encapsulated in task III. Essentially, the adjustment to life without this dependable person, thing, substance, or pattern will be challenging as there are numerous adjustments to be made. Help your clients first explore and acknowledge the dependencies and then move toward adjusting. Consider the following as conversation starters:

> "When you think about losing _____ (i.e. drug, relationship, pattern, behavior), what else are you losing? What came with the _____ that will also be missed? What are you thinking about trying to move forward in its/their absence?"
>
> "Part of an addiction is the reliance on external things—let's talk about the ways in which you relied on _____. What's it like to let go of that or to try and let go of that and find other ways to meet your needs?"
>
> "How capable to do you feel in handling life on your own without _____ to depend on?"
>
> "How do you feel about learning to depend on yourself?"
>
> "There are two terms that might be helpful to us when we talk about your recovery. The first is *primary loss*—this is the actual thing or person that's going away or lost. The second is *secondary loss*—this refers to all the things that change in response to the primary loss. For instance, if I lose my job, I lose my income. If I lose my husband, I lose a helper. If I lose heroin, I lose the ability to numb out. If I lose sobriety, other recovery efforts could be impacted (i.e. employment, family healing, etc.). Think about your life and let's identify your primary and secondary losses around recovery. Let's take time to appreciate everything on your plate as you're working on this."
>
> "I know that ending the relationship has been really difficult for you. Let's think about all that you've lost; it wasn't just him/her/them. You might have also lost your hopes for the future (if they were tied to the relationship), happiness, routine, emotional support, financial resources, and sense of safety. It can be hard to lose anyone, but it's even harder when you relied on that person for important things. Tell me about it."

Mediator 3: How the Person Died

When thinking about addiction and recovery around this mediator, from one end it's worth taking Worden's model as it was written around actual deaths that might be experienced. It's also worth considering a metaphorical take on the death of an identity. I've gone two directions myself clinically around this idea and would recommend either for your consideration:

Version 1: I've discussed the idea that recovery marks the death of the "addict" identity. I've encouraged some clients to view recovery as a death and rebirth in terms of how they understand themselves. In doing that, we (counselor and client) want to preserve bits and pieces of the previous life/identity that can be useful in the new one. We explore what was worthy and capable in the "addict" identity that could be resurrected in the new life. Likewise, what was more centered on pain and unhealth that we might work to leave behind in 'death.' Some examples of capabilities that existed within the addiction included persistence, tenacity, grit, resilience, loyalty, solid attempts at meeting needs and self-regulation, awareness, and hope (however fleeting it may have felt for some). I've focused sessions (both group and individual) on how to move forward in terms of how one is living without leaving those qualities behind; it becomes the search for their presence in one's character over the search for their presence in one's behavior. Things to leave behind might be self-doubt, hopelessness, acting without thoughtful consideration/impulsivity, and one-sided relationships that largely didn't serve the client but another instead (i.e. either a person or the addiction personified).

Version 2: I've reflected with clients about their pre-addiction self and the identity that was surrendered or lost to the addiction. This angle promotes the recapturing of the lost elements of self—in short, let's (counselor and client) work to bring back some of the things they lost to the addiction and reincorporate or reinvigorate them into their daily life and self-understandings. This approach also allows clients to reflect on a different time of life, for better and for worse, and to search for new insights that may have been missed initially or long-forgotten. Some examples have included self-regard, self-concept (a sense of who they are), fun, relaxation, mutual versus one-sided relationships, and hope.

Both versions have suited different clients differently, and sometimes I don't use either depending on the person I'm working with. But I can honestly tell you that they have been some of my favorite clinical conversations. The reason why is because they are more abstract than concrete much of the time. Recovery, and treatment more specifically, should be based on insight, exploration, and identity at its base. When we move to worksheets and scripted/

standardized models of helping we lose the nuance; we lose the individuality of who our clients are. Conversations around meaning, identity, and the more existential bits of life, addiction, and recovery restore that individual-focused care and for me, that's clinical gold.

As I stated much earlier in this book, I really believe that recovery (not just abstinence, but true recovery—see Chapter 2 for a detailed definition if unsure about what this means), relies on the application of existing skills and qualities in a healthier context. We don't need to scrap who a person was during an addiction in order to create a 'better' version of who they are. *They are already worthy.* Their life and behaviors need to come in line with that truth and that is hard work cognitively, emotionally, and spiritually.

From Worden's original mediator, talk about stigma, deservingness of grief, sudden and unexpected losses or shifts in one's life, violence and traumatic losses like safety and hope can result. Consider the multiple losses experienced by some—both internal as noted above and external (i.e. loss of friends or family, housing, health, freedom/incarceration, money, etc). Also, consider the sometimes-ambiguous nature of addiction-related loss—those that we just can't quite put a finger on (refer to Chapter 2 for an expanded definition of ambiguous loss). Remember Worden's note that with disenfranchised grief (again, defined in Chapter 2) there tends to be a lack of support for the mourner. This could slow down the movement in and through tasks II, III, and IV. This mediator from Worden provides the seedlings for meaningful, existential conversations centered on recovery; don't miss the opportunity to have them.

Mediator 4: Historical Antecedents

As a carryover from the previous section/mediator, the pasts of our clients can be invaluable in understanding who they are currently. Past losses, grief responses, and change processes can provide insight into what helps, what hurts, and overall which direction to move in when someone is working to make a major shift in their life. For some clients, there may be a backlog of hurts. That is, they have not partially or fully grieved previous losses and that may slow down or complicate the adaptation to more recent grief.

This reminds me of dental complaints when reducing or stopping use (hang with me here and keep reading!). Many clients I've worked with who have had long-term use of opioids (heroin and oxycontin in particular) have found that dental pain increases as they reduce and ultimately cut out use. Why? The dental problems aren't new, but they have been covered up by the pain-relieving effects of the substance, sometimes for years. Now that behaviors have changed around use, old pains creep back in and invade the present. Grief can operate in the same way. As some clients move closer toward recovery, old pains can creep in and invade their minds and hearts. Remember to take an inventory of the past as it relates to the present. Consider the following questions/invitations when initiating these conversations:

> "Are you having any memories or thoughts creeping in from the past since you've started treatment (or thinking about treatment)? If so, tell me about them. If not, are there any you anticipate coming up?"
>
> "What might the use have been covering up or numbing that might come back? (think thoughts, feelings, or memories)."
>
> "When engaging in your behavior/pattern/use, did you do so with the intention of blocking certain parts of your past? Was the addiction a coping skill/attempt for something else? Help me understand."
>
> "Where have you found your mind taking you these days now that _____ (i.e. addictive pattern or substance) is taking up less room in your life?"
>
> "How have you grieved before? What do you know about how you handle loss?"
>
> "Do you tend to face loss and the emotional fallout head-on or do you tend to avoid and protect yourself? Whichever you do (even if a third option entirely), does it work/help? If it does, for how long?"
>
> "How has your life to this point influenced you? Which relationships or events that have shaped you into who you are now? Which have shaped what you do in response to emotional pain or loss more generally?"
>
> "How has your life to this point prepared you for recovery? If it hasn't, what do you think has been missing?"

Mediator 5: Personality Variables

It makes sense that personality variables will factor into how someone approaches addiction, recovery, and the losses associated with both. Worden and Bowlby focused on age and gender, coping style, attachment style, cognitive style, ego strength (self-esteem and self-efficacy), and assumptive world (beliefs and values). Let's briefly consider each variable's role in the addiction and recovery context. Please refer to earlier in this chapter for a more detailed account of each variable.

Age and Gender

Again, consider the carryover from the previous mediator. Look at the history of how clients were socializing around coping (how have they/ have they been taught to do it?), emotional expression (what, when, and how much is allowed of each emotion?), levels of self-efficacy (are they capable on their own or is someone else supposed to help when in distress?), self-esteem (how has their worth been defined and what about them has been valued?), etc. Lessons from the past will often factor into who someone is now. Explore them. What did the client learn about who they are and what their identified gender implies? Consider generational gaps around all aspects (i.e. past and current understandings of gender roles, allowed or denied emotional expression, etc.). Most importantly in this context, think about how those lessons have translated to one's addiction. What rules might they be operating under that directly influence use or engagement with an addictive pattern? For example, if a client was taught that men don't cry and if they do, it's a sign of weakness, that emotional constriction might lead to numbing of emotions (through substances or behaviors). If a client was taught that self-sufficiency is paramount, they may struggle to ask for help or acknowledge shortcomings; these may present as barriers in treatment.

Point is, age (and generation) often corresponds with what the world teaches us. I'd argue that the same is true for gender identity; how we identify often shapes what we're taught. Consider those messages and lessons in recovery when applicable.

Coping Style

Worden laid out three functions of coping in his original model: problem-solving coping, active emotional coping, and avoidant emotional coping. When working with clients around addiction and recovery, consider client needs and deficits in coping. If clients are using ineffective problem-solving strategies (i.e. they don't work and yet they're repeatedly used), use psychoeducation to broaden their options. Also, explore the experience of trying to fix or resolve something and repeatedly failing to do so.

If clients do well with reframing and finding the so-called silver lining, encourage them to apply those skills to their addictive and recovery processes. Worden believed, and I would agree, that for growth to occur, redefinition must also occur. Redefine (you and the client together) the negatives into functional things (i.e. use was an attempt at coping or survival versus self-destruction or sabotage). Find the strength where others see weakness (i.e. they are alive and they have endured difficult circumstances; they are resilient not weak) and foster hope where it seems there isn't any left (i.e. they are trying and that alone implies that they want to be somewhere different in life; it's a matter of when and how, not if).

Active emotional coping is about balance—acknowledging and valuing the positives and negatives. Accepting support from others is also central; processing one's view on reaching out as well as their experiences when they have will also be useful (Did it help? Did someone respond to their request for help or not?). Worden believed that accepting help from others ultimately helped build one's self-esteem (presumably because one is seen as worthy of help by others) and self-efficacy (they may see options of how to support another).

Finally, if clients are engaging in avoidant emotional coping (via avoiding emotional pain or negative states), they may find long-term well-being elusive. Basically, avoidance is effective, but only in the short-term; distraction (i.e. substance use, workaholism, gambling, unhealthy relationships, etc.), blaming (self or others), denial, and social withdrawal will only work for so long for most people. Eventually experiences, thoughts, feelings, or all of them will have to be reckoned with. Clients may benefit from psychoeducation on coping options, self-regulation, accessing and utilizing social supports, and self-care. They may also require trauma care/reprocessing and/or more specific mental health treatment to attend to suppressed problems.

Attachment Style

More broadly, around grief, a secure attachment style lends to pain that's manageable. Over time, a continuing bond is possible if sought. Essentially, a secure attachment style makes it more likely that someone will be able to walk with their pain rather than be trampled by it. Thinking about someone working to leave an addiction behind, it makes sense that people with secure, safe, and reliable relationships in their life will be better able to manage the pain of addiction-related loss. The emphasis placed on social supports during recovery (and I believe appropriately so) echoes the strength in secure bonds. Likewise, it makes sense that insecure attachment styles may not only complicate addiction-related grieving but also inform addictive patterns. Let me explain.

The anxious/preoccupied (aka anxious/ambivalent) attachment style is characterized by external emotional regulation and a negative view of self. Basically, a person relies on something or someone outside of themselves to define their worth and help manage emotions. Substance use and/or other addictive patterns can be thought of as an external means of emotional regulation. Think about it: if someone wants to numb away emotional pain and relies on oxycontin, for instance, to do it, that fits the bill. If an individual is consumed by fears of rejection and drinks heavily to manage such fears, that also fits. For a person who wants to feel powerful and significant, gambling can produce that effect for some, particularly when in the presence of others who celebrate wins or console losses (i.e. table games). Workaholism and advancement can provide a sense of external validation, acceptance, and worth for some people that is unmatched internally. It makes sense that people with this style could get caught up in addictive patterns; the external validation meets an important internal need.

If someone loses a job, tries for sobriety and recovery or is incarcerated (and therefore forced into sobriety), or experiences a breakup or death of a partner or loved one, the external source of validation is lost. As Worden noted, when a regulatory figure is lost, high levels of distress may present and can lead to complicated, prolonged grief. Someone is up a creek with no paddle—their emotional guide/manager is now gone, and they are left to navigate the current alone and have little to no confidence in their ability to do so.

There may be a fixation on the lost relationship (in this context the substance or pattern). The continued relationship with the lost person/pattern/substance might start to take priority over current relationships and an imbalance between reminiscences and current life may take hold (think rumination or obsessive focus on use or past actions) (Stroebe et al., 2010). Avoidance of the pain is likely (Worden). Another response may be substitution—latching onto another pattern, substance, or person to fill the gaps of the lost one. The idea that someone is changing seats on the Titanic is apt here; substance switching (i.e. heroin to cocaine) may occur, rebound relationships, or the intense drive that fueled workaholism may transfer to treatment activities or hobbies, etc. New activities filled with old patterns. Helplessness in the face of great pain and discomfort speaks to low levels of self-efficacy; the sense that one is incapable of emotional regulation in the absence of the person, object, or pattern.

Another layer with this style is the tendency for anger as a means of protection from anxiety. Anger is a powerful distractor/deflector from worry; for clients who present as angry in sessions, be curious as to the source. Explore fears, worries, and discomforts; hesitate strongly to punish this coping skill and work to understand the agitation instead. As Worden and Stroebe et al. noted, clients might aggrandize the lost attachment figure— that may manifest as a client glorifying a substance or addictive pattern and downplaying or omitting the negative aspects. This behavior is also protective against underlying fears. If one focuses on the positive, one is also distracted from the negative. Work toward a balanced remembering and accurate depiction of what this substance/pattern was like in the client's life; welcome the positive memories and gently work toward acknowledgment of the negative ones as well.

Clinical efforts that focus on rebuilding life in the absence of the lost substance/person/pattern and focusing more on self-regulation are worthwhile (Stroebe et al.). Essentially, help clients to recognize, build, and internalize their capabilities; help them look within rather than without. For individuals who relied on a substance, person, or pattern to regulate negative emotions or create positive ones, help them to see their capability. They found a way (that worked!) to manage their emotions; remember that something does not have to be healthy to be effective. Start by looking for the effective management of emotions, no matter how unhealthy. They (and we as providers) are shortchanging themselves if all they see is the addiction—see the effort to manage pain/emotions and celebrate their persistence in doing so. Then, importantly, work to transfer those inherent strengths and efforts (i.e. persistence, awareness of emotional need, and determination to do something about it) to healthier versions of regulation. Skill-building and learning to foster a stronger self-concept and sense of efficacy will appropriate targets.

Individuals with an avoidant/dismissing attachment style may be particularly challenging in a treatment or peer support setting (i.e. AA, NA, or SMART Recovery), primarily due to the dismissal of others and fierce self-reliance. It may be challenging for such individuals to buy into the idea of counselor or peer support; both require some degree of mutual reliance and support. Certain aspects of the addiction may be easier, or at least far less distressing, for this style to let go of. For instance, social connections or the people associated with the addiction may be of little concern when moving toward recovery. The loss of the regulatory substance or addictive pattern may be tough though. If someone has found a way to self-regulate via that substance or pattern and has eliminated the need for other people (i.e. self-selected isolation or withdrawal), they may be slow to loosen their grip on those behaviors if the alternative is a greater reliance on the outside world. Worden noted that individuals with this style might struggle with adjusting to the world following the loss. He attributed this to difficulty in acknowledging the meaning and impact of the loss.

Consider devoting time to the therapeutic alliance first and work to build a safe space for this client; this truly means meeting them where they are at and not expecting much, if any, buy into our points of view. Elements of choice and emphasis on improving their self-reliance may be more welcome than invitations to broaden one's social support system (and that includes us as providers). Invite clients to self-reflect on the meaning of this new stage of life and what the changes might mean for how they operate and cope.

The avoidant/fearful attachment style might struggle with recovery efforts as well. Consider that this style often brings a high level of fear around rejection. The desire for meaningful relationships is present, but the belief they are likely to be so is often low. Individuals may find substances/addictive patterns safer and more reliable when compared with people—social withdrawal is protective for such individuals (Worden); it prevents a negative relational interaction. No-shows for appointments or other treatment obligations may be higher for individuals with this style; again, strongly fight the urge to punish and instead work to understand the potentially protective nature of the behavior. When thinking about this style, it may be helpful to remember the adage that the best offense is a good defense.

As Worden noted, individuals with this style may experience fear in response to loss and present with depressive symptoms. Be on the lookout for low mood and protective behaviors early on in sobriety and recovery efforts. Help clients recognize the meaning behind their actions and to lean into the treatment process as much as they can tolerate. As with the previous style, emphasis on first improving self-reliance may be more welcome than invitations to broaden one's social network. The counselor would be tasked with proving their worth as a provider (never a bad thing) and demonstrating the consistency, respect, safety, and stability in the clinical relationship that was missing in the past.

Cognitive Style

Knowing that clients (and all people) are likely to have a skew (in this case, either positive/glass half full or negative/glass half empty) when coming into treatment, inviting conversations—either in individual or group settings—about a few things may prove useful:

1   What insight they have into it. That is, do they know that it's skewed and which way it leans? What are their thoughts about how that's impacted their life up until this point?
2   Checking in with them about expectations for their recovery attempt. Do they tend to have hope and a belief that they can ultimately achieve recovery? Or do they believe that this will be yet another chance to prove to themselves and the world that they can't move beyond their patterns? Are they somewhere in between—a place I think of as 'tentative hope?'
3   Their tendency, or lack thereof, to ruminate on perceived problems or hang-ups. Do they find themselves turning their thoughts over and over again around loss or anticipated loss? Recall that Worden believed that rumination around loss could prolong the grief process and stall someone's efforts to process the pain of what they're feeling. Also recall that Worden hypothesized that some people ruminate as a way of holding on to something they're hesitant to let go. Talk to clients about what they're scared or hesitant to let go. I firmly believe that meaning can be found here. Explore the functions (i.e. usefulness) of their behaviors and patterns. See what they provided to the client and talk about what gaps will remain if they were to stop or change their behaviors or ways of thinking.

Work to understand rumination as a signal that something needs to be talked or thought through. I would even suggest that providers avoid teaching clients to eliminate or distract from the rumination on a long-term basis. Invite those thoughts in when the day or week allows for it (i.e. schedule it; I often suggest taking 15–20 minutes before bed) and see what's there; what are one's body and mind trying to tell them? Encourage clients to guess and to look for meaning where there is seemingly only pain or annoyance (rumination often brings both). Reconnecting with the self is a primary goal of recovery in my mind; this is one way to facilitate it. Learning and devoting time to asking one's body and mind what it needs and then listening the best one can.

Ultimately, examining one's way of thinking was critical from Worden's perspective. Avoiding depression and unrelenting grief through an exploration of meaning, processing pain, and moving forward in the presence or absence of both (meaning and pain) are ultimately the tasks here. I agree that these are useful aims and have experienced many clients muck their way through these processes. I'm a believer in setting everything on the table—that is, being transparent with clients about what might help along the way or set them back. Discussing one's cognitive style early on can bring awareness to both client and provider and give context to any self-defeating or self-promoting (i.e. hope) thoughts that arise throughout the recovery attempt. Taking time to look metacognitively (that's a big word for thinking about your own thoughts) at thoughts can be useful in recovery as it allows a person to understand that their way of thinking might need some work.

Ego Strength: Self-Esteem and Self-Efficacy

Worden understood this mediator as a sort of battle against self-doubt. With a death or significant loss (losing a substance or addictive pattern qualifies), he believed that people could begin to question how they see themselves and their ability to impact their world. Self-doubt = tougher internal and external adjustment to life without addictive patterns. Makes sense doesn't it? As a provider, focus on the impact of the loss and how clients internalize it. Put more simply, talk to clients about how confident they feel in surviving and making changes in the absence of their substance or pattern. Consider exploring (in individual or group settings) some sources and impact of self-doubt:

- If applicable, where'd they learn they aren't entirely capable? This is exploring the origins of self-doubt. Has it been self-generated (i.e. coming from their own heads and hearts)? Or imposed (i.e. someone or many people have told them they are failures, weak, forever a "junkie," etc.)? Sadly, be open to clients when reporting that previous or current counselors have contributed to their self-doubt. Listen carefully and learn from what they share.
- Is the doubt related only to recovery efforts or has self-doubt been around a long time? Do they see it factoring into their reasons or need for use/addictive patterns? What has the substance, behavior, or pattern done to help in this area? Does it distract them from those feelings? Numb them? Bring a sense of power and significance that is otherwise missing? (Again, what's the function or purpose of the use/pattern—what's it/they provide?).
- How much space does self-doubt take up in their heads and hearts? Is it an overwhelming feeling, a nagging thought in the back of their mind, or non-existent?
- What do they (clients) need to hear, believe, or experience to change how they see themselves? Again, does it swing external or internal—that is, do they need to hear, see, or experience something with or from another person or do they need to work something out entirely inside themselves?

From my view, this is one of the most important mediators when it comes to recovery. Ultimately, it boils down to two things: (1) How much a client believes in their capability to do something different and to sustain that change (self-efficacy), and (2) To what degree they believe they are worth the effort (self-esteem). For clients who struggle in one or both of these areas, learning to adjust to a life without their addictive pattern or substance may feel overwhelming. If a change process itself is more painful than the thing one is changing from, few people are likely to stick it out. Losing coping skills (i.e. substances, addictive behaviors, familiar but unhealthy people, distraction, numbing, etc.) can cast doubt on one's ability to survive a change. The "how" of survival is missing. Clients need new coping skills that have proven to work before letting go of the older, less healthy ones. Remember that when it comes to coping, we're trying to pull a sort of switcheroo. A near-simultaneous acceptance and use of new coping skills while shedding or losing reliance on the old ones.

We're working to help people believe in their ability to change and their worthiness of a different life. Don't lose sight of that worth piece. This is, in my mind, largely accomplished through the relationship. Treating clients with the respect they deserve (ALL the time, not only when they are progressing), being flexible and patient (change is *very* hard), expressions of grace, kindness, and sharing of our hope in small doses. Actually, telling them, not just thinking in our own heads, that they deserve a better life because their presence matters in this world and in your world (again ALL the time, not only when they are progressing). Expand on what you see in them and what you value about knowing them.

This sort of self-disclosure is supported by theory, in particular, gestalt therapy (Perls, 1969). Using the here and now in the relationship to infuse our external perspective around worth can feel good for the counselor too. Just don't overdo it and never lie. If you struggle with a client, you can either share that in a useful way with the same intent in mind, for instance,

> I struggle sometimes sitting with you when you're using because I know I'm only seeing one version of you. I would love to get the chance to see who you are underneath your behaviors/patterns. I hope at some point you feel safe enough to share that person with me.

or say nothing and wait for the right moments. One of my favorite things to say to clients working toward recovery is "I see how hard you're working. Even when it doesn't pan out all the time, I notice, and I see you trying."

Remember that the function of the use is important to consider when clients are working to make those internal adjustments. Through the suggested conversations/questions above, you and they can begin to understand how much they relied on the substance or pattern to supply confidence (or distract from lack of it). If the level of reliance was relatively low, the emergence of self-doubt and erosion of confidence in recovery may not be salient. If the level of reliance on a substance or pattern to supply confidence and cover-up self-doubt was high, those should be expected themes during recovery and need to be attended to regularly.

Assumptive World: Beliefs and Values

Worden believed that when a death or loss challenged one's assumptive world, spiritual adjustments suffered. Remember that this is not so much tied to religion or faith, as it is to our belief in the world (i.e. predictability, stability, safety, order, the goodness of people and the world at large, and when applicable, the trust in a higher power). When thinking about how this piece fits into the recovery conversation, think about (and perhaps ask your clients—again individually or in groups) the following:

- How do they define a meaningful life? Is it okay if their definition (in their mind) differs from how others define it? Has their addicted life been meaningful or devoid of meaning? Have they ever felt a deep sense of meaning in life?
- Do they see a meaningful life ahead, even if they still need to work out the details? This is essentially hope, but in a broader sense—is the change worth it? Will life be better and do they believe it will last? What do they need to lose or gain to increase their chances of recovery working out? What are they wanting or needing that they currently lack to feel fulfilled by their existence?
- How does the client see the world? Is it one where second chances (or third or fourth, etc.) are allowed and possible? Or is it one where your damned and defined by your past?
- If they follow a religious/faith tradition, do they believe in redemption or forgiveness? Are forgiveness or redemption a given or are they earned? If the latter, do they believe they have or can earn it? Do they believe themselves worthy of either? What's the meaning either way—if they do earn it, how much does that matter? If they don't earn it, how much does that matter?
- Perhaps the clients themselves don't put much stock in any religious/faith tradition, but others in their life do. How do they experience the impact of others' beliefs on their life?
- Is there any resentment toward a higher power for the course their life has taken? Any gratitude? How do they explain their life course in the context of their beliefs? Do they find their belief system useful to them moving forward or is it more a source of pain?

Ultimately, explore the meaning of life and how their substance, pattern, and recovery efforts fit in. The way one sees the world can create or buffer bumps on the road. If one is rooted in the belief that the world is good and they can, at some point, find a way to meaningfully experience it, triggers may be less influential/tempting. Conversely, if they believe that they are damned and forever defined by their past, hope may be less powerful than any trigger that comes along promising relief. These are important themes and can be informative guides to individualized treatment. Cater to the world that the clients believe they occupy and help them to understand the impact of such a belief system.

Social Mediators

Social support matters. While that may seem painfully obvious, some-times the world only remembers that in the short-term. This, I've found, is true for providers as well. We sometimes forget that the *entire* period of recovery can be hard, not just the beginning. I have found myself slip-ping into the comfortable illusion (and to be frank, complacency) that my 'late-recovery' groups have fewer needs than my 'early recovery' groups. Truthfully and importantly, they have *different* needs.

This complacency or illusion is referencing the honeymoon effect that can be seen with grief; that early period of time after a loss where intense attention and care is paid that slowly dwindles over time. That slowing of support, attention, and other's simply remembering that something big has shifted in their life can leave some people feeling unseen or forgotten. Other people may see the slowing or lack of overt support as evidence that the support should no longer be needed (i.e. they should be moving on and less impacted by the loss). As providers, we need to remember that change takes time. Don't forget that support should take time too. Support should be chronic, not acute. Help your clients remember this too. Capabilities will grow and challenges will change; the level and type of support needed over time will vary person to person. Allow for that variability and don't forget to ask what your clients need from you, from others, and them-selves. I find patience is a common answer to all three. Sometimes we need to be patient while we adjust.

As Worden noted, support is not the answer, it's one critical com-ponent. People can be supported and still be in pain. Help your clients remember that too. The goal of support is not a lack of pain or hardship; it's not being alone in one's pain and hardship. I think of support as a life ring (the big white floating rings with ropes attached that lifeguards sometimes carry). You might still be stuck in the water, but you're not alone and you're not unseen. There's someone else there as a witness, holding on to the end of the rope so that you don't go completely un-der. And if you do, it'll be noticed. You won't drown alone. You'll have someone diving in after you or alerting another that additional help is needed. Comfort is a funny thing; sometimes it truly is the absence of pain or fear and at other times it's knowing that those things will simply be noticed and that they'll matter.

Counselors can be comforting, supportive, and still hold firm boundaries. We can hold the rope attached to the ring of support without ever getting in the water ourselves. We can notice and advise, but we don't have to risk drowning ourselves. *Support is not saving*; it's an additional muscle (emotional or physical) while someone else finds a way out of difficult circumstance. Remember that too.

Worden talked about three areas of support that he saw as central to how someone responds to loss: support satisfaction, social role involvements, and religious resources and ethnic expectations. Placing each in the context of recovery, they boil down to this:

1 Support Satisfaction

  People on the receiving end of support need to actually notice it and recognize it as support—not as a means to control or manipulate their choices. I have seen control labelled 'support' many times in my counseling life. For instance, when clients are threatened with discharge for positive drug tests. Some facilities or providers will say that such a policy 'supports' recovery in that it draws a firm boundary. I would suggest such policies reinforce the idea of conditional support, that is, "we have your back if you behave the way we want you to." I strongly favor unconditional support and counselor accountability. Instead of removing someone from treatment, perhaps we could instead be curious about what we (client and counselor) have missed or not yet attended to in the recovery efforts. We can support them during the times they may feel like they're drowning. We can stand on the shore and actually throw the life ring and hold on tight. We can support while they continue to try and save themselves. Alternatively, we can say through policy that effectively "if you can no longer tread in the water, you'll drown."

  A concept from Relational Cultural Therapy (Jordan, 2000, 2017) called *mutual empathy* is especially relevant here. Mutual empathy is not a simple exchange of empathy back and forth between counselor and client. Instead, it's the idea that both people are impacted by one another and that impact matters. The client should be able to see and be impacted by our empathy for their experiences. They should be able to pick up on and really connect with our empathy for them (Jordan, 2000, 2017). It should be evident that we care and we shouldn't hide it. Invest in your clients and allow them to see your investment. Really work to connect (and of course, maintain professional boundaries). I highly recommend reading more into Relational Cultural Therapy, particularly as it relates to connection and healing within the therapeutic relationship. Jordan (2017) is a wonderful place to start.

2 Social role involvements

  Essentially, the more social ties and roles a person has, the better the adjustment to great loss. This is fairly intuitive; the more you are invested in life, the less alone you might feel. The more you interact and involve yourself with others, the more those others are likely to notice if you are struggling. Remember that roles can vary and include being a friend, parent, partner, employee, volunteer, pet parent, etc.

For some people working toward recovery, connection may feel unfamiliar at best, and terrifying at worst. Processing any fears, hesitations, or doubts may prove useful in addition to social skills training (i.e. assertiveness, but also how to make friends, how to be a friend, etc.). Teaching someone what makes a healthy relationship and how they'll know; help them find the good parts of who they are and help them learn to freely offer those parts to others. Help clients learn to talk about themselves and what they value. Encourage clients to risk social involvement—that is, volunteering. Believing they have something to offer may also be unfamiliar for some—help them remember what they have to give and encourage them to give it over time.

3   Religious resources and ethnic expectations

Despite the name, don't pigeonhole yourself into thinking that this piece has to revolve around a religious tradition. This part can help some clients to memorialize what they're losing or have lost. As mentioned earlier in the chapter, learn about the culture of your client and which aspects of it they find meaningful around loss. Some may find ceremonies in which they say "goodbye" helpful; others may seek an enduring connection and work to integrate what's been lost into a new identity moving forward. Some cultures and people highly value the past, others look ahead to the future. Talk to your clients. Ask what they find useful when transitioning in life; do they want to hold on or let go of the old ways? Are they somewhere in between? Do they want tangible reminders of their past (i.e. pictures, collages, journals, or other artifacts) or do they prefer to rely on memory and less tangible means of remembering? As per usual, rely on your client to inform you.

Concurrent Stresses

Here's another chance for me to remind you to go back and refresh your brain around secondary losses! What it really boils down to is this: if the primary loss comes with a bunch of secondary losses, a person is expected to have a tougher time adjusting. Worden's seventh mediator here also points out that concurrent stress (i.e. stress happening at or around the same time as the loss) can complicate the efforts to change. The implications for recovery efforts here are numerous. If clients are working on or struggling with any of the following, they may also struggle with adjusting to a life without a substance, behavior, or pattern:

- Housing
- Finances
- Employment

- Legal involvement/probation/suspended sentences
- Relational troubles or lack of healthy relationships
- Mental health
- Domestic violence
- Trauma
- Transportation
- Parenting
- Lack of confidence/self-esteem/self-efficacy
- Other deaths or losses
- Mandated treatment rather than voluntary
- School or academic stress

And the list can go on and on…

Consider that any of these listed (and many more that are not) could result from the primary loss of a substance, behavior, or pattern (that would make these secondary losses). They could also be distinct from the loss of substance, behavior, or pattern and simply be occurring at the same time as recovery efforts (that would make them concurrent). Either way, give clients credit for all they may be dealing with. Have patience and help them have patience too. One single change can take time; multiple changes can take a LOT of time. Give grace and acknowledge the enormity of what many clients are up against.

References

Ali, J. I. (2010). *Mourning me: An interpretive description of grief and identity loss in older adults with mild cognitive impairment (MCI)* (Unpublished doctoral dissertation). University of Victoria, Victoria, BC, Canada.

Attig, T. (2001). Relearning the world: Making and finding meanings. In R. A. Neimeyer (Ed.), *Meaning reconstruction and the experience of loss* (pp. 33–53). Washington, DC: American Psychological Association.

Boelen, P. A., & van den Bout, J. (2002). Positive thinking in bereavement: Is it related to depression, anxiety, or grief symptomatology? *Psychological Reports, 91*, 857–863.

Boerner, K., & Heckhausen, J. (2003). To have and have not: Adaptive bereavement by transforming mental ties to the deceased. *Death Studies, 27*, 199–226.

Boss, P., Roos, S., & Harris, D. L. (2011). Grief in the midst of ambiguity and uncertainty: An exploration of ambiguous loss and chronic sorrow. In R. A. Neimeyer, D. L. Harris, & H. R. Winokuer (Eds.), *Grief and bereavement in contemporary society: Bridging research and practice* (pp. 163–176). New York, NY: Routledge.

Bowlby, J. (1980). *Attachment and loss: Vol. 3. Loss: Sadness and depression.* New York, NY: Basic Books.

Bowlby, J. (1982). *Attachment and loss* (Second ed., Harper torchbooks; 5087). New York, NY: Basic Books.

Bugge, K. B., Darbyshire, P., Rokholt, E. G., Haugstvedt, K. T. S., & Helseth, S. (2014). Young children's grief: Parents' understanding and coping. *Death Studies, 38*, 36–43.

DiBase, R. J. (2012). *Disenfranchised grief: Oncology nurses facing the challenge.* Retrieved on May 11, 2018 from http://www.cancer.org/acs/groups/content/@ greatlakes/documents /image/acspc-036055.pdf

Doka, K. (1989). *Disenfranchised grief: Recognizing hidden sorrow.* Lexington, MA: Lexington Books.

Doka, K. J. (Ed.). (2002). *Disenfranchised grief: New directions, challenges, and strategies for practice.* Champaign, IL: Research Press.

Dowdney, L. (2000). Childhood bereavement following parental death. *Journal of Child Psychology and Psychiatry, 41,* 819–830.

Folkman, S. (2001). Revised coping theory and the process of bereavement. In M. S. Stroebe, R. O. Hansson, W. Stroebe, & H. Schut (Eds.), *Handbook of bereavement research: Consequences, coping, and care* (pp. 563–584). Washington, DC: American Psychological Association.

Fraley, R. C., & Bonanno, G. A. (2004). Attachment and loss: A test of three competing models on the association between attachment-related avoidance and adaptation to bereavement. *Personality and Social Psychology Bulletin, 30*(7), 878–890.

Jordan, J. V. (2000). The role of mutual empathy in relational/cultural therapy. *Journal of Clinical Psychology, 56*(8), 1005–1016.

Jordan, J. V. (2017). *Relational-cultural therapy (Theories of psychotherapy series),* 2nd ed. Washington, DC: American Psychological Association.

Klass, D., Silverman, P. R., & Nickman, S. L. (Eds.). (1996). *Continuing bonds: New understandings of grief.* Washington, DC: Taylor & Francis.

Melhem, N. M., Moritz, G., Walker, M., Shear, M. K., & Brent, D. (2007). Phenomenology and correlates of complicated grief in children and adolescents. *Journal of the Academy of Child & Adolescent Psychiatry, 46*(4), 493–499.

National Child Traumatic Stress Network, issuing body. (2012). *Guiding adults in talking to children about death and attending services.* Washington, DC: National Child Traumatic Series Network. Retrieved on March 5, 2019 from https:// permanent.access.gpo.gov/gpo46098/talking_points_about_services.pdf

Neimeyer, R. A. (2001). *Meaning reconstruction and the experience of loss.* Washington, DC: American Psychological Association.

Neimeyer, R. A., & Sands, D. C. (2011). Meaning reconstruction in bereavement: From principles to practice. In R. A. Neimeyer, D. L. Harris, & H. R. Winokuer (Eds.), *Grief and bereavement in contemporary society: Bridging research and practice* (pp. 9–22). New York, NY: Routledge.

Nolen-Hoeksema, S. (2001). Ruminative coping and adjustment to bereavement. In M. Stroebe, R. O. Hansson, W. Stroebe, & H. A. W. Schut (Eds.), *Handbook of bereavement research: Consequences, coping and care* (pp. 545–562). Washington DC: American Psychological Association Press.

Perls, F. (1969). *Gestalt therapy verbatim.* Lafayette, CA: Real People Press.

Prigerson, H. G. (2008). Traumatic grief as a distinct disorder. In M. S. Stroebe, R. O. Hansson, H. Schut, & W. Stroebe (Eds.), *Handbook of bereavement research* (pp. 613–646). Washington, DC: American Psychological Association.

Rnic, K., Dozois, D. J. A., & Martin, R. A. (2016). Cognitive distortions, humor styles, and depression. *European Journal of Psychology, 12*(3), 348–362.

Schnider, K. R., Elhai, J. D., & Gray, M. J. (2007). Coping style use predicts post-traumatic stress and complicated grief symptom severity among college students reporting a traumatic loss. *Journal of Counseling Psychology, 54,* 344–350.

Sood, A. B., Razdan, A., Weller, E. B., & Weller, R. A. (2006). Children's reactions to parental and sibling death. *Current Psychiatry Reports, 8,* 115–120.

Stroebe, M. (1992). Coping with bereavement: A review of the grief work hypothesis. *Omega, 26,* 19–42.

Stroebe, M. S., Schut, H., & Boerner, K. (2010). Continuing bonds in adaptation to bereavement: Toward theoretical integration. *Clinical Psychology Review, 30,* 259–268.

Stroebe, M. S., Schut, H., & Stroebe, W. (2006). Who benefits from disclosure? Exploration of attachment style differences in the effects of expressing emotions. *Clinical Psychology Review, 26,* 133–139.

Stroebe, W., Stroebe, M., Abakoumkin, G., & Schut, H. (1996). The role of loneliness and social support in adjustment to loss: A test of attachment versus stress theory. *Journal of Personality and Social Psychology, 70,* 1241–1249.

Winokuer, H. R. & Harris, D. L. (2012). *Principles and practices of grief counseling.* New York, NY: Springer Publishing Company.

Worden, J. W. (1996). *Children & grief: When a parent dies.* New York, NY: Guilford Press.

Worden, J. W. (2009). *Grief counseling and grief therapy: A handbook for the mental health practitioner* (4th ed.). New York, NY: Springer.

Wortman, C. B., & Silver, R. C. (2001). The myths of coping with loss revisited. In M. Stroebe, R. O. Hansson, W. Stroebe, & H. Schut (Eds.), *Handbook of bereavement: Consequences, coping, and care* (pp. 405–429). New York, NY: Cambridge University Press.

Zisook, S., Paulus, M., Shuchter, S. R., & Judd, L. L. (1997). The many faces of depression following spousal bereavement. *Journal of Affective Disorders, 45,* 85–94.

11 Four Stages of Grief and Variants of Pathological Mourning and Considering the Four Stages and Variants in the Context of Addiction and Recovery

Bowlby's (1969, 1980, 1994) ideas have been incorporated into many theories on grief over the years. Earlier, you read about adult attachment styles in relation to the Continuing Bonds Theory, internalizations within the Mental Representations Theory, and personality variables and attachment principles that are found in Worden's Four Tasks of Mourning; all are connected to Bowlby. Since many of his ideas have already been discussed and connected to these various approaches, I will not do so again here. I do however want to walk through the four stages of grief as proposed by Bowlby and Parkes (1970) (Note: I have seen these four referenced as both "stages" and "phases"). Following that, additional perspectives from Bowlby's work around mourning and loss will be presented, particularly his ideas around *healthy* and *pathological* mourning.

Four Stages of Grief

The four stages are as follows:

1 Numbness, shock, and denial
2 Yearning and protest
3 Despair, disorganization, hopelessness, and low mood
4 Reorganization and recovery

The first stage, per this model, captures one's immediate reaction, and comes with a sense of unreality (Bowlby & Parkes, 1970; Mallon, 2008; Parkes, 1996, 2006). Think of this as someone trying to take it all in and process the loss now before them. Some may struggle to comprehend what's happened and both their senses and their mind may fail them (i.e. feeling numb or in total disbelief). The shock of such a blow may bring that sense of unreality and questions/statements such as:

> "This can't be happening."
> "It can't be real."
> "This is a joke."

"Are you being serious?"
"This isn't funny."

A sense of impermanence may also be conveyed:

"It/they'll be back again. It/They're not really gone forever."
"I don't believe you." Or "You're lying."
"This isn't real. It's not as bad as it seems, and it'll go back to normal soon."

This stage may also bring silence as some will not have words to express these feeling states or have a desire to speak about them:

"Just leave me alone."
"Stop talking to me."

Moreover, during this initial stage/phase, the loss may seem impossible to accept. Somatic distress may also present and result in complaints of physical pain. According to Bowlby and Parkes, it can be problematic if people don't move beyond this stage *at some point*.

If they remain in stage one, they will remain stuck in their pain with little understanding of the emotional impact of the loss (because they run from it). I think of this as similar to someone running into the ocean but as soon as a wave comes toward them, they retreat to dry land. They're running from the actual experience of the ocean; they're retreating to safety every time the water comes close. There's no real harm, per se, in running. But the feel of the water, the sensations it brings, and the excitement of one's ability to swim in it are missed. When people continuously run from their emotions for fear of drowning in them, they miss out on both the sensations (i.e. pain, joy, relief, fear) *and* recognition of their ability to stay afloat.

Part of our job as counselors is to help clients learn to swim in a sea that seems impossible, at first, to swim in. Practically, this looks like a validation of emotions, assisting clients with identification, understanding, and communication of their feelings, and increasing awareness (and ultimately utilization) of their internal and external resources.

The second stage centers on yearning and protest and it's pretty much what it sounds like. Individuals may protest the reality of their situation and yearn for the lost object to return. The hole left by the loss is noticed, often painfully so. Emotional responses may ebb and flow between longing for the lost object and anger at its absence. Crying, anxiety, and tension may be present and what's lost may be intensely missed. Concentration may be difficult, and one may present as irritable, frustrated, and preoccupied.

A sense of guilt might also be present, particularly when one feels they didn't do enough to prevent the loss or lessen its impact. Blame might also be a common theme if others were involved and had power to influence the outcome. In the case of death, the decedent's presence may be felt or sought (Bowlby & Parkes, 1970; Mallon, 2008; Parkes, 1996, 2006).

People may seek to regain a sense of comfort by filling the gaps left by the loss. Others might present as preoccupied with the lost object and look for reminders or ties to the past, so they don't forget. This reminds me of the idea that it's okay to revisit the past, but we don't want to live there. Bowlby and Parkes believed that if people didn't eventually find a way to move beyond this yearning and searching, their life would become and remain stagnant.

Despair, disorganization, hopelessness, and low mood characterize the third stage (Bowlby & Parkes, 1970). In short, reality has landed. There is an acknowledgment that things have changed and that those changes are permanent. One feels completely out of sorts and is unsure if that feeling will end anytime soon. People fall into a pit and don't see a way out. Not surprisingly, they feel badly.

The word that best captures this stage for me is *scattered*. Emotions are winning over logic and feelings of helplessness and hopelessness can be intense. For some, there may be an underlying fear that life will never make sense again in the absence of the lost object. People can feel aimless and unsure of what to do next. Isolation may present and people may retreat into their thoughts, getting stuck in ruminative patterns. Individuals who become stuck in this stage can experience anger, unrelenting negativity, and hopelessness (Bowlby & Parkes, 1970; Parkes, 1996, 2006).

The fourth stage focuses on reorganization and recovery. This stage is marked by new perspectives and returning hope. One is able to acknowledge that life can continue following the loss and takes steps toward that end. New patterns are developed and implemented, and life begins to take on a new shape. Essentially, people become less scattered and begin putting the puzzle pieces back into place so that the larger life picture makes sense again. This may involve a so-called letting go of the past (Bowlby & Parkes, 1970; Parkes, 1996, 2006). It may also involve an investment in the future. This is reminiscent of the continuing bonds theory and emotional relocation of loss.

Ultimately, Bowlby believed the loss was relocated, not forgotten. The loss moves to a different part of our brain. The loss no longer consumes the conscious mind; life continues and the loss fades into background noise. The loss is still there, it still has influence, but it's not running the show any longer.

Mallon (2008) made an important point when reflecting on this model. At the time of its creation in 1970, Bowlby and Parkes did not consider cultural differences in grief. This again reminds us that we cannot and should not put people into boxes.

Grief isn't standardized (aka there isn't one right way to do it) because people aren't standardized. The way one person reacts to a loss will be different than another reacting to the same loss. Don't ever forget that. Allow for variation in responses and do not expect grief to be neatly laid out into sequential stages. Use these ideas as loose guides, as jumping-off points for exploration into one's personal experience. Clients ultimately determine the exact direction and scope of their grief process.

Variants of Pathological Mourning

Bowlby differentiated between "healthy" and "pathological" mourning as follows (1994):

- *Healthy* = processes that in time leads to full, or nearly full, function being restored (i.e. a renewal of the capacity to make and maintain loving relationships) (p. 186)
- *Pathological* = processes that in time leads to an impairment of function to a greater or lesser degree (i.e. diminished capacity to make and maintain loving relationships) (p. 186)

Bowlby described four variants, or patterns, of pathological mourning in adults (1994). To put it simply, he believed there was an expected response pattern when someone was up against a significant loss. As you read, keep in mind that these variants were not meant to exist in isolation. These patterns could be experienced in combination with one another and could result in, or coexist with, other states of being familiar to counselors such as anxiety and depression.

Variant one was all about instinct. Instinct drives us to focus on the lost object and to yearn for it. This instinctual yearning is paired with an "angry effort to recover the lost object…" (Bowlby, 1994, p. 185). He believed this response pattern could contribute to one's ability to eventually let go of the lost object and move on toward greater functioning.

To Bowlby, "healthy" mourning included yearning, crying, and preservation of thoughts, feelings, and actions associated with the lost object. It also included aggression. The idea was that all of these parts had their place in recovering the lost object; in short, they were useful. He noted that the combination of yearning, crying, aggression, and memory might work to recover a temporary loss. When up against a permanent loss, however, this combination would ultimately fail. Since the lost object could not be recovered, a "healthy" response would also include a gradual end to these behaviors.

A pathological, "unhealthy" response would be the continuation of them (i.e. yearning, crying, and preservation of thoughts, etc.) when no change or recovery is possible. In short, someone holds on even when it's clear that it won't work; life stalls and they do not move on and reorganize and regroup within their new reality. They remain stuck in the past and remain preoccupied with the lost object. They also hang onto the emotional fallout. They may continue to "weep" (p. 189) for their loss and present as irritable to self and others.

Another aspect considered pathological was the inability to accept and express a strong desire for reunion (1994). Over time, the unexpressed urge and desire would become repressed and thus, persist in the background. In sum, this first pathological variant is characterized by an *unconscious yearning for the lost object*.

The second variant was *unconscious reproach against the lost object combined with conscious and unremitting self-reproach*. Basically, there is intense and unrelenting anger and criticism directed both outward and inward; one is angry at the lost object, the world (i.e. revenge is sought), and at themselves (Bowlby, 1994; Freud, 1917). The point of all this anger, according to Bowlby, was to achieve a reunion with what's been lost. Bowlby believed this angry response to be characteristic of "healthy" mourning. Put simply, he saw aggression as effective; it had the potential to get the job done. If the point was to reunite with the lost object, an angry response increased the likelihood that it might happen—anger provided energy and vigor. Once reunited, anger could serve as a warning to not become lost again.

Think of an example where a child wanders off in a busy store. When the parent and child are reunited, the parent yells at the child to pay attention and stay close to not go missing again. They may also express their fear and panic at noticing the child had gone missing. The anger is meant to be protective and precautionary. It's the same idea here for what's been lost—if one gets mad, there's a chance it won't be lost again.

But what use is this anger if something cannot be retrieved or reunification is not possible? Per Bowlby, this lands one into "unhealthy," pathological territory. The expression of anger becomes futile and prolonged because it can't work; reunion isn't possible, so the anger is all that remains. That anger can be directed at others, the self, or at the lost object itself. Importantly, Bowlby noted that the pathology or unhealth isn't linked to the existence of the anger, but in the misdirection of the anger. Accepting the angry feelings and helping people sort out where to direct their anger and reproach was important.

The third variant was the *compulsive caring for others*. Essentially, to bypass the pain, all energy is put into caring for others that are hurting. This isn't just kindness, it's compulsion. People may surround themselves with others who have experienced significant loss or are otherwise perceived as helpless. It's a distraction and energy is diverted away from one's own emotional pain and focused on another. Bowlby believed that the yearning for the lost object and the anger previously discussed could also be transferred onto these 'others' and an overlap of the variants was possible.

One additional angle worth noting here is Bowlby's point that at times, this variant may be useful in a practical sense. For example, if one's mother dies and the individual fills that role as caretaker for others in the home (or any circumstance around role fulfillment), they are bypassing their pain, yes, but they are also helping with the adjustment to the loss. This potential expression is reminiscent of previous discussion around the restoration-oriented activities in the DPM and/or the external adjustments in Worden's Four Tasks of Mourning.

The fourth variant then was the *persistent disbelief that the loss is permanent*; also known as denial. Bowlby believed that denial was part of a larger picture. He also believed that people had awareness, at some level, that something had been lost. The denial allowed for the absence of an instinctual response (i.e. anger, redirection of attention, etc.). Denial sounds to be protective of the ego from this point of view. In short, it's not bad, it's meaningful. Despite the importance and meaning attached to this pattern though, for Bowlby the pathology lay in the restriction of experience. As he so clearly stated, "grief is only partially experienced because loss is only partially admitted" (1994, p. 202).

Important to note here is that Bowlby's work was predominantly around losses in childhood, and particularly the loss of a parent (often the mother). He noted that in his experience when adults responded to loss via one or more of the four variants, they had often experienced a significant loss in earlier life. He also noted that children often grieve in similar ways to adults; therefore, the variants are not age-restricted (Bowlby, 1994). Finally, it's important to remind the reader that Bowlby has written volumes (literally) explaining his theories and this is just a small snapshot. Please refer to his works for expanded discussions and ideas around these concepts.

Considering *the Four Stages of Grief* in the Context of Addiction and Recovery

Stage 1: Numbness, Shock, and Denial

Think of this stage as someone trying to get a sense of the loss(es) now before them and being somewhat overwhelmed at the experience. Some clients may struggle to comprehend or even identify what losses they have sustained, and both their senses and mind may fail them (i.e. feeling numb or in total disbelief).

Making the shift from a life dominated by addictive patterns to one without is quite a change and the sense of the losses can be huge. For instance, losing one's coping method, relationships tied to the addiction, routine, sense of control, certainty, and/or power, etc. Literal deaths might have occurred—some might have been directly related to an addiction (i.e. overdose) while others may have overlapped with the timeline of an addiction (i.e. someone important died while the client was immersed in their addictive patterns).

When someone moves toward recovery, there can be a tendency to look to the future rather than the past, a focus on gains rather than losses. As hopeful as looking forward can be, it can discount what one is moving away from. If clients (or counselors) are too forward-focused, they may not realize or attend to the losses that come with ending an addictive pattern. Importantly, clients might not realize all the ways their use/pattern contributed to their life, for better and for worse, until they lose it. Thus, the full measure of what is now lost may not be known until change begins. When those losses eventually land, they can be jarring. As counselors, try and appreciate how hard that can be.

Numbness, shock, and/or a sense of unreality could present in a multitude of ways:

- Denying the severity of their use/pattern
- Refusal to discuss or acknowledge associated losses
- No-shows for sessions or repeated cancelling (avoidance)
- Rejecting the idea that harm has been caused (to themselves or others) due to the addiction
- Reports that one feels "nothing" or appearing unfazed by significant losses or life circumstances
- Shutting down and disconnecting from an interaction
- Laughing out of context
- Dissociation/spacing out

Stage 2: Yearning and Protest

There's no big leap to be made here. On ending use or an addictive pattern, clients may discover that they long for it. They may miss the substance or behavior intensely and desire to return to the old ways (it doesn't mean they will). They may seek comfort from old sources as they work toward new patterns. Letting go of what worked can be difficult.

Individuals may protest the reality of their situation and express anger at the absence of the lost object. The lost object in this context might be a drug, person/relationship, choice, power, trust, a behavior such as gambling or eating, a job, money, and so on.

Some clients may present as irritable and prickly because they know that there's no going back, at least not without consequence. I have found this to be true for many clients, but particularly for mandated clients. Whether the mandate for change came from the courts or one's family or friends is no matter, the resulting loss of choice, power, and sense of freedom often leads to irritability in my experience. Some examples of protests I've heard include,

> "Don't tell me what to do. I don't want to be here [in counseling]. I didn't choose this. _____ forced me to come."
> "I'm not that bad off. I know what I'm doing."
> "I hate heroin and what it did to my life."

"I hate feeling this way [withdrawals]; I hate heroin so much, but damn do I want to shoot up."

"How did my life get this way? At least when I'm high I don't notice how big of a disaster I am."

"How could they fire me?! I only drank at work one time. They had no right to let me go over one mistake."

"It's not my fault. None of this is my fault. I wish people would just leave me alone."

Clients may seek to regain a sense of comfort by filling the gaps left by the loss. In the addictive context, this might look like substance or behavior jumping (i.e. heroin is no longer used, but alcohol has taken its place, or one stops using illicit substances altogether and begins compulsively overeating).

Others might present as preoccupied with the lost object and look for reminders or ties to the past. An application of this idea in the recovery context is when clients retell "war stories" about their substance use. Retelling old stories maintains a connection to the past. The continued identification as an "addict" can keep some from moving forward into recovery. Longing for the identity and certainty that addiction provided (for some) can be hard to let go of.

Many clients will yearn for what they've lost, both the presence and absence. What I mean is that some clients will yearn for the presence of a substance, a high associated with relationships, feeling powerful, feeling in control, etc. and will protest the absence of such things in recovery. Likewise, some clients will yearn for the absence of pain, loneliness, uncertainty, fear, etc. and protest the presence of these in recovery.

This stage is a fascinating one when applied to the addiction and recovery context. There are many meaningful discussions to be had—don't miss them. Help clients explore and gain insight into what they long/yearn for—it's a useful endeavor as it essentially makes a list of things that need to be accounted for or gained in treatment.

Don't punish preoccupation, expect it. Remember to look beyond the initial craving to what's being craved.

For example:

- Is it really heroin being craved or the numbness that came with it?
- Is it really an "unhealthy" person they're yearning for or companionship?
- Is it the gambling or the sense of power and significance that came with winning?

Remember to search for the meaning behind the yearning. What are they actually seeking?

Don't take cravings or yearning at face value. Look deeper and identify the need. If clients long to feel powerful again, client and counselor can discuss the experience of powerlessness and find healthier and more long-lasting ways to feel significant in the world. If clients yearn for the absence of loneliness, counselor and client can examine both current and past relationships and the role addiction played. It may be that the addiction brought community or regular interactions with other people who used or dealers. New community might need to be built or the client may need support in identifying and asking for what they need from current relationships. It might also be that the drug or pattern numbed the pain of loneliness and now it has come back into awareness with sobriety and/or recovery.

There are multiple possibilities and that's the point. Don't miss out on these conversations by avoiding the losses. Somewhat ironically, so much can be gained by examining what's been lost.

Stage 3: Despair, Disorganization, and Hopelessness

I understand this stage to mean that the shock, numbness, and denial from stage one have dissolved and the reaction has arrived. The full measure of what is now lost has taken shape and for some people, the response can look despairing, disorganized, and hopeless. This is by no means all clients, but for those that do experience this stage, it can be intense. There can be a deep sense of pain that has no defined end point.

Consider the following examples:

- A client reporting loneliness and despair at the realization that their relationships connected to their addiction can't continue. They report that they are "alone" in the world. Additionally, they feel stuck in that aloneness. They do not know how to make friends or reengage in relationships that don't have an addictive component. They feel lost and disorganized, unsure of their next move.
- A client reporting a pregnancy loss during their active addiction and mourning the loss of the child they envisioned and experiencing intense guilt over their role in the death. This client had a late-term loss that was reportedly connected to severe malnutrition. The malnutrition was connected to her cocaine use. Sobriety brought the realization that her behaviors contributed to the loss and when she no longer used to avoid it, that landed like a ton of bricks. She felt like she "murdered my baby." Denial was replaced by despair and disorganization; she didn't know what to do with such intense feelings. The pull to use in order to numb the guilt and sadness was fierce. The client knew she didn't want a relapse but had not yet developed alternate coping skills. She languished in her pain while trying to decide on the next steps.
- Consider clients who despair when their efforts don't result in immediate change. When someone does all the "right" things and still struggles, despair and a sense of aimlessness (or disorganization) can

result. This might sound like: "I'm not getting better. Nothing is changing. What if I'm doomed to this life?" Without adequate support, these feelings can devolve into hopelessness.

Be realistic with clients. Loss is hard and one may not have a clear path in front of them to resolve it. Sit with clients in that confusion and invite the questions that may be swirling in their heads to enter the room. Empathize with how hard uncertainty can be; normalize the presence of hopelessness. Remember that emotions might be winning over logic. Support and acknowledge the client's experience and reactions and *really* listen. Listen with the intent to understand their feelings; fight the urge to "fix" their situation or talk them out of their emotional response (i.e. "It's not as bad as you think," "You're remembering it wrong," "It wasn't your fault," or "Find the silver lining. You're too focused on the pain."). Allow the pain and work to understand both its source and impact; reorganization comes later.

Stage 4: Reorganization and Recovery

As the name implies, this stage focuses on reconstruction. Clients are working to piece together their life. This stage is about adaptation and growth. Clients have a sense of their pain and what they are dealing with thanks to the previous stage. Here, they do something with that knowledge and insight.

New skills are acquired and implemented (i.e. coping, relational, job/vocational skill, etc.) and many clients look less scattered, and as a result they get a sense of direction, and for some, a sense of purpose or return. Renewed hope is evidenced by a focus on the future. Clients begin to change their relationship with the past, becoming informed by it rather than defined by it. Readers who have or currently work in the field might draw similarities with this stage and mid-to-late recovery.

Counselors can help this reorganization process along in several ways depending on client need:

- Gently introducing additional perspectives. For instance, one doesn't have to forget the past to heal. Lessons can be drawn from past experience to inform future choices. Help clients make those connections; help them value where they've been as much as where they're going.
  - Assisting clients in transforming their pain and applying new meaning. Meaning reconstruction will be discussed in a future chapter as well. For now, remember that the meaning one attributes to an experience can determine its impact. Help clients enter recovery with a survivor identity versus an "addict" identity. Focus on what skills they already possess while they work to acquire and use new ones.

- As counselors, help clients understand that integrating a loss into one's experience isn't the same as forgetting. It's making the loss a part of us; something that continues to inform our lives. It becomes a passenger in the car, rather than the driver. Reduce the pressure some clients feel to forget or completely cut ties with the past; rather, shoot for integration and learning.
- Helping clients identify and engage with available or potential relationships. For some clients, that might involve learning how to socialize without substances or addictive contexts (i.e. gambling).
- Assisting clients with vocational exploration. Some clients might want to return to the workforce, pursue education, or change careers. Helping clients reorganize their life in a way that supports recovery is an important aspect of our work.
- Providing ongoing encouragement and reminders of their ability and worth. Change is hard and occasional reminders of their ability to persist may be helpful for some.
- Remember that clients are working to reorganize their cognitions, emotions, and behavior. As counselor, don't become too focused on behavioral change. Embrace the whole person and check-in on thoughts, feelings, *and* behaviors as clients work to live differently.

Considering the *Variants of Pathological Mourning* in the Context of Addiction and Recovery

Any time there's a dichotomy of health around emotional processing (i.e. healthy vs. pathological mourning), my red flags rise, and I am cautious. Let me begin then by stating that health versus unhealth (or pathology) is more of a continuum than a true dichotomy. Health from Bowlby's perspective was when patterns led someone in a direction that is likely to restore functioning, and in particular, to a place where safe, loving relationships were possible and plausible. Unhealth/pathology was when patterns sustained impairment and reduced someone's ability to form and maintain safe, loving relationships.

Thinking about the four variants in the context of mourning the loss of a substance, related relationship or object, or an addictive pattern or behavior, several ideas and connections come to mind.

Unconscious Yearning for the Lost Object

I can't overstate how much I appreciate Bowlby's perspective on aggression and the instinctual response to loss. I have known many clients who are angry when entering treatment. When exploring those feelings, loss is often a familiar theme. Some have lost control or the ability to choose for themselves (think mandated clients). Others have lost important relationships or the trust of someone they love. Some have lost self-respect, and others have lost a person to death. Loss is part of addiction and as noted in Chapter 2, it can come in many forms. Let's consider how *unconscious yearning for the lost object* might play out in this context.

To recover something, one has to be aware of its absence. For some people, this awareness lies predominantly in the background or the unconscious part of our minds. Our instinct then drives us to recover what's been lost. But what happens when the loss was productive; meaning the lost object or person was a source of unhealth. What happens when someone unconsciously yearns for something that was bad for them (i.e. substance, abusive or unhealthy relationships, addictive patterns)?

First and foremost, remember that per this approach, we're designed to grab at what we've lost so this yearning makes sense; it's not unexpected. Think of it as a reflex. For example, I recall a former client saying

> I had a terrible day at work and somehow ended up at my dealer's house even though my recovery was going pretty good. It was like muscle memory; my body drove me there. I don't know what my mind was doing.

While this kind of response is not necessarily unexpected, it *is* considered pathological in the sense that this type of yearning doesn't serve the person in the long run. Moving back toward things that lead to unhealth is inherently unhealthy. Thinking about what was yearned for here though yields several possibilities. The 'lost object' being desired could have been:

- the oxycontin itself
- the comfort or promise of emotional numbing (which was achieved through oxy use in the past)
- the familiar routine of going to the dealer's house when feeling stressed
- the friendly interactions with their former dealer and need for connection in a time of stress

The client, having had a very bad day at work, reacted to the negative emotional state by doing what they did in the past. There was no conscious planning according to the client, they just got in their car, started driving, and that's "where my body took me." Once they tuned-in back into their conscious experience, they realized that they did not want to use and rely on old methods of coping (namely oxycontin use). Importantly, unconscious yearning does not always lead to behavioral setbacks. This client's conscious mind was able to notice the desire to cope with stress (via oxycontin), use refusal skills when offered the pills, and ultimately left and went home without using. The unconscious yearning was overridden by conscious thought in the end due to the client's ability to be mindful.

Talk to your clients. Talk about what's been lost. Talk about what's missed when it comes to addiction. Work to bring the unconscious yearning to the forefront—make it conscious. When we have awareness of our thoughts, we have more power to choose action or inaction. Restoring a sense of power and choice should, in my humble opinion, be a central theme in treatment. Focus on exploring the whole experience of recovery—the good, the bad, and the ugly. Tell the "glory stories" and the "war stories." Reflect on the good that was found in the "bad" (i.e. pain relief, euphoria, illusion of connection, etc.). I made this same argument earlier in the text, but it's worth repeating.

Allow clients to miss the "bad" stuff. Invite them to yearn out loud and process what it means to yearn for something that one knows is bad for them. Talk about how our mind can compete with itself—the unconscious which often tells us what we want, and our conscious mind which often tells us what we need. There's no shortage of meaningful content here. *Don't miss it.*

Second, don't think that clients have learned nothing from counseling if they end up in precarious situations or do actually lapse back into old patterns. The instinct to recover what's been lost can be strong and operate in the background outside of awareness. Self-awareness combined with new skills (like the ones we often teach in counseling) may still win in the end even if the unconscious yearning leads the person back toward past behaviors. Finally, remember that Bowlby believed it was healthy to hang on to old thoughts, feelings, and behaviors related to the loss as long as they promote growth.

Help clients connect the dots between their desire to preserve old patterns and the need for change. Metaphorically, it's like a person that refuses, or is reluctant to, upgrade to a new car because their old one still works (i.e. it's a beater, but it runs). It's technically functional, but it's not the safest, nor the most comfortable option—and it could die at any given moment. The world might try to convince that person to let go and move on to a better vehicle because the old car is unsafe, old, rusty, worn, and not meeting current needs. The world may focus on the function and safety, while the owner may focus on the memories and connection to the vehicle. As counselors, we don't need to say "stop focusing on those bits, see the possibilities. You could have something so much better!" Instead, we can empathize with the desire to hold on to something that is maybe no longer worth holding on to. Something akin to…

> *I can tell that this is a car* (or time in your life) *that's full of memories and that you're having a hard time letting go. There were a lot of good times and you also worked hard to maintain this thing through the tough times. Let's focus on all the energy you put into this car* (or behavioral pattern) *and what you did that kept it going this long. Those are the things worth keeping and reinvesting in your next vehicle* (or stage of life). *Let's examine the investments you made and figure out which ones paid out in the end.*

It's taking time to acknowledge that the past may be hard to let go of, that the world might not understand the struggle to let go, and that there can be value in preserving and remembering the old patterns and behaviors. Helping clients sift through their old patterns and helping them determine which thoughts, feelings, and behaviors to preserve is part of our job, and a cool one at that. This part of the mourning process is healthy (per Bowlby) when we help clients bridge the past and the future by applying old patterns (i.e. stubborn perseverance, decisiveness) to newer, healthier contexts.

Unconscious Reproach against the Lost Object Combined with Conscious and Unremitting Self-Reproach

In case the reader is unfamiliar with the word 'reproach,' let me begin by defining it. A reproach is a criticism or a rebuke. Reproach against a lost object would be placing blame on the thing that's lost. For example, getting angry at a dog for breaking its leash and running away or getting angry at someone for dying by suicide or an accidental overdose. The blame, criticism, and associated feelings are directed outward at the person, thing, or object that's lost rather than at the self. Self-reproach would be getting on your own case and criticizing your actions, inactions, beliefs, feelings, etc. For example:

> "I should have known."
> "I should have stopped this."
> "Why didn't I say anything?"
> "Why did I let go (of the leash)?!"
> "Why wasn't I stronger?"
> "Why was I so stupid?" etc.

When facing a loss, these types of questions and statements can be fairly common. With regard to our focus here on addiction and recovery, I can tell you that I've heard many in my time with clients and even said some myself.

Consider how this second variant manifested in my experience. I have had one client die by suicide in my career so far and I hope he's the last. That death was more than a decade ago, but I can remember how badly I got caught up in the idea that I missed something in our sessions and that his death was somehow my fault. There was a large amount of conscious self-reproach. I analyzed everything I did and felt a simmering anger that I couldn't quite place. Over time, I realized that some of that anger was directed at my deceased client. I was mad at him for dying (*unconscious reproach against the lost object*).

From Bowlby's model, this anger toward my client and the intense self-criticism could be explained as an attempt to regain what I'd lost. Since my client was dead, he was not recoverable, but my confidence as a clinician, my sense of self-efficacy, and my memories of him were. The anger made the memories stick; it cemented them into my personal and professional memory. Without the anger, I think his memory may have become part of the overall tapestry of client memories, not a distinct story in and of itself.

The legacy of that anger and the vividness of my memories have served as a warning to never underestimate one's desire to die when recovering from a depressive episode and consumed by physical pain. I am a more vigilant professional and that has protective qualities for the other people I work with. My professional world was changed by his life and his death. It was a wonderful privilege to know him and sit with him through his pain, and it remains a privilege to remember him years later.

Thinking about clients who enter treatment angry. For some, that anger can quickly fade once trust and safety are established, but for others it sticks. As in my experience, the anger may serve to reunite the client with something they've lost. They may be fighting (near literally) to hang on to something they are being forced to let go of. This is not a sign of unhealth (per Bowlby), however challenging; it's part of a healthy mourning process. Consider some ways this can show up in a treatment context:

- The anger might repel other people and make it less likely that others will try to help. Anger can isolate because frankly, it's not pleasant to be around it much of the time. Anger can protect us from outside influence. If someone is threatened by, or not interested in, others' opinions on their behavior, health, life overall, anger might re-unite them with the so-called 'lost object'—in this case the freedom to choose for themselves, power, and/or control. The anger may deter someone from treatment because it's deterring them from change and/or giving up some control. It's a fight for independence and choice from this perspective (aka not wanting to lose them).
- If someone has tried to become sober or enter recovery and *been unsuccessful*, anger directed at their substance or at *themselves for perceptively failing might support their continued fight for a healthier life* (i.e. "I hate who I've become and I should be stronger than this. Why am I so weak? Get it together!"). It might also perceptively justify a return to old ways (i.e. "I can't do it, it's too damn hard! Why bother?! I'll always be a junkie.").
- If someone has tried to become sober or enter recovery and *been successful*, anger may still present. Through sobriety, treatment, and/or recovery they may have been reunited with their self-respect, pride, sense of resilience, past relationships, employment, health, etc. Some formerly 'lost objects' may have come back (reunified). Anger toward the past, oneself, others, etc. might serve as a warning to not become lost again. This idea may be useful in helping clients persist when treatment gets hard. It might also help understand why people are sometimes angry during periods of success or progress.

No matter which scenario the clients may be in, our job is to help find the meaning in the anger, to understand the purpose of its presence. Begin by identifying what was lost and then explore the reactions (anger and others) the client is experiencing. Take time to explore the anger they are aware/conscious of and also the anger that may lie beneath the surface, in the unconscious. Make connections and find the meaning of those feelings.

- Is it really anger at the self for "failing" again (i.e. lapsing or relapsing)?
- Is it anger at the drug and the chemical grip it has on one's mind and body?
- Is it fear that the progress/changes might slip away, and they may revert to old behaviors?
- Something else entirely?

Talk to your clients, examine what's been lost, and find the meaning in how they've responded. Then, use that information to inform their survival efforts (if not yet ready for recovery) or recovery efforts moving forward.

Compulsive Caring for Others

Recall that in this variant, people may surround themselves with others who have experienced a significant loss or are otherwise perceived as helpless (for example, another person living with an addictive pattern). This compulsive caring is thought to be a distraction as energy is diverted away from one's own emotional pain and focused on another. Avoidance is a common coping strategy, and I have seen it many times in the addictive context. There are two things to remember when we consider this variant:

1 Avoidance is not a four-letter word. It's not a bad thing ... it is a thing.
   - Resist the urge to label it "good" or "bad." It is simply a thing people do. We want to understand its purpose and respect the protective nature of it. Don't penalize or reprimand clients for avoiding "the issues." Work to understand the avoidance and diversion of attention from their own pain. Ask and then listen.
2 Bowlby was not trying to pathologize caring or kindness. He was presenting an option for how someone might respond to loss.
   - The potential pathology with this variant was that when one *only* cares for others and ignores the self, trouble can ensue. Primarily, the problem (per Bowlby) lies in the avoidance of one's own pain and experience. This is reminiscent in some ways to the grief work hypothesis noted in Chapter 2 that emphasizes the need to work through the pain of loss in order to 'move on.' From that perspective, bypassing the pain and actively avoiding one's feelings is pathological (aka doesn't serve the person in the long run).

When in the counselor role, use caution if you feel the impulse to tell people they *must* face their pain. Remember that when we think of coping strategies, both healthy and unhealthy versions exist. For instance, if I cope with distress via exercise, the initial judgment might be that it's a healthy means of coping. Exercise is good for us, right? But what if I exercise compulsively and wear my body down in the process? The health of the behavior becomes debatable; not because of the behavior itself, but because of the pattern of expression. Avoidance is similar. Wanting to avoid pain is human and healthy in terms of survival instincts (i.e. if I can avoid what hurts me, I'm in a better position to survive it). Avoidance of one's experience to the point that one doesn't acknowledge or attend to the pain *at all* can be problematic. The behavior itself (aka avoidance) is not unhealthy, but the pattern of expression can be.

We (counselors) do not determine what the most effective methods of coping are; we offer clients options, perspectives, information, and support. Remember that what works for one may not work for another. If a client presents with a compulsive need or pattern of caring for others in the wake of an addiction-related loss or during a recovery attempt, it might serve as an important coping skill. Mandating they drop it would be akin to saying, "stop coping, you're doing it wrong."

Also, remember that Bowlby did not believe that this compulsive caring for others was all bad. He believed that this was an expression of one's yearning for what they've lost and an attempt to regain a sense of completion. In the recovery context, this might present as someone focusing most or all of their energy on the welfare of others and seemingly ignoring their own recovery needs. Simply saying "focus on yourself" will likely fall short. Again, search for the meaning in the behavior.

Explore the needs, wants, and how this behavior pattern checks, or attempts to check, those boxes. Also, check-in on the function/purpose of the behavior. For example, if someone is engaging in caretaking behaviors of another who is stuck in an addictive pattern, and as such, appears to be ignoring or avoiding their own recovery needs, ask "why?"

Be considerate of your tone here; an accusing, patronizing "why?" (i.e. asking in such a way that one is made to feel stupid for engaging in the behavior) might only produce shame rather than invite self-reflection. An example of this type of *why* question might be: "Why aren't you focusing on yourself? You need to focus on you, not other people." A lot depends on the tone of voice when asking. *Try this:* say this last question out loud and apply a patronizing, slightly accusing tone to it and see how it sounds to your ear. Hopefully, you see my point. A genuine, sincere, curious "Why are you putting so much energy into caring for others and so little into caring for yourself?" (i.e. asking in such a way that the client knows you care and that you want to understand) might yield more self-reflection and spark discussion. To Bowlby's point, you might also get a concrete, rational answer like, "I'm focusing on everyone else because they need me to," or "I have to make them see that I'm not useless. That I actually can add to their lives. I need to be seen as worthy in their eyes again." (This second sentiment was conveyed by a former client).

The first example speaks to role fulfillment; that is taking on roles that were previously filled by the lost object or person. The latter speaks to the idea that some may care for others to prove their worth and lessen the burden for their loved ones. The caring can become unidirectional and totally other-focused because, for a long time, all eyes, energy and attention were on the client. The cared-for becomes the caretaker.

Ultimately, this variant is about adjusting to loss; sometimes people adjust through the compulsive caring for others. Sometimes people moving away from an addiction will be intensely other-focused. Please, don't shame, punish, or miss the value here. All behavior is purposeful.

Strive for balance with these clients. There's no need to give up caring for others; we just don't want the client to be left in the dust. Help them understand their compulsion, appreciate the meaning contained within it, and help them shift over time so that their needs are also met. Again, balance.

Persistent Disbelief that the Loss Is Permanent

Recall that this title is a fancy way to say denial. I have heard this word "denial" used repeatedly by a multitude of clinicians around addiction. Sadly, it is often said with derision. For example, imagine the following statements being said with irritation or contempt in one's voice: "They're just in denial" or "You [client] need to stop denying how bad this is. This could kill you and you've really hurt people who love you."

I agree with Bowlby's perspective that denial is rarely, if ever, complete. Meaning that most people who present as denying the severity of their situation DO know they are in a bad spot. People are aware they've lost something (i.e. health, respect, relationships, safety, ability to cope without substances, etc.) but are protecting themselves by keeping those losses out of full awareness. It's instinct.

Even if we think of denial as 'conscious deception,' it remains protective. Would you want to face the facts head-on that you've hurt yourself, people you love, and that you might not be able to fix it? I wouldn't. People sometimes protect by shielding themselves.

Rejecting the permanence of loss serves us in the short-term. It's reminiscent of the avoidance seen earlier in variant three. The idea that "If I can avoid what hurts me, I'm in a better position to survive it." In this variant, it becomes "If I can deny the hurt, maybe I won't notice the pain."

Do not punish or admonish your clients for how they protect themselves. Forcefully resist the urge to respond with frustration, exasperation, or strong confrontation. Instead, work to understand what they are protecting themselves from. Really think. Turn up your empathy and try to imagine why they would deny their situation.

When working with a client that denies, I find it helpful to think about the following questions:

1   What if recovery isn't truly better than active addiction? That is:
     •   What if 'facing' the pain isn't worth it in the end? (from the client's perspective)
     •   What if all that work just brings more pain?
     •   What if some of the things that would make a person feel whole can't be recovered?
     •   Would I want to face that reality and sit with that realization?
2   Could they function if the denial went away or would they be overwhelmed by the reality of it all?

The answers to these will, of course, vary widely depending on who you're working with. The point of such questions is not so much to get an actual answer but to help the counselor think about why denial might be present, to begin with.

Bowlby believed that restricting one's experience was the real problem here. That grief was only partially experienced because only part of the story was being acknowledged and told. Ultimately, appreciate the utility of the denial. Don't rip it away from people, understand its purpose and work to create a therapeutic relationship that allows for safe exploration of "reality," whatever it's perceived to be. By reducing the threat, you may also reduce the need to protect.

References

Bowlby, J. (1969). *Attachment and loss: Vol. 1: Attachment.* London, Hogarth, New York, NY: Basic Books.

Bowlby, J. (1980). *Attachment and loss: Vol. 3. Loss: Sadness and depression.* New York, NY: Basic Books.

Bowlby, J. (1994). Pathological mourning and childhood mourning. In R. V. Frankiel (Ed.), *Essential papers in psychoanalysis. Essential papers on object loss* (pp. 185–221). New York, NY: New York University Press. (Reprinted from "JAPA," 11, 1963, pp. 500–541).

Bowlby, J., & Parkes, C. M. (1970). Separation and loss within the family. In E. J. Anthony (Ed.), *The child in his family* (pp. 197–216). New York, NY: Wiley.

Freud, S. (1917). *Mourning and melancholia, standard edition of the complete psychological works of Sigmund Freud.* London: Hogarth Press.

Mallon, B. (2008). *Dying, death, and grief: Working with adult bereavement.* Los Angeles, CA: Sage Publications.

Parkes, C. M. (1996). *Bereavement: Studies of grief in adult life* (3rd ed.). London: Routledge.

Parkes, C. M. (2006). *Love and loss: The roots of grief and its complications.* New York, NY: Routledge.

12 The Six "R" Processes of Mourning and Considering the Six "R" Processes in the Context of Addiction and Recovery

Rando (1993) believed grief and mourning were different and echo what was described in Chapter 2. Grief was defined as a reaction to a loss; Rando believed this reaction was largely involuntary. As noted in Chapter 2, grief responses were thought to be comprehensive and included psychological, behavioral, social, and physical reactions to the perceived loss.

Mourning was viewed as an active, ongoing process toward accommodating a loss; more specifically, mourning behaviors are coping behaviors (Rando, 2000, 2015). In this model, people cope (aka mourn) by moving through six processes that focus on personal readjustments. These processes are intended to help people heal and reach a point where they can remember with less pain. Essentially, for current life to coexist with memories—remembering the past while reinvesting in the present. The six processes (each begins with an "R") occur in the context of three phases of mourning. During each of the three phases, certain "R" processes are accomplished.

Let's outline the three phases and the tasks completed within them:

Phase 1: Avoidance
Rando used the term "avoidance" for what most others call "denial." This phase is characterized by an inability or unwillingness to fully acknowledge the loss. This reminds me of the notion that sometimes it takes a while for the heart to accept what the head already knows. People in this phase might acknowledge that the loss has occurred, but have trouble fully accepting the reality of it.

Only one task is associated with this first phase:

1 Recognize the loss. It's what it sounds like. Individuals need to understand with their head and their heart that a loss has happened and that it *is* reality (Rando, 1993, 2000, 2015).

Phase 2: Confrontation
Basically, what was out of awareness is now in. The avoidance is gone, and the grief reactions are front and center. This phase is about finding ways to understand one's experience and to process the grief response.

Three tasks are associated with this phase:

1   **R**eact to the separation: People feel what they're feeling. The emotional response is felt and embraced. People work to understand what they're feeling. Of importance, there is no implication that the emotions must be sad or negative; Rando left that door open to a multitude of emotional responses. Recognition of the secondary losses attached to the primary loss also happens here.

2   **R**ecollect and reexperience: The recollect component of this is centered on balanced remembering. People work to remember the person they've lost and they remember both the good and not so good aspects of that relationship. Per Rando, these recollections can be fuel for a continuing bond/ongoing relationship (should one be sought) with who they've lost. The reexperiencing aspect centers more on the point that the departed will continue to exert influence on one's life (again, if that ongoing influence is sought).

3   **R**elinquish old attachments: This task focuses on the gradual processing of one's loss. Basically, over time (sometimes a long time) people process the impact of the loss and its meaning in their lives. This task may also include discussions of imagined futures with the deceased; futures that will no longer play out due to the loss.

Phase 3: Accommodation

This phase is about getting back in the game; people are no longer sidelined by their loss. People find meaning in life once more and begin to reexperience moments of joy (and many other emotions) (Rando, 1993, 2000, 2015).

Two tasks are associated with this phase:

1   **R**eadjust to the new world without forgetting the old world: This task is centered on figuring out how to fill the gaps left by a loss and filling them. This involves internal adjustments and accommodations. For instance, accepting new identities that may have emerged from a loss or reflecting on how the lost person changed them/ helped them develop. People are coping well with the loss in this task and that's evidenced by their increased sense of self-efficacy (i.e. "I can and am surviving this") paired with continued remembering/ sustained memories. One's life continues, but links to the past are retained. This is similar to the internal adjustments from Worden's model and the restoration-oriented activities from the DPM.

2   **R**einvest emotional energy: This is essentially what it sounds like; people find new places such as relationships, hobbies, work, etc. to reinvest their energy. This builds on the previous R where life begins to carry on. This isn't about a replacement of what's been lost; it's about reinvesting in life and finding renewed purpose and/or direction.

Considering *the Six "R" Processes of Mourning* in the Context of Addiction and Recovery

Rando's (1993, 2000, 2015) assertion that grief is an involuntary and comprehensive experience with psychological, behavioral, social, and physical components is significant. It serves as a reminder to assess and work with the whole person. It also reiterates that grief is to be expected following a loss; therefore, we should be asking about it rather than waiting for it to present externally. The perception of loss is subjective so be careful not to define someone's reality for them. Essentially, you don't have to agree that your client lost something for them to experience grief. If *they* perceive a loss, that's enough. As per usual, meet the client where they are at rather than where you think they should be.

Mourning is understood in this approach as an active coping aimed at accommodating a loss (aka filling the gaps left by the loss); that's right up our alley in addictions work. Coping skills can dominate conversations when working on addictive patterns, and this model simply extends the conversation by incorporating grief responses. Counseling work becomes a combination of coping with the absence of a substance or behavior *and* the reaction to those losses (aka grief); it's rather seamless. Counselor and client focus on both aspects rather than filling gaps alone.

Rando's goal for these processes is still sound in the addictive and recovery context: make personal readjustments so that one can remember with less pain. The goal is not forgetting, but coexistence with the past. Remember and reinvest in the present and future. This ties into one of the central arguments of this text: allow and encourage a balanced remembering (pros and cons) around one's addictive history and use it to fuel recovery efforts. Understand the past, retain the lessons, and apply them as life goes on.

Recall that the six processes (each begins with an "R") occur in the context of three phases of mourning. During each of the three phases, certain "R" processes are accomplished. Let's again walk through the three phases of mourning and the six R's, applying them to the addictive and recovery context as we go.

Phase 1: Avoidance

Remember that the avoidance phase is essentially denial by another name. The inability or unwillingness to fully acknowledge a loss is typical here. I have encountered this many times over in my work with clients. It presents in a variety of ways. Some examples include:

"I'm fine. I'll be fine without it." (heroin)

i   Losses included predictability/routine, friends who still use, and coping mechanism for physical pain

"They'll come back to me; they're just trying to prove a point." (partner broke up with them following a lapse)

i   Losses included trust/trustworthiness, relationship, stability, and social support

"It was just one time. I don't want to talk about it; I feel ashamed enough already." (following a lapse with alcohol after two months of sobriety—the client had been quite proud of this two-month milestone)

i   Losses included pride, hope, self-efficacy, "sober" label

"I only spent $150.00. I've done way more damage in the past." (client gambled after an ultimatum from the partner—stop or they'd leave)

i   Losses included money, trust, self-control, perspective (not recognizing that the number of dollars didn't matter so much as the loss of control)

I often experience the avoidance phase as half acknowledgment; the circumstances are within a client's awareness, but the impact isn't being felt or appreciated fully. It's like having information but not having a sense of the implications. For example, knowing that heroin is no longer an option, but not fully appreciating all that's tied to it—those secondary losses (i.e. social network, pain relief, numbing, relaxation, predictability, etc.).

A sense of limited awareness describes this phase in my book. People are either half acknowledging, or not acknowledging at all, the permanence or scope of their primary and secondary losses. They're avoiding the full reality of the situation and they can stagnate (remain stuck) in this avoidance.

The task associated with this phase is to **R**ecognize the loss (Rando, 1993, 2000, 2015). Efforts are geared toward a full acknowledgment of what one is up against. An acknowledgment that the loss is real (primary loss), and that life will likely change because of it (often due to secondary losses) is needed according to Rando's model.

The completion of this task can be a useful starting point in counseling because it gives a decent map of what needs to be addressed over the course of the treatment. If counselor and client have a good sense of what pieces are missing in the puzzle and how much those matter to the larger picture, they can start to create new pieces to fill those in. If people have a sense of how much a particular loss is impacting their life, they can begin processing and ultimately accommodating/adapting to that loss.

As counselors, we can help clients complete this task through gentle lines of questioning and exploration. Help clients identify the primary and secondary losses. Ask about their thoughts, feelings (physical and emotional), and behaviors on those losses:

- Are they noticing an impact? If so, in what ways?
- What are they thinking about the loss and their new reality?
  - Are they thinking about it at all or pushing it out of awareness?
- What are they feeling?
  - Are they feeling anything or is it all numbing/distracting? How do they feel about the prospect of allowing those emotions in?
- What are they doing?
  - Is their behavior aiding the avoidance of the loss or new reality (i.e. isolation or distraction behaviors)?
  - Is their behavior reflecting an acknowledgment of their situation even if their words are not (i.e. Going to places associated with the loss but stating that nothing is missed or longed for)?

Be curious and encourage awareness. Help clients consider the areas of impact and strive for an honest assessment of their losses and the impact they've had on their world. Again, the goal is an acknowledgment that life is now different. We need to first acknowledge we're in a race in order to run it. Acknowledgment is the starting line.

Phase 2: Confrontation

Once there is a full acknowledgment of loss, the emotions follow. This second phase aims to increase the understanding of one's experience, validate what's being felt, and to process through the emotions toward meaning. Recall there are three R's in this phase: **R**eact to the separation, **R**ecollect and reexperience, and **R**elinquish old attachments.

When processing one's **R**eaction to the separation, allow clients to feel whatever they feel. If clients are missing their substance or addictive pattern terribly, welcome that longing into the session. If they're excited at the prospect of sobriety and recovery, welcome that excitement and hope into session. Allow for, normalize, and welcome a broad range of emotional responses into sessions. Permit clients to feel what they feel, rather than what they've been told they *should* feel.

I remember several clients who hid their fears and sadness about leaving behind certain addictive elements (mostly relationships and the coping functions of their substance/pattern) because they were told that they should be thrilled, relieved, excited, hopeful, grateful, "jumping for joy," etc. about their recovery attempt. In their reality, they felt scared, unsure, skeptical, hopeless, sad, discouraged, and more. Encourage clients to be open about their emotions and help them sit with those in a new way. That means introducing new or revising old coping skills; that's particularly true if one of the main reasons for using was emotional numbing. Work hard to remember that clients may be new at this and need guidance on how to feel and identify what they're feeling. Exercises around mindfulness, emotional vocabulary/labeling, containment, and acceptance may be useful.

Recognition of the secondary losses attached to the primary loss also happens in this first R. Talk with clients about the associated losses and help them think about the spread that comes with significant loss. Encourage clients to appreciate the magnitude of the loss and change that often comes with a recovery attempt. Remember that many people are not just losing a substance or addictive pattern. They are also losing coping skills, relationships, certainty, routine, perceived control, sense of purpose, perceived comfort, some level of freedom, etc. They are of course going to gain a lot in recovery, but let's have no illusions that those gains come quickly. Losses come quickly and gains come slow. That's reality. Allow for clients to react to their losses and help them grieve/process what's happening. Consider the following options for starting such conversations:

- When we think about loss, the main thing we've lost is called a primary loss. For instance, you're losing (or trying to lose) an addiction—that's the main thing you're losing—the primary loss. But there's also a term called secondary loss. Basically, it means that when we lose something meaningful, we lose other things too. Examples here could be relationships, routine, pain relief, the high, etc.—basically things tied to the addiction that will also change or go away once recovery is established. Have you noticed other changes or losses now that you've started moving toward recovery? Let's take some time to think about them together.
- How big a hole, do you think, this change/loss is going to leave in your life? Is it a welcome change or a scary prospect? Maybe some of both? Do you feel prepared to handle it currently? Talk to me about where you're at.
- How are you feeling about losing one of your main methods of coping (if applicable)? Have you thought about what you'll do instead? How are you feeling at the prospect?
- What's something that you wish you could keep about your current life? What's something you're looking forward to losing?
- Describe what you're losing here (in moving toward recovery).
- Help me understand what emotions come up when you think about the scope of loss or change. Does it feel overwhelming? Doable? Are you surprised by any of your reactions? Talk to me.
- How have these losses impacted your thinking? What about your body? And your insides, your spirit? Let's take some time to explore what you're experiencing and how you're feeling about all these. Remember that the changes and impacts don't have to be negative. Be open to whatever you're feeling.
- Describe what your body feels like now that _____ is gone or _____ has changed. Is it an improvement? If yes, please describe. If no, please describe.

- Are you fearful of anything now that your substance (or pattern) is missing? Talk to me about it.
- Are you hopeful now that your substance (or pattern) is missing? Tell me.

Notice that balance is present in these questions; high and low points are included, and positive and negative emotions are inferred. This balance highlights one aspect of the **R**ecollect and reexperience process—the second R in this phase. People work to remember what they've lost for better and for worse. I have observed that reviewing the memories of the lost relationship, identity, behavioral pattern, etc. in an addiction treatment context can get mixed reviews from clinical staff. What I mean is that some clinicians discourage sharing around fond memories of use, opting instead to only allow for negative recollections (this is particularly true in group settings). Likewise, I've seen other clinicians discourage the telling of "war stories" around the profoundly negative aspects of use. Let's consider the utility of both types of memories.

For some clients, the positive memories will fuel a continuing bond, an ongoing connection that will motivate, support, or sustain them as life continues. For example, remembering how hard things sometimes were and yet also remembering that one managed to survive; this can evolve into valuing one's resilience. Remembering supportive relationships with other people who used or with those who practiced unconditional love during a period of addiction may evolve into a search for those relationships in recovery. Knowing that support is possible when things are hard and that there are people out there who will support them is powerful for some. Remembering the euphoria and the joy, release, relaxation, energy (whatever it was) that the high brought can be reframed as well—the physical body and the emotional state can be manipulated. Learning how to do that from the inside out through breathing, mindfulness, exercise, and other self-regulatory behaviors can re-instill a sense of control; one does not have to rely on external factors (i.e. drugs, sex, gambling, eating, etc.) to change their physical and emotional state.

For others, the negative memories may also fuel a continuing bond, an ongoing connection that reminds them of where they've been and where they don't want to go back. Positive memories are not the only ones that serve us. Holding onto negative aspects can keep us on track and remind us that moving in reverse is not a good idea. Think about all the ways that this idea plays out in life—you touch a hot stove and you remember the burn. That memory and associated fear likely keeps you from touching another hot stove. I know that I'll never personally eat raw oysters again because the experience was so unpleasant that it's burned in my memory. The negative associations keep me from going back. Consider this with addiction; remembering the pain, stress, financial pressure, health complications, or legal trouble addictive substances and patterns paired with, might make one reconsider going back when triggered. At the very least, someone might pause, and pauses can be powerful. In that space, they can engage a newer coping skill or think through what they're feeling in the moment. Positive and negative memories can serve us, work toward balanced remembering and making those memories meaningful.

This idea pairs with reexperiencing. This component centers on the influence the lost object will continue to exert in one's life. Temptation and triggers are on par for the course with addiction; the brain takes time and repetition to change. It makes sense that the old patterns will continue to exert influence and that sometimes that influence will dominate. Remember that losses come quick and gains often come slow. Help clients recognize how their former behavioral, thought, and emotional patterns are exerting influence over their present life. Validate the difficulty in quieting these urges and reminders while working to strengthen their new coping repertoire.

The final R in this phase is **R**elinquish old attachments. Remember that this process focuses on the gradual processing of one's loss. The word gradual is notable here. Clients might be acutely aware of their losses in the first session and it might take time for them to come into awareness. One neat aspect of this R to my mind are discussions around imagined futures. Basically, if it was a person that died, people may struggle to accept that the future they imagined having with them is no longer possible. Think about that with the loss of an addiction, there may be struggle depending on the loss ("I don't know how I'll go on without it [meth]. Without it, I'm useless. What am I going to do now?"). Conversely, there may be joy or relief knowing the imagined future isn't likely to play out (i.e. "I'd probably die or get locked up if things kept going as they were. I dodged a bullet."). Consider some ways to explore these ideas in session:

- Talk to me about how life will look different in sobriety and recovery— for better and for worse. How do you see your life changing?
- When you were using or stuck in your pattern, how did you imagine your future? Did you think you had one? Was is a future you looked forward to or dreaded?

Be open to any answer here; fight the assumption that futures with use included are perceptively bad. Some clients, particularly those in the early stages of a recovery attempt, may have preferred a future with use included. That may change over time and it may not. The point here is to help clients process their feelings and to find meaning now that the future they imagined is no longer possible. Keep your eye on the goal.

- How about now as you attempt sobriety and ultimately recovery, do you think you have a future? How is it different from what you perhaps imagined it to be? Is it a future you look forward to or are there elements you still dread?

Here too, be open to any answer; continue to fight the assumption that sobriety brings peace. For some it will, for others it will bring turmoil and gaps to fill. While recovery efforts will work to fill those holes over time, a sense of hope and peace may take time to emerge and settle. This R is ultimately about finding meaning in letting go of one's former expectations—letting go of the future they thought they'd have and embracing the one that is now likely. Winokuer and Harris (2012) added that searching for meaning after loss is nearly universal. Looking at negative events as opportunities to learn is one way to facilitate meaning-making. Reframing loss and striving to learn about oneself, others, or working to add to a world that now feels like it's lacking can bring a sense of coherence and help the world make sense again.

Phase 3: Accommodation

This phase seems to align with mid and late recovery. Essentially, life starts to feel more settled and the adjustment isn't so fresh any longer. As with the original model, clients will not feel as sidelined by their addiction as they take active steps to fill in the gaps left by it. The plans for coping are now being implemented and clients may report success, or at least progress. The search for meaning and the derivation of it becomes more prominent and clients may experience a greater emotional range (aka they'll feel a variety of emotions) with joy becoming more familiar.

Recall that two tasks are associated with this phase: **R**eadjust to the new world without forgetting the old world and **R**einvest emotional energy (Rando, 1993, 2000, 2015).

Readjusting to the new world without forgetting the old pretty much sums up the entire intent of this book in a nutshell! The idea that clients need to and can readjust to their new reality without forgetting or shunning the old is significant. Rando was on to something here (in my humble opinion). Rando believed that this R could be accomplished through a review of the relationship, reconciling different aspects of the person, and finding ways to integrate these new aspects into a composite picture of the deceased/lost person (Boerner & Heckhausen, 2003; Rando 1993). I'll note where I see each of these happening as we consider this R more fully.

The internal adjustments and accommodations related to death in the original model are not so far away from what's likely to be helpful with addiction. For instance, accepting and exploring new identities that may have emerged from a loss and/or reflecting on how the lost object or person changed them or helped them develop. The road to recovery is often filled with identity work. Shifting from the identity of "addict" to something else can be empowering, but also scary.

Reflecting on the ways the addiction shaped one's identity, thoughts, feelings, and behaviors can help clients see that their core being is still, and I believe, has always been intact (*reviewing the relationship*). Think of an egg. The shell may be cracked, but the insides are still intact. Here's another way to think about it: addictive patterns shape identity by seemingly burying who one actually is. People get buried in unhealth. Part of recovery then is digging the self out of that hole and seeing what's still intact down there. Find the strength and the lessons amidst the unhealth. This is reminiscent of previous discussions related to the application of the Continuing Bonds Theory and attachment principles in the addictive context (Stroebe, Schut, & Boerner, 2010).

Recall that in this R, one's life continues but links to the past are retained. Help clients hold onto useful links. Look for the lessons, the takeaways. Help clients realize the skills they used to survive their addiction and then apply them to present recovery efforts. What did they learn about relationships, the world, and themselves during their addiction? Explore what the addiction has taught them, for better and for worse, and apply that insight to their recovery (*reconciling different aspects of the person*). For example, clients may have learned that:

- they can endure great hardship and still survive
- they trust too easily
- they have the potential to be quite loyal and dedicated to people and/ or a way of being (and their loyalty may have been misplaced during active addiction)
- substances, addictive behaviors, and the brain are powerful, and sometimes willpower alone isn't enough to change behavior
- they are worthy of love no matter their addiction status
- they are capable of giving love no matter their addiction status
- they are tenacious and creative
- they make poor decisions when tired or distracted
- they've hurt others, sometimes badly/their life impacts the lives of others

Any one of these could be useful in recovery. Remembering that one is a survivor when they're hurting, believing in one's ability to persevere and acknowledging how hard change is, leaning on their tenacity and creativity, and acknowledging that trust can be problematic when misplaced can all be the seeds of growth in recovery. Recognizing that one has always been deserving of love and that one is also capable of adding to the world, not just taking, is significant and novel for some.

As was stated earlier in the text, reminiscing on and retaining a connection to the former "addict" identity may *promote* recovery rather than threaten it. Some people need reminders, either tangibly or internally, that represent where they've been so that they don't go back. Other people might benefit from the development of compassion and empathy for their former selves. Work to increase awareness of strengths that existed during the addiction when there seemed to be none and appreciate their survival value (i.e. tenacity, grit, resilience). Look at the whole of who they were when addicted, not just the negative aspects (*integrating these new aspects into a composite*).

Help clients relate differently to their past selves and connect the dots of how the lessons they learned during their addiction can now serve them—essentially taking the good from the bad. Rando believed that people needed to acknowledge the implications of the past while moving forward in the present (Boerner & Heckhausen, 2003; Rando, 1993). Here, this translates to not forgetting the past, but shifting perspective in order to promote growth as life continues after loss—readjust to the new world without forgetting the old.

Some options for how to explore these areas were offered by Neimeyer (2001) and are reminiscent of the empty chair technique from Gestalt therapy. Clients could write a biography of the lost person—in this context it might instead be the lost identity (Boerner & Heckhausen, 2003; Neimeyer, 2001). This could assist the client (and counselor) in getting a more accurate picture of that identity/person. It lends to a more detailed exploration that adds chronology—meaning that one's story could be understood across the timeline of their addiction. Letters could also be written to the former identity/former self (i.e. "Dear addicted self, …" or "Dear Julie") or an aspect of oneself or one's addiction (i.e. "Dear heroin…" or "Dear anxiety…" "Dear Mom and Dad…"). Another variation would have the client write to their past 'addicted' self and then respond from their 'recovering' self. I've used these kinds of letters many times over the years (see Appendix C for examples).

Reinvesting emotional energy, the final R in this phase, represents a shift from past to future. People are reinvesting in their life and the loss(es) aren't taking up as much space as previously. Again, this is not forgetting, but rather a culmination of the previous R's: people understand their experiences differently and can now work on applying those insights and takeaways to their life. Focus shifts from learning to living. Finding renewed purpose and direction are hallmarks here.

For many of the clients I've had the privilege of working with, the return of purpose is a significant marker of recovery. I recall a former client who returned to school during recovery saying, "My life is finally more than chasing a high. I get to finally be someone my kids can be proud of." For him, finding purpose as a student, a 'contributing member of society,' and a father proved to him that he was moving in a different direction; his emotional reinvestments were paying out.

References

Boerner, K., & Heckhausen, J. (2003). To have and have not: Adaptive bereavement by transforming mental ties to the deceased. *Death Studies, 27,* 199–226.

Neimeyer, R. A. (2001). *Meaning reconstruction and the experience of loss.* Washington, DC: American Psychological Association.

Rando, T. A. (1993). *Treatment of complicated mourning.* Champaign, IL: Research Press.

Rando, T. A. (2000). On the experience of traumatic stress in anticipatory and post death mourning. In T. A. Rando (Ed.), *Clinical dimensions of anticipatory mourning: Theory and practice in working with the dying, their loved ones, and their caregivers* (pp. 155–221). Champaign, IL: Research Press.

Rando, T. A. (2015). *Coping with the sudden death of your loved one: A self-help handbook for traumatic bereavement.* Indianapolis, IN: Dog Ear Publishing.

Stroebe, M. S., Schut, H., & Boerner, K. (2010). Continuing bonds in adaptation to bereavement: Toward theoretical integration. *Clinical Psychology Review, 30,* 259–268.

Winokuer, H. R., & Harris, D. L. (2012). *Principles and practices of grief counseling.* New York, NY: Springer Publishing Company.

13 Loss and Adaptation Model and Considering the Loss and Adaptation Model in the Context of Addiction and Recovery

Horowitz (2005/2006) believed that adaptation was a natural outcome of any kind of loss. In this model, 'closure' is believed to be present when a self-defined normal level of functioning has returned and there's an ability to remember without impairment. More specifically, if one can feel normal (as they define it), actively remember what they've lost, and continue living without those memories interfering, they're in an adaptive place (Horowitz, 2005/2006; Novak, 2018; Rothaupt & Becker, 2007). In classes, I often talk about healing as being able to live with pain rather than being consumed by it; having it become a *part* of your life rather than *all* of your life. I seem to be in line with Horowitz in terms of the healing target we shoot for.

Horowitz proposed four stages of loss: *outcry, denial and intrusion, working through, and completion*. While each was considered typical, it was acknowledged that they do not always occur in sequence (i.e. stage 2 does not always follow stage 1) and some might not occur at all depending on the person (Horowitz, 2005/2006). This content may feel familiar as you read; some components are quite similar to previously discussed theories. In particular, the third stage of *working through* is very similar to tasks II and III in Worden's model that centered on processing the pain of grief and adjusting to life without the lost object (Rothaupt & Becker, 2007; Worden, 1991). Let's walk through each stage:

Stage 1: Outcry

This stage is marked by the expression of emotion when someone realizes they've lost something of value. This can look quite different depending on the person. Emotional outcry may present as uncontrollable screaming and emoting out loud, in public. It might also be much quieter and private. Yet another version is suppressing or containing the pain, so it feels more manageable. Whichever way it swings, this stage is typically exhausting; this level of emotion takes a good deal of energy. This stage also tends to be brief (Horowitz, 2005/2006; Novak, 2018; Rothaupt & Becker, 2007).

Stage 2: Denial and Intrusion

This stage is represented by movement between periods of denial and intrusion. The denial piece of this stage might well be called evasion.

Individuals distract from, avoid, and evade their loss and can do this so effectively that they might forget for a bit that they've lost something. This effect, if it happens, is of course temporary. It's notable, however that guilt might result from the sense that the loss is no longer dominating their thoughts or hearts. This break from the grief was seen by Horowitz as a positive in the sense that life was starting to coexist with the pain. In other words, the pain was becoming manageable rather than overwhelming. The intrusion piece is characterized by periods of time when the loss is unavoidable, and the absence is intensely felt.

This is similar in some ways to the oscillation of the DPM discussed earlier; recall that the DPM sets the expectation that people will move back and forth between focusing on the loss and trying to adapt to it (Stroebe & Schut, 1999; Stroebe, Schut, & Stroebe, 2005). Horowitz (2005/2006) also believed this movement between denial and intrusion was normal and adaptive. While this model does share this similarity with the DPM, there are notable differences which we will discuss shortly.

Stage 3: Working Through

Life starts to come back online during this stage. Grief and pain might still be very fresh, but people become more engaged in life activities as they continue to process it. Adjustments are made to account for the loss here as well. I think of this as filling the gaps left by the loss. New relationships may meet the needs of old ones; new hobbies may fill the time that was once filled by the lost object. If people are not yet ready to engage in these new endeavors, they might begin thinking about them and planning. This might include things like thinking about joining a social group, resuming a hobby, going back to school, reengaging in relationships that have become distant, etc. The denial and intrusion from the last stage don't take up as much space anymore (Horowitz, 2005/2006). Essentially, life becomes louder than the loss and less attention is paid to the absence; it begins to shift to background noise. The loss is still thought about and the associated feelings are still felt, but life continues; people find ways to continue living (Novak, 2018; Rothaupt & Becker, 2007).

Stage 4: Completion

The name is apt here; this stage signifies the conclusion of bereavement. Horowitz (2005/2006) believed that bereavement had reached its end when memories of the loss no longer dominated everyday life. Importantly, Horowitz noted that the process could be complete *enough*; basically, it's a subjective definition, not a textbook one. From this model's perspective, the completeness of someone's grief process is measured by their ability to live with the memories. It's not forgetting, and the loss may be on one's mind to some degree every day. The difference is that it no longer impairs them; the emotions are manageable. Life begins to feel normal again as the loss shifts to the background and is no longer front and center. Reminders of the loss such as anniversaries may trigger higher levels of thought or emotion, but they are periodic. If someone frequently feels held back or otherwise impaired by their loss, they may still be in an earlier stage. This process can take months or years depending on the person and the loss (Horowitz).

As previously noted, there are some similarities between this model from Horowitz and Stroebe et al.'s Dual Process Model. Some differences are also important that one needs to be aware of. For instance, Horowitz believed that complicated grief was another, natural, expression of grief and bereavement. Briefly recall that complicated grief is a painful and impairing state where acute grief symptoms are prolonged and one struggles unsuccessfully to rebuild a meaningful life after loss (Shear, Boelen, & Neimeyer, 2011) (refer to Chapter 2 for a more detailed definition).

The DPM in contrast stated that complicated grief was not a natural expression of grief and represented an outlier experience that presented a threat to one's grief process. Specifically, it was thought that complicated grief could halt one's natural processing and keep them at a standstill, immersed in the pain (Bonanno & Kaltman, 2001; Horowitz, 2005/2006; Novak, 2018; Rothaupt & Becker, 2007).

Other differences between the theories include the delineated stages in Horowitz's compared to the stage-less model from Stroebe et al. (2010) (recall that the DPM purports an oscillation between orientations). The oscillation in the DPM allows for freedom of movement, and the lack of structure in the grief process may be appealing for some; grief can be self-paced and personal. Others may prefer the more structured movement offered by Horowitz's Loss and Adaptation Model. Importantly, both models believe that grief is unique and that the stages from Horowitz and the oscillation from Stroebe et al. (2010) are guidelines, not mandates on how to grieve (Novak, 2018).

Considering *the Loss and Adaptation Model* in the Context of Addiction and Recovery

Thinking about the Loss and Adaptation Model in the context of addiction and recovery, there is a lot to consider. One primary point to consider is the semi-structured stages combined with the idea that grief is unique and personal. It's a slight paradox and approaching someone's grief process from this lens may require periodic reminders that moving about, skipping, or circling back to the different stages is somewhat expected and considered normal (Horowitz, 2005/2006). Remember that the stages are intended as guidelines for how grief may unfold, not mandates.

Stage 1: Outcry

Remember that per Horowitz, an outcry does not have to be loud (Horowitz, 2005/2006). Different people emote differently, and this model allows for a variety of presentations. Recall that this stage is marked by the expression of emotion when someone realizes they've lost something, or perhaps many things, of value. Thinking about this in the addiction and recovery context, the outcry will depend on the loss itself as well as the circumstances around it.

Our job as counselors is to support our clients in their form of outcry and examine the primary and secondary losses in determining what the outcry is in response to. Please look for the meaning in the outcry and encourage your clients to do the same. Consider the following areas of exploration:

- Which emotions are being expressed?
  - Anger, sadness/sorrow, regret, longing, excitement, relief? Be open to a range of emotional responses.
- What are the emotional responses related to?
  - Are they related to the past and what is now missing? Are they in response to the realization that life is now different and that the change might be permanent? Are the emotions stemming from a rejection of the new reality (i.e. disbelief that something is lost despite other people's assertions)? Excitement and anticipation for the future now that something has been lost or left behind? Something else entirely?
- What do the emotions imply?

  Depending on which emotion(s) presents during the outcry, they might signal pain, lack of control, frustration, relief, deep sadness or hopelessness, fear, insecurity, or doubts that one can continue living in the aftermath of loss, etc.

With each emotional expression, there is a story and a meaning. Explore the meaning of the emotions and work to understand the impact the losses and accompanying emotions have on their recovery efforts. Help clients to connect the dots; what they are feeling tells them something about the place the lost object held in their life.

The outcry, when examined, can help identify gaps that now exist in someone's life. Counseling can help clients fill or adjust to those emotional (i.e. finding a new identity or regaining a sense of control), relational (i.e. forming new relationships), and physical gaps (i.e. basic needs such as housing, etc.). Encourage the expression of emotion, validate what is expressed, and keep an ear open for the meaning attached to the emotion and to the loss(es). There is a good deal of insight to be gained here; try not to let it slip by unnoticed.

Consider an example: A client was mandated to counseling (with periodic drug testing) by the court system after an arrest for heroin possession with the intent to sell. The client presented to counseling and expressed anger, frustration, and a feeling of injustice related to their sentence. The client complained about having to attend counseling and was vocal about his belief that it would be of no help.

At first glance, this outcry/presentation could be written off by the counselor as the client complaining and blaming others for their circumstances. It could also be labeled "resistance." Please use your critical thinking abilities and look again. Remember that things are not always as they seem; that's particularly true with anger. Behind all anger is some sort of pain.

This client may feel angry that their routine has been disrupted or that they are being forced to change (aka they feel out of control). It's also possible that they are sad and afraid that their income has been compromised (what if selling heroin put food on the table?). They may also be angry that someone else is determining what is best for them and they would prefer to choose instead. Examine the outcry and value what's been lost, what's being communicated and felt.

During counseling, in the relapse prevention group in particular, the client was encouraged to examine their anger toward their sentence and what was lost when the sentence was imposed. The client was initially confused about what the potential loss might be and was encouraged to elaborate on their anger. The client felt most angry that someone else was deciding what their life was going to be for a period of time (i.e. the judge).

When the sentence was imposed, he lost control. The client linked control to his transition from heroin user to heroin dealer. He described wanting to have more "quality control" over what he used and decided the best way to do that was to become his own supplier. Through exploration of the sentence, we ended up talking about shifts in his use patterns, triggers, and eventually he connected the need for control back to his early years. This client grew up in a home with an authoritarian father, whom he routinely rebelled against. Essentially, he wanted to be in control because he rarely felt like he was. Losing control triggered a strong desire to regain it and that led to some unhealthy choices in his life, including heroin.

Any efforts aimed at recovery would have to consider that need, want, and active effort to get and retain control. This insight translated to a few things in our recovery efforts:

1   Giving the client choices whenever possible in session.
2   Finding the right fit for social supports.
    •   For instance, the client previously had a sponsor from NA who believed the best way to support someone was to give advice. The client saw this as the sponsor telling him what to do, so he

disengaged from the relationship. Identifying people who could instead offer their experiences from which the client could draw his own meanings, or someone simply willing to listen was preferable. It was a stylistic difference, but it mattered.

3   As counselor, I had to filter his behaviors toward me through this control insight. For example, if he didn't show up for a session, I used the time to examine our previous interactions and see if the control pattern could explain the absence (i.e. if something came across as me taking control away). This would then come up for discussion in the next session.

4   Perhaps most importantly, helping the client to explore the ways he was grabbing for, or trying to keep control, and how sometimes it backfired. Most notably, using heroin to control his physical state (primarily physical discomfort) led to SUD, which ultimately led to dealing, which led to his arrest and a sentence he was unhappy with. His attempts at control had brought him to a place where he no longer got to choose. His previous attempts to stay in control left him out of control.

Consider another example: A client seeks counseling voluntarily and states they want to change their use because they've recently had a friend die from an overdose. The client says very little in session about their feelings and yet is quite focused on making progress and reducing their own use. This focus and intensity may represent another form of outcry. The reaction to the loss is more active behaviorally and quieter verbally.

Examine the outcry and the messages being communicated. Fear, pressure, sadness, shock, hope, motivation, and more could be contained in this version of outcry. Do not assume that because you are not hearing a lot, that there is little being felt or experienced. Look for communication, not just talking. Consider the body language, the intensity or drive to get well/change, level of dissatisfaction with setbacks, etc.

One more example is a client who has had their children removed from the home due to their addiction and related behaviors. They push away and distract from their pain near completely, containing it so well that it only comes into awareness (and into session) with effortful prompting. While all versions of outcry tend to be tiring, this version may be downright exhausting (for the client and counselor); containing a high level of emotion can feel similar to a dam holding back a body of water. There's constant pressure to do the job well in order to prevent a flood.

Please fight the urge to label this "resistance" if it should arise. That is, seeing a reluctance or hesitance to talk about something as a resistance to our attempts to help them; it can be better understood as containment. When we look at clients this way (as resistant), we miss the meaning of the outcry and are often reduced to frustration with the distraction and containment efforts. I have seen this dynamic play out more times than I can count in alcohol and other drug abuse (AODA) treatment settings. When clients don't change at the pace that the facility (or some other stakeholder) deems appropriate, clients are often labeled resistant, and it all goes clinically downhill from there. Be better than that; use your clinical training and skill to understand the meaning behind the presentation.

Remember that people emote in a variety of different ways. At the very least, reframe "resistance" as the client resisting pain or discomfort. Depersonalize it; don't blame or write-off a client when they seemingly resist your efforts to help. Instead, examine the intent of the behavior and value (and help the client value) the protective nature of it. Remember that from this model's point of view, this type of presentation can represent an outcry of emotion; it might just look different than what an outcry of emotion is expected to look like. Be curious, look to both body and verbal language to assess what's being felt, and be on the lookout for meaning in their expressions.

Stage 2: Denial and Intrusion

From a counseling point of view, this stage might be one of the most frustrating when working to help someone understand what they've been feeling. The frustration can come from clients evading discussion or acknowledgment of what's been lost, their reactions to it, and its implications. It's imperative that counselors remember that this type of distraction, or evasion, is normal; it's also important to note that we often label this type of behavior "denial." Horowitz used this term as well. Be careful of how you use this word, however. Words carry meaning and I have found that very often saying someone is in "denial" comes with an implicit pressure to break that denial. To confront them with the "reality" of their situation so they can deal with it. Be careful and use empathy. This hearkens back to my point around the use of the term "resistant"; words matter and our responses to behavior also matter.

Counseling is not all pain, all the time. At least it shouldn't be (in my humble opinion). Instead, counseling is a place to express whatever feelings are impacting you, and to begin understanding how these emotions and the meaning attached to life events are impacting or could impact one's life.

Meet denial with curiosity and gentleness. Be curious about what it's like to have a break from the intensity of their grief:

1   How are they able to tuck away their emotions and do it so effectively?
    •   Understanding the ins and outs of those containment skills might be quite useful to draw on later; information and insight around how one currently copes can be a great help to future efforts at coping.

2   What was it like to seemingly forget (or fail to acknowledge) for a period of time that something has been lost?
  • Comforting? Scary? Guilt-inducing? Freeing? Something else entirely? Hopeful (perhaps one day it won't feel so big)? Explore that.
3   What was it like when the loss came back into awareness?
  • Comforting? Shame-filled? Guilt-inducing? Confusing? Something else entirely? Explore this too.

Contrast these times of denial to the times when the memories, emotions, and/or thoughts couldn't be avoided. Remember that Horowitz believed this movement between denial and intrusion was normal and adaptive. Explore the experience of being consumed or overwhelmed by something and the intensity of the absence:

1   What is it like to move back and forth between periods of unawareness and intense absence?
  • How do they cope? How do they explain this back and forth?
2   Is it viewed as a positive or negative sign from their point of view?

There are intriguing, insight-building conversations to be had here.

Stage 3: Working Through

I have always felt that working through could be a fill in the blank. Such as working through *and going strong*, or working through *the pain*, or working through *and getting stuck*, or working through *and actually getting somewhere*! My point is that this sounds like an active stage, and it is. People start to reengage in life and grief and loss elements start to become less prominent. This is not a time of forgetting, but a time of adjustment. People are learning to live with their loss. *Live* being the key word there. I said in the previous chapter that I think of this stage as filling the gaps left by the loss so that life can continue. Think of your clients and how often you have likely seen this too. People may begin to reengage in old hobbies that fell by the wayside during addiction. Or old relationships are repaired or rekindled as recovery is being built. New relationships might be formed if old ones have been lost or changed over time. New skills are learned to supplement what has been weakened by the loss of the substance or behavior (or any other type of loss). This could include coping skills, formal education, a job change, reengagement in the workforce, exploration of what "fun," or even what "pain" is when sober.

If clients are not ready for this type of reengagement, they may begin thinking about it. They may ask for more information from outside (or internal) groups, how to make friends or repair relationships, begin working on their resume, or ask for information on parenting, begin showing up more regularly for appointments, etc. The absence begins to take up less space. It's not forgotten, but it is not alone; other elements of life begin to creep in and take root. Life continues in the presence of the absence (Novak, 2018; Rothaupt & Becker, 2007).

Counselors can be a source of information and support during this stage. Work to find balance with your clients. Help them understand that life and pain can coexist and point out times when you see that happening in their lives. One of my favorite sentence stems for this is "Have you noticed…?" For example:

1   Have you noticed that you're still hurting but that you had fun?
2   Have you noticed that you enjoyed time with friends and you still remember that he died? You didn't forget him by focusing on other people for a bit.
3   Have you noticed that you were uncomfortable (physically or emotionally) and that you still did it? That's important. You tolerated something you weren't sure you'd be able to tolerate.
4   Have you noticed that you had fun without _____ (i.e. gambling, drinking, meth, etc.)? What's that like to think about?
5   Have you noticed that your kids still love you even though they didn't get to come home with you? And have you noticed that you still love your kids even though you're currently struggling?

And the list can go on…. help clients to notice the efforts, movement, and progress they make in the presence of their pain. Balance is key.

Stage 4: Completion

From Horowitz's (2005/2006) perspective, bereavement has reached its end when memories of the loss no longer dominate everyday life. Recall that he also believed that bereavement could be complete enough—that individuals could find a balance between the new reality and remembering the old and move forward with life.

This idea is quite applicable to recovery for many people. The effort to remember and forget all at the same time, but ultimately forging ahead into a new, healthier territory. This target feels achievable: finding a way to live with the memories (emphasis on *live*).

Managing the impact of the memory is an important target here, having the memory be a memory and not a trigger.

Consider some options for assessing and processing this stage:

1   How often do you find yourself thinking about the use (or other addictive pattern or behavior)?
2   When you think about the past, how long does it stick around? Do you find yourself thinking about _____ (insert memory) frequently or every now and again?

3   What happens in your mind and body when you remember? Which emotions come up and how intense are they? Are you able to notice, acknowledge, and manage the emotions that arise without returning to old patterns (i.e. particularly addictive ones)?
4   Do you tend to focus on where you were or where you are now?
5   Do the memories feel like a ball and chain holding you back or are you able to carry them with you as you move forward? If you feel trapped or held back, what do you think needs to happen in order to move forward?
6   What's it like to look back and not be held back by what you see? What's that mean about you that you're learning to live with your past, rather than be defined by it? If you're not quite there yet, do you believe it's possible to one day live with the memory and not be defined or plagued by it?

Explore the changing relationship with the past and/or their ability to carry it differently. Encourage clients to notice that what used to take up a lot of mental and emotional space may be shifting more toward the background. In measuring success or change, we often look to behavioral changes. Be sure to look at behaviors, yes, but also the internal shifts that have happened or are happening.

References

Bonanno, G. A., & Kaltman, S. (2001). Toward an integrative perspective on bereavement. *Psychology Bulletin, 127*(4), 554–560.

Horowitz, M. (2005/2006). Meditating on complicated grief disorder as a diagnosis. *Omega: Journal of Death and Dying, 52*(1), 87–89.

Novak, K. (2018). *An examination of grief and bereavement theories in human service practice.* Retrieved November 4, 2019 from https://www.advisorycloud.com/board-of-directors-articles/an-examination-of-grief-and-bereavement-theories-in-human-service-practice

Rothaupt, J. W., & Becker, K. (2007). A literature review of western bereavement theory: From decathecting to continuing bonds. *The Family Journal: Counseling and Therapy for Couples and Families, 15*(1), 6–15.

Shear, M. K., Boelen, P. A., & Neimeyer, R. A. (2011). Treating complicated grief: Converging approaches. In R. A. Neimeyer, D. L. Harris, & H. R. Winokuer (Eds.), *Grief and bereavement in contemporary society: Bridging research and practice* (pp. 139–162). New York, NY: Routledge.

Stroebe, M. S., & Schut, H. (1999). The dual process model of coping with bereavement: Rationale and description. *Death Studies, 23*(3), 197–224.

Stroebe, W., Schut, H., & Stroebe, M. S. (2005). Grief work, disclosure, and counselling: Do they help the bereaved? *Clinical Psychology Review, 25*, 395–414.

Worden, J. W. (1991). *Grief counseling and grief therapy: A handbook for the mental health practitioner* (2nd ed.). New York, NY: Springer.

14 Psychological Perspective on Dying, Mourning, and Spirituality and Considering the Psychological Perspective in the Context of Addiction and Recovery

Marrone (1997, 1999) offered a perspective on bereavement with emphasis on psychospiritual transformation and the role of spiritual and religious changes for some people when adapting to loss. Don't let the word 'psychospiritual' intimidate you if you've never encountered it. Essentially it refers to an integration of the mind and spirit when working to enhance our mental health (think whole person-type philosophy).

Keep in mind that not all clients will identify spirituality as a salient area for themselves, but some others surely will. This model paid attention to responses to loss (specifically death) and the existential changes, spiritual growth, and transformation that might occur. Basically, Marrone believed loss could change how we viewed the world and our place in it. Four phases addressed differing responses to loss: cognitive restructuring, emotional expression, psychological reintegration, and psychospiritual transformation. More on these later.

One element that's important to be aware of when considering this approach is what Marrone called The Spiritual Experience. Part of this experience was described as an emerging awareness ... "of a higher power, higher intelligence, purpose, or order in the universe" outside one's control, but one which is used as a guide for living (Marrone, 1999, p. 497). Imagine this: you live your life as a passenger in a car and the driver of that car takes you where it/they think makes the most sense. Think of this spiritual experience as the opportunity to pick a new driver for the car. Your current driver may be leading you in directions that you have no interest in, don't serve you well, or interfere with happiness. The spiritual experience might bring awareness that your car is moving in an errant direction and could offer a new driver that can steer you elsewhere.

This new awareness and connection may lead to questions about how one has been living up until that point. It's reminiscent of an existential crisis—questioning the meaning of life and one's role in the world. Think of this as wondering if how you've been living and what you've believed to be true, is actually true. Another element of the spiritual experience can be the feeling of being reborn through death (or threatened death). Ultimately the new or enhanced spiritual awareness is seen as a positive which can lead to positive changes in thoughts, feelings, and behavior (Klass, 1995; Marrone, 1997, 1999). This contentment results in the person feeling more authentic and like life has more meaning. Additionally, individuals can feel like their thoughts and intentions have been reset; their thoughts in general and behavior toward others becomes "right and true" (Marrone, 1999, p. 497). It's like righting a ship that was previously drifting away at the mercy of the waves. Life comes back online and begins heading in a meaningful, positive direction.

Spiritual awareness can be tied to various areas including:

i   religious beliefs
ii a bond with a higher power or deity
iii a philosophy
iv dedication to a cause such as the relief of human suffering or making the world a better place
v   seeing oneself as a work in progress and believing that your progress will have a trickle-down effect on the next generation (i.e. others will learn from your mistakes)
vi a strong desire to leave a legacy (most notably through children or one's life work)

Marrone (1999) believed that this spiritual experience and awareness were important parts of the grief and bereavement process for some people. This brings us back to the four phases mentioned earlier. Remember, they are intended to address differing loss reactions people may have. They include cognitive restructuring, emotional expression, psychological reintegration, and psychospiritual transformation.

1   Cognitive restructuring
    This phase is focused on cognitive restructuring that allows for acknowledgment and acceptance that the loss has occurred and is permanent (Marrone, 1999; Rothaupt & Becker, 2007). This phase is near identical to Worden's (2009) first task of mourning which also centered on accepting the reality of the loss and the need for acknowledgment and acceptance. Ultimately, the aim of this phase is assimilation of the new reality. Don't let the phrasing confuse you; this is simply saying that people need to digest their new reality and incorporate the new truths into the way they live.
    Marrone also talked about the interaction between religious beliefs and cognitive assimilation. Some people will lean on their faith for comfort, support, or for an explanation as to why the death or loss occurred. Such strategies reflect an attempt to integrate the experience of loss into one's current understanding of the world (i.e. let me

try and make sense of this based on what I believe to be true and seek support in ways I think will work). Taking this approach, assuming one has a faith they ascribe to, has its upside. Marrone pointed out that invoking traditional beliefs around God, a higher power, or some other being that controls one's fate makes it possible for life to continue (1999).

2   Emotional expression

This phase included the challenge of feeling and allowing those emotions in, identification of feelings, acceptance, and "giving some form of expression to all of the emotional turmoil, cognitive confusion, and physical pain that may be experienced" (Marrone, 1999, p. 498; Rothaupt & Becker, 2007).

This description from Marrone is one of the best I've read on emotional expression because it's so comprehensive. It captures the struggle to feel, label what's being felt, accepting that the emotion is present for a reason, and then figuring out what to do with the big ball of pain, confusion, and turmoil, as he put it. This phase can feel enormous for some people depending on the nature and scope of their loss.

3   Psychological reintegration

Think of this third phase as the development of supports to aid in the adjustment to the new reality (Marrone, 1999; Rothaupt & Becker, 2007). It boils down to coping. The development and integration of new coping skills, or the strengthening of old ones is central here. The goal is an increased ability to deal with the new reality in the wake of loss.

When a person has endured a loss, in responding to the loss it may be wise to take stock of what's left, gather the resources available to you (i.e. social supports), and work to find new resources to aid in your response or recovery effort. A synonym for reintegration is restoration; this phase is largely about psychological restoration and enhanced psychological stability after loss.

Marrone also talked about how one's religious views on death can influence the response to loss. Specifically, he noted that for individuals who viewed death through a religious lens, it was often seen as a transformative process rather than a permanent ending devoid of meaning. Since meaning was found in the presumed transformation, individuals had an easier time adjusting to the loss. The people with religiosity had a framework to understand death; those without it might spend more time reflecting or questioning in their search for meaning. Neither approach (i.e. religion or not) is better, but there are notable differences in the potential responses to loss.

4   Psychospiritual transformation

The last phase encompasses a lot. It involves a "profound, growth-oriented, spiritual or existential transformation that fundamentally changes our central assumptions, beliefs, and attitudes about life, death, love, compassion, or God" (Marrone, 1999, p. 498). It may help to simplify this a bit. Through loss, one's understanding of the world and their place in it may shift. Questions may arise and/or beliefs may be solidified. Consider some questions or areas of reflection that may arise from loss:

"What does my life mean?"

"What's my purpose and am I even close to fulfilling it?"

"Why did I survive, and another did not?"

"Why me?"

"Why is God punishing me?" or "How could a loving God allow this to happen?"

"God is with me and I'm not alone in this."

"I can do this. I'm a survivor."

"I can trust that people will help me when I need it."

"They're gone, but the love and memories are not."

Notice that Marrone labeled this transformation as 'growth-oriented.' Loss can initiate a transformative process which changes the mourner, at times, in fundamental ways. This means that some people will find growth on the other side of loss, not just pain. This phase encapsulates the idea that perhaps loss can add to life, just as it takes away. It's a hopeful idea.

Considering *the Psychological Perspective* in the Context of Addiction and Recovery

When something like death or significant loss challenges existing beliefs, new meanings, a revised self-concept, and new ways of living can emerge. As counselors, there is incredible opportunity to explore the impact of addiction-related loss(es). Assist clients through exploration of patterns and ironies (i.e. using to reduce short-term pain, but increasing long-term troubles; trying to fit in by changing oneself), lessons learned from life (i.e. if one is worthless or worthy), exploration of their strengths and potentials (i.e. do they believe they have any), belief systems (i.e. whether they're alone or supported, if past determines future), etc.; curiosity, reflection, questioning, gentle encouragement, and validation would be primary.

Finding a connection after loss, religious or not, can feel like a breath of fresh air or like a new shoulder to lean on. Having, or seeking connection can support a do-over, a reset of perspective. Life comes back online and searching for (and finding) meaning following a loss can lead toward a more authentic, meaningful, and healthier life (Marrone).

When thinking about responses to the loss of an addiction (or any loss tied to an addictive pattern), consider that some clients may be trying to simply right the ship and survive the storm. Their reactions may not seem to propel them forward, but rather keep them standing still. For instance, following a significant event like arrest, overdose, or fight with family, someone may take active steps to become sober yet make no changes to friends, job, housing, or overarching attitudes toward life.

A significant change has happened (i.e. sobriety attempt)—the ship is no longer actively sinking—but it's not moving forward to safer territory. It's standing still and the storm is still raging. Some clients may believe that God is helping them survive, while others may feel God has abandoned them, and yet some others may feel they were alone to begin with and that a God-like figure is irrelevant. It's a matter of perspective. As counselors we can facilitate the exploration for meaning; from this model, conversations might center around The Spiritual Experience previously detailed.

Recall that a piece of The Spiritual Experience was an emerging awareness of something bigger than the self (a higher power of sorts), a renewed purpose, or finding order amidst chaos. From this new awareness came direction, sort of a road map for life. Consider the analogy of the car and the driver offered earlier: people live life as passengers in a car and the driver of that car takes them where it/they think makes the most sense.

In this context, the driver might be a substance like heroin, a compulsive behavior pattern (i.e. compulsive gambling or shopping), a controlling partner or family member, and/or a flawed set of cognitions that make someone feel worthless or weak. One follows the lead of the driver and they're taken on a ride that's billed as scenic and comfortable but turns out to be lacking direction, going down maladaptive roads, all without the proper supports to maintain the car. It's a wonderful metaphor for addiction.

To change course or the car, one first needs to be aware that they don't like the vehicle they're traveling in, don't care for the road they're going down or destination they're heading toward, and that other options exist for new destinations. In short, change begins with an insight into the need for change.

Applying Marrone's model to this addictive/recovery context, that might translate to a relinquishing of control to a newly discovered or re-discovered higher power. It might also mean new awareness which allows a person to question their current state, emotionally respond to what they find, and choose a different course with renewed purpose. It may also mean that someone begins to understand why they went down the unhealthy roads to begin with and bring greater self-understanding and compassion, finding order amidst a chaotic past (or present).

Understanding what's happening and analyzing the impact of the current action on one's life and well-being is a good starting point for doing something different. In this model, The Spiritual Experience is like the light coming on so one can see better. Emerging awareness allows for questions around one's current state, emotional reactions to what's happening, and ultimately choice for where to go next. It really is reminiscent of an existential crisis—questioning the meaning of life and one's role in the world. Think of this as wondering if how you've been living and what you've believed to be true, is actually true.

How people view the world can also provide meaningful structure after loss, addiction, and into the realm of recovery. Whether one believes the world is mostly good or mostly bad, if they believe they have a lot of or very little personal control, if luck exists or life is entirely self-determined, and whether justice exists for all or just some will be impactful (Marrone, 1999). Even if a person's beliefs around any of those areas are merely an illusion, when left unchallenged, such beliefs provide a framework for how people approach life. For instance, if I think I have a good deal of control over what happens to me, I won't sit back and wait for someone or something else to initiate change; I'll steer my own ship, so to speak. Conversely, if I believe that I am largely out of control in life, I may wait for someone or something else to guide me or simply complain about being stuck and having no way out. When working with clients around loss, it can be quite useful to understand how they view the nature of the world (i.e. good vs. bad), level of control in determining one's destiny, and any spiritual or religious elements the client identifies as salient. Clients who find spiritual connection or disconnection in their addictive process and/ or recovery efforts may have an added support system to lean on.

The process of recovery has the potential to be transformative; the death of addictive patterns also brings the potential for new meanings, new understandings of self/self-concept, and new ways of being in the world. There are several implications for counseling and recovery/efforts here. Consider some areas of exploration with clients:

1   Examining the assumptive world (again, what they believe to be true) will be useful during the cognitive restructuring phase.
    *   Have elements of the assumptive world been challenged or strengthened during addiction? How about during recovery? Has their view on life or others shifted? If so, how? Are those changes helpful or hurtful?
2   Considering (or perhaps reconsidering) how much control one has over their addictive pattern; is it real or illusory? What might it mean if perceived control is really an illusion?
    *   More broadly, do they believe they determine their fate or are they at the mercy of outside forces?
    *   Do they want to take more control over their life or are they interested in perhaps relinquishing some of it?
    *   Do they believe they are responsible for their actions or are they governed by outside (i.e. environmental or spiritual) forces?
3   Are people or the world–at–large seen as safe or unsafe? How do they know the difference between a safe and unsafe person?
4   Do they view themselves as alone? If so, is that preferred or lamented?
5   Do they have an internal, self-generated support system or is support sought/received through others in the world (possibly a spiritual relationship)?

- Either way, how do they access and utilize these supports when they're struggling?
- How about when they're succeeding (or is support only sought in · times of struggle)?

6   Are people with addictive patterns or behaviors 'bad' people? If yes, is redemption possible? If no, Is self-forgiveness possible?

- If an explanation exists that challenges or removes the shame (or blame) which often accompanies addiction, are they open to letting that shame or blame go? What would it take to transform their view on what an 'addict' is (i.e. good person who is hurting/ surviving vs. bad person who is doing bad things)?

Help your clients to look for and welcome new insights. Help clients navigate their internal worlds when the insights are scary, sad, and possibly traumatic. Assist them in finding supports in the external world as well. For clients seeking new or renewed connections to a higher power, encourage them to explore the religious or spiritual communities in your area. Alternatively, they might explore the local AA, NA, Overeaters Anonymous, etc. groups. For clients who are interested, but hesitant to attend in person, they may consider participating in online forums for such groups to get a flavor of the culture, the level of spirituality/higher power-focus, and the group norms.

Finally, let's consider Marrone's four phases in the addictive and recovery context:

1   Cognitive restructuring

This phase is focused on cognitive restructuring that allows for acknowledgment and acceptance that the loss has occurred and is permanent. When thinking of losing an addictive pattern, substance, person, environment, health status, freedom (or any other type of addiction-related loss), acknowledging that reality has changed is an important step for some people. The process of creating or moving into a new reality depends on accepting the old reality is no longer an option. It represents one of those weird ironies in life: letting go allows you to hang on.

Some clients will lean on their faith for comfort, support, or for an explanation as to why an addiction or addiction-related loss(es) occurred. I have encountered clients who believed God led them down the addictive path for a reason and that finding redemption through recovery was part of their faith journey. Some others felt abandoned by God or betrayed or ostracized by their faith community during active addiction.

For clients with existing or evolving religious or spiritual belief systems, examining the impact of external control (in this case a God-figure) on their life and recovery could prove fruitful. Some clients may lean solely on their faith until they feel capable of leaning on others or standing on their own. Believing someone is at the wheel when the car feels out of control can be powerful; religious or spiritual beliefs (for those that ascribe to them) can give structure to the pain and assurance that the pain is not without meaning or explanation. I read that as hope.

Counselors may find that this phase pairs well with group processing. Clients actively trying to digest their new reality and finding ways to navigate it might benefit from the experience of others. Note that this does not only mean positive experiences. Hearing the trials and hardships of other clients working to adjust to a new reality might be as, or more beneficial than hearing stories of success. Hope can come in unexpected packages; knowing you're not alone in your struggle can go a long way. An initial connection around challenge or despair can be paired with active efforts to overcome and/or adapt to struggles.

For some clients, mere engagement in communication around shared experience can represent the seedlings of personal growth; don't miss that! If someone has retreated to addictive patterns in the past when hurting and they can learn to shift that toward communicating with others about shared pain or frustrations, that is a remarkable exercise in social skill development. Integrating the faith perspective here could be helpful for some clients as well; finding community with a deity or faith with a community may serve the same supportive purpose.

2 Emotional expression

This phase has a definite seat at the table when thinking about the loss of an addiction or addiction-related loss. Challenging, and perhaps more importantly, inviting clients to feel and allow their grief in is paramount. As has been acknowledged throughout this text, many people have their losses denied, devalued, or ignored by the larger world when addiction is attached. Encourage clients to feel and express (when ready) their emotional turmoil, confusing thought processes, and the physical toll the loss(es) have taken.

Consider some of the following questions and invitations as prompts:
- Take a few minutes and just sit with your thoughts. What comes up? What, if anything feels unsettled in your head or heart about moving away from _____ (insert addictive substance or pattern)?
  - Is there anything that you've lost that perhaps you haven't given credit to? Meaning, something that you've pushed out of awareness that maybe deserves attention?
  - Have you noticed any grief around leaving _____ behind?
- How did you expect this loss to feel (again, insert substance or pattern as appropriate)? Does it feel that way or is it something different? What do you think of that? What's your reaction?

- What do others in your life expect this change to be like? Easy? Hard? Impossible? Inevitable?
  - What's it like negotiating other people's expectations around your recovery?
- Have you taken time to notice your feelings around this change (or change attempt)? What have you found?
  - Or Why don't you take some time and see what you find/feel? There's a lot going on and a lot to consider. Take some time to consider it.
  - Or Let's do that together. Tell me how you're feeling about leaving these patterns behind? How do you feel about what comes next?
- How's your body doing? When people work to change anything, the body can take a hit. What have you noticed? Tell me about it? What do you think your body is trying to tell you?

3 Psychological reintegration

Once clients have acknowledged their new reality and gotten a sense of their emotional response to it, this model shifts gears toward coping with the adjustment. Strengthening, renewing, and/or creating support systems is of primary focus in this phase. In many ways, this aligns with what we try to do in counseling. Assisting with the adjustment to loss(es), the new reality, and working to ensure clients have the resources available to them, internally and externally, to adapt and survive.

A personal favorite in this phase is the taking stock of what remains after a loss; it's a useful starting point. If attention is going to be paid to what needs to be added to support adaptation, it makes sense to begin with what remains. Consider the bits that survived the loss from two angles: (1) internal (2) external.

The internal assessment would consider the individual's traits and what has survived the loss. The external assessment considers outside supports and elements which may have survived the loss. For example, let's imagine someone who has ended methamphetamine use and to that end, also ended a relationship with their romantic partner who is still engaging in use.

Internal elements/supports which may have survived the dual loss (substance and relationship):

- Self-awareness, particularly around the idea of remaining in an unhealthy relationship dynamic when attempting a big change
- Tenacity/grit/determination
- Self-love or self-worth (to some degree; evidenced by an effort to be healthier)
- Love for romantic partner (love can of course remain when relationships end; also note that just because one loves something does not mean they stay)

- Intelligence and ability to distinguish between helpful and unhelpful dynamics
- Hope (to some degree; evidenced by attempt at change)
- Curiosity (about potentials for future)
- Sense of commitment (may shift to self rather than commitment to others)
- Religious or spiritual faith (if applicable)

External supports/elements which may have survived the dual loss:

- Friendships or acquaintance relationships from the now-defunct romantic relationship
- Financial resources (potentially)
- Housing (potentially)
- Family relationships (potentially)
- Employment (potentially)
- Physical health and safety (potentially)
- Pets (animals sometimes act as emotional supports or provide companionship)

After the initial assessment of what's left, talk with your clients about what needs to be added to aid in their transition into recovery. Enhanced psychological stability is a goal here. Increased stability often comes with increased resource awareness, availability, and utilization. That means that one needs to be aware of the resource and then know how to access and implement them (this is true for internal and external resources). For example, the client above may first need to acknowledge their emotional awareness (resource awareness), then learn to listen to their inner side, trusting that they can move in the right direction without another person's guidance (resource access), and then taking actual steps in that direction based on those insights (resource implementation). In the example of enhanced self-awareness and self-trust, there is another useful application: self-acceptance or internal validation of losses that have been rejected or devalued by others. Learning to lean on and trust oneself may be the central components of this phase (and recovery) for some.

Other clients responding to loss may have more external needs. If the loss of relationship also resulted in loss of housing, financial contributions, and friendships, attention will need to be directed at rebuilding and reestablishing those areas. The results of the internal assessment could aid in this effort. For instance, if self-awareness and self-determination are high, clients may require less assistance in their external-focused efforts. Instead of the counselor or case manager searching for housing with the client, a referral might be made with the client the sole actor in seeing it through. Conversely, if a client is

206 Models and Theories of Grief and Loss

struggling to find or lean on their internal strengths or abilities, additional assistance may be needed to accomplish initial goals. Getting a sense for the internal and external bits that survived a loss can help guide intervention efforts and ultimately support recovery.

4   Psychospiritual transformation

Psychospiritual transformation shifts one's understanding of the world and their place in it. Loss can prompt this shift, and I suggest that a recovery attempt can as well. By now I gather that the reader has noted my belief that recovery attempts are filled with potential loss; as such, this assertion simply echoes that belief. A person's attitudes and beliefs about the self, life, love (for self and others), God, and more can be transformed through loss (Marrone). From where I sit, it seems most appropriate for a counselor to be more of a witness to shifts of this magnitude. Helping the client explore and ponder these areas after loss and at various points throughout recovery efforts could prove useful/insightful. Consider some of the following questions clients may consider to this end:

- What have they or could they contribute to the world? (i.e. their purpose for being)
- How might their impact on the world be different in recovery than it was during active addiction?
- What was the world's (or God's) level of support during their successes and perceived failures; what meaning can be derived about the world when thinking about how the two might compare?
- What was the level of self-acceptance or self-forgiveness/grace extended to oneself during periods of success or perceived failure. What might the differing levels of support imply? (i.e. one's worth is absolute or perhaps it's conditional)
- Does my loss or experience need to be valued by anyone else for it to matter to me? Who determines meaning in my life?
- Is love conditional or unconditional? Have I ever known unconditional love? Have I ever extended it to myself or another?
- Can one fail and still be considered a success? Can one succeed and still be considered a failure? Who decides?

Recall that Marrone viewed this transformation as growth-oriented. Loss can initiate a transformative process which changes the mourner, at times in fundamental ways. Recovery can as well. A change of such magnitude is bound to have ripple effects. Help clients search for the meaning in their growth and their loss; learn to (and teach clients to) appreciate the changes in perspective, meaning-making, purpose, and self-concept when working with addiction and addiction-related loss. Recovery is about so much more than just straight behavioral change. Loss can be painful, but as Marrone often noted, it can also transform us and bring us back to life.

References

Klass, D. (1995). Spiritual aspects of the resolution of grief. In H. Wass & R. A. Neimeyer (Eds.), *Dying: Facing the facts* (pp. 243–268). Washington, DC: Taylor & Francis.

Marrone, R. (1997). *Death, mourning and caring.* Pacific Grove, CA: Brooks/Cole/ Wadsworth.

Marrone, R. (1999). Dying, mourning, and spirituality: A psychological perspective. *Death Studies, 23,* 495–519.

Rothaupt, J. W., & Becker, K. (2007). A literature review of western bereavement theory: From decathecting to continuing bonds. *The Family Journal: Counseling and Therapy for Couples and Families, 15*(1), 6–15.

Worden, J. W. (2009). *Grief counseling and grief therapy: A handbook for the mental health practitioner* (4th ed.). New York, NY: Springer.

15 Growth-Oriented Models as Applied to Addiction and Recovery

Some additional models, three in particular, are also worth discussing. Each incorporates or builds on elements previously discussed and as such, are presented in a briefer form. The Conceptual Model of Positive Outcomes of Life Crises (Schaefer & Moos, 2001) and the Model of Loss Resolution and Growth (Nerken, 1993) are growth-oriented and focus on the potential for personal growth and adaptation in the aftermath of loss. The Model of Family Bereavement and Mourning (Walsh & McGoldrick, 2004) acknowledges the challenges experienced by families during grief and the processes that foster resilience and allow for healing after loss. Each is detailed in brief below with translations to the addictive and recovery context interspersed throughout.

Conceptual Model of Positive Outcomes of Life Crises

Another model worth considering centers on successful adaptation and the emergence of personal growth out of bereavement (Schaefer & Moos, 2001). More pointedly, the idea that a significant loss can be the trigger-point for increased coping skills and personal growth. This runs counter to the idea that grief and bereavement lead to personal deterioration and impaired functioning.

Schaefer and Moos (2001) wanted to understand the systems that contributed to personal growth out of significant loss. Their model, as with all previous ones, was written around death and bereavement. As I continue, I'll add in considerations for the loss of an addiction, addictive pattern, or other addiction-related losses.

First off, this model asserted that a person's preexisting environmental and personal resources, that is, what they had in place before any loss, would influence the loss itself and their response after a loss (Schaefer & Moos, 2001). This is fairly intuitive—if you're highly resourced you might be able to avoid certain losses (i.e. the ability to pay for healthcare or having social supports to access treatment compared to those who have neither). Likewise, what you have at your disposal is what you're likely to lean on following loss. So, resources count, and they can influence both the loss and the response to loss from this perspective.

Schaefer and Moos also believed that one's preexisting resources could contribute to positive outcomes after a loss, life crisis, or transition. For readers who have experience working with people with addiction, you have likely found this to be true (I certainly have). The more resources, supports, and coping skills a client has as they move toward recovery, the more likely they are to make ground. Same goes for clients coming into treatment; more resources typically translate to increased access to treatment and better follow-through. Having a somewhat stable foundation to begin standing on and seeing a correlation between that foundation and personal growth is also fairly intuitive.

Breaking down the resources a bit, they split them into two categories: *personal and environmental*. Personal resources included self-confidence, resilience, and existing coping skills. Environmental coping skills included financial resources, the home environment, community supports, relationships with social support from family, friends, and coworkers (Schaefer & Moos). They also detailed characteristics of the event, which could be a loss, life crisis, or significant transition, and how those elements could impact someone's response. Event-related factors included the nature and timing of a crisis or loss, the context in which it occurs (i.e. think supportive context vs. not), and its suddenness and controllability. For the last bit, I think of mandated clients. Some people do not move toward treatment or recovery by choice. Sometimes it happens through a court or family mandate. For example, the suddenness of an arrest (factor 1) could remove one's control (factor 2) and both of those factors are likely to influence the response to the imposed recovery attempt. One might be angry, saddened, feel powerless, experience withdrawals, feel relieved, or something else entirely. The response will vary person to person, but having a sudden change that you didn't choose is going to influence the response, as will a planned change that one has a lot of say in. The context of loss and event-related factors matter in terms of one's response.

Interestingly, Schaefer and Moos believed coping to be both a process (that is, something we do) and outcome (that is, something we achieve). They asserted that through coping with a loss using both preexisting coping skills and newly acquired ones, a person is enhancing their coping repertoire. This repertoire can then be a resource for future losses. If you're totally confused, let me simplify. Adding to and practicing the coping skills one has makes them better prepared to respond to loss in the future. By coping and learning new ways to cope (process), one becomes better at coping (outcome).

The implication of the last point is perhaps more important than it sounds. This is saying that through pain and coping with pain comes growth. This relates back to the earlier point that this model viewed significant loss and one's response to it as an opportunity for personal growth, not personal deterioration. *We grow through loss.* I find this point particularly hopeful when applying it to the addictive and recovery context. Mostly, the idea that people grow through pain and that when we hurt, it's as much an experience that requires reflection on the past as it is an opportunity to look toward the future. These ideas can support validation of a client's pain and loss, and at the same time, validate that they are not stuck or stagnant. Even in their pain there is learning to be gained and meaning to be derived that can facilitate life; again, from loss can come growth. Through losing, we can gain. This last bit could be a slogan for substance use recovery—through losing, you gain.

Schaefer and Moos (2001) described two categories of coping: *approach* and *avoidance*. Approach coping included the tendency to analyze the crisis in a logical way, reappraise it in a more positive light, and take actions to solve the problem or seek support. This sounds an awful lot like cognitive behavioral therapy to me; helping clients to analyze the thoughts around a loss or crisis, reframing or restructuring cognitions, and behavioral change to enhance one's life and emotional-support resources.

Avoidance coping included attempts to minimize the problem, seek alternative rewards, express emotions, or decide that nothing can be done to change the situation (Schaefer & Moos, 2001). These are reminiscent of addictive characteristics: minimizing pain and downplaying the problematic nature of patterns, finding alternate means to feel good or reduce pain, or giving up because the crisis or loss is too big to influence (i.e. hopelessness that change is possible). Emotional expression is also lumped in with avoidance coping and an example of this might be someone expressing anger only and denying the coexistence of sadness, disappointment, resentment, etc. Emotions are present, but there is an avoidance of the underlying emotional experience.

Moreover, Schaefer and Moos believed that one's successful adaptation to a loss and the personal growth experienced in the aftermath was dependent on resources. The combination of existing skill sets (i.e. pre-loss coping ability) with environmental supports while working to develop new coping strategies was key. This is a sensible road map for counselors. Get a baseline assessment of the skills your clients come in with and check for effectiveness. Consider the following talking points:

- Have you thought about or identified the losses you've experienced? If yes, tell me what you've come up with. If not, let's do that together.
- Tell me about what you've done in response to your loss? How have you coped?
  - What thoughts have you had?
  - Which emotions have come up?
  - How intense have those emotions been?
  - Have you had any thoughts or feelings that have surprised you?
- How about behaviors?
  - What have you done or acted on since your loss?
  - Do you connect this behavior to what you've lost, or do you understand it as something else?

- Do you find that your coping skills have worked? Are they effective?
  - If yes, how so? Tell me about the changes you've noticed.
  - If not, how so? Talk to me about what's still missing (i.e. hope, relief, hope, etc.) or what's lingering that you'd rather have gone (i.e. sadness, regret, etc.).
- Let's talk about the personal resources you have available.
  - How confident do you feel in general? How about related to the loss(es)?
  - Do you feel capable of handling this loss(es)? In times where your confidence may waver, do you have anyone who can re-assure you? Are you able to tell them or ask them for what you need?
  - Do you consider yourself resilient? If not, do you think this is something you can develop?
- Let's talk about the environmental resources you have available.
  - Do you have enough money to get what you need? Has the loss(es) impacted that at all? If so, is it a temporary effect or a permanent one?
  - How has this loss(es) impacted your home life? If you've noticed changes, have they been positive ones (i.e. an abusive or trigger-ing presence leaving the home, reunification with children once recovery has stabilized) or negative (i.e. a supportive person leav-ing the home or pressure to find new housing)?
  - Have you felt supported by your community? If so, in what ways? If not, can you identify any ways in which your community could help?
  - Have you felt supported by your family, friends, or coworkers (if applicable)? If so, in what ways? If not, can you identify any ways in which they could help or support you better?
  - Have you thought about ways you can support others? Do you believe you have anything worth offering to another person?

Remember, the world at large, and sometimes helping professionals take a deficit approach. Assuming that a person with a SUD is resourceless and paints a bleak picture devoid of hope, focus then on what the clients bring to the table, even if the skills require some reworking. Consider skills that are operating in an unhealthy way and see if they can be reframed into a healthier light. For example, the tenacity to sustain an addiction to a substance (i.e. constantly sourcing your drugs and finding ways to afford continual use) can be a helpful resource in pursuing recovery. The ability to endure when faced with ongoing challenges is a tremendous asset in recovery. Assess for and talk about the skills your clients are walking in with, whether and how they're working, and what they still need. Getting a sense of available resources and coping strategies at the start is important in determining where to go next.

Model of Loss Resolution and Growth

This model was predicated on the idea that grief work was self-work and that with loss, one has the opportunity to redefine themselves (Nerken, 1993). I believe the same is true with addiction-related loss and recovery. This model was largely focused on self-concept and how the self responds to loss, recovery, and growth. Select elements of this model are discussed in the following pages and translated to the addiction and recovery realm. If you find that Nerken's ideas connect with you, I strongly recommend reading his original work.

Nerken distinguished between two parts of the self: the core self and the reflective self. The core self was made up of our talents, ideas, opinions, dreams, feelings, and overall identity (1993). The reflective self created meaning. Basically, it took the bits and pieces which existed in the core self and interpreted them into something meaningful. Here's a food metaphor: the core self was the pile of ingredients; the reflective self made them into a meal.

The two selves were always talking to one another and interacting. The reflective side interpreted feelings sent from the core along with other information from the world, made meaning from it, and then sent it back to the core where feelings would respond (Nerken, 1993; Rothaupt & Becker, 2007). If this seems confusing, that's okay. Take a minute to digest it. What we feel and believe about things (i.e. our core self) ultimately depends on what we think about what's happened; this perception comes from the reflective self. Once the self has a sense of what it believes and feels, it can act. Behavior is determined by what we believe to be true (Nerken).

Following loss, the reflective self takes information from the core self and interprets it. Beliefs that existed in the core might now be questioned by the reflective self. While one's core might not be changed or damaged, it can be interpreted differently after a loss. For example, someone who felt capable of making decisions with the advice of a trusted advisor might question their capability if this advisor is lost. The actual capability of the person has not changed, just their perception of it. One's core can remain intact. The perception is what needs changing.

In this model, grief is about meaning-making and that happens in the reflective side (Nerken; Rothaupt & Becker, 2007). Help clients examine how their losses have impacted their perceptions of self. Help clients appreciate that even with the presence of an addiction, they have a core that might be filled with useful things that can fuel recovery. Help change their perceptions of their capabilities. For instance, if a substance is lost, that does not also take away their ability to cope with negative feelings, it does mean another form of coping must substitute it, but it doesn't eliminate their ability, it changes the means.

The task is renegotiating the relationship between the core and reflective self. Basically, finding ways to interpret the core differently so that new meaning is made. Remember the core is comprised of one's talents, ideas, opinions, dreams, feelings, and overall identity. Back to that food metaphor. I have the same pile of ingredients, but instead of pizza, I want lasagna. I need to rearrange the ingredients for a new outcome. For people with addiction, they may need to rearrange their ideas, beliefs, dreams, etc. for a new outcome. The core does not need to be thrown out, just reinterpreted.

Here are some additional points to consider about Nerken's model. As noted earlier, he believed that grief work was self-work. When a person loses someone or something of great value, it can feel like a part of the self is also lost. Think of a time when you may have heard this sentiment expressed. It may have sounded something like:

"When she died, she took a piece of me with her."
"I was never the same. It's like a part of me was lost forever."
"I don't know who I am anymore without it/them."
"Who am I? I'm not sure I know how to live without its/their presence."
"I'll never be the same."
"How will I cope? Or I can't cope."
"What do I do now?"

People can become so preoccupied with what they've lost that they forget about other areas of life. To the outside world, this can seem like selfishness. For readers with clinical experience or loved ones with addiction, ask yourself how many times you've heard accusations of selfishness when an addictive pattern is in full swing; it's one piece of the stigma surrounding addiction. I've heard it countless times—people with addictions only care about themselves and are selfish. Consider this alternate perspective: taking time for the self, especially after an important loss, is not selfishness, *it's survival* (Manning, 1984; Nerken, 1993). As a counselor, and honestly just as a human in the world, try and let that point sink in. If selfishness can be viewed as a symptom of survival efforts, there's an opportunity there.

Counselors can help clients identify the function/purpose of the so-called selfish behaviors and attitudes (i.e. what they were/are trying to survive) and work to broaden their options for survival. For instance, some clients don't ask for help when facing challenges, trusting only themselves. However, having more people in your corner likely increases chances of survival compared to going it alone; more people means more resources much of the time.

Explore how clients understand and define themselves with emphasis on the survival elements of their self-concept. If you're unfamiliar with what a self-concept is, it's pretty straightforward. It's one's self-definition and is filled with beliefs about the self ("Self-concept," 2020). For example, if a person believes they are incapable of handling emotional pain, low self-efficacy will likely be part of their self-concept. In contrast, if a person believes themselves capable, that capability will be reflected in their self-concept. Part of the task in counseling and recovery is revising and updating the self-concept.

Help clients think about how they survive when things get hard; talk about how the addictive patterns likely fit into those survival efforts. Reframing can be quite useful here, particularly with addiction. One of my favorite client stories is about a former client who initiated and maintained an injection heroin habit while incarcerated in federal prison. Part of his self-concept included an inability to cope with his circumstances (hence the heroin use), whereas I reframed it as skillful survival. Is injecting heroin the healthiest choice? Certainly not. But the resourcefulness and creativity that allowed him to do it under intense supervision can work to his advantage. This man not only found a heroin connection but managed to fund his purchases through drawings/artwork and crafted his own injection equipment from a combination of paperclips and cheap pens. Where he saw only an 'addict,' I saw tenacity, creativity, and skill; this combination fueled an effort to survive with less pain. Don't discount your power as a helper here; help clients redefine what they see when they look at their thoughts, feelings, and behaviors. Is/was it selfishness or survival? That's an important question. Help clients find the answer.

Ultimately, Nerken made the point that the experience of grief will touch and influence the self. When clients lose something of significance, their reactions can shed light on their self-concept. Revising the self-concept is essentially helping someone change what they see when they look within: strengths, weaknesses, or some of both. Revisions might be aimed at moving from self-defeating, self-deprecating beliefs about self toward empowerment and enhanced capability. Think of it as a car with aftermarket parts. Let me explain:

If I take a basic car right off the lot, I have a car that was designed by someone else. The limits were imposed by the designer, and I had little, if any, control over the final product. But, once I drive that car off the lot, I can redefine its limits by upgrading the motor, adding different tires, and/or modifying the suspension. I can also change the outward appearance to better match the new insides, and more. I can take a car not designed for racing and make it capable of it. I could also take up an old car that has been non-functional for years and restore it to working order (i.e. reviving what was thought to be useless). Both require time under the hood, resources, and knowledge, but they're both possible.

Take this metaphor and apply it to people. A person's self-concept may be filled with external judgments (think of these as the designers of the car)—could be from parents, siblings, peers, etc. If those judgments fuel someone toward capability, change might not be needed. If someone had confidence and resilience instilled in them, we don't want to take those away. But if one has been told or shown they are less than, incapable, worthless, a burden, etc. there is room for improvement (i.e. modifications/upgrades). In counseling, we can help clients modify their original parts and reflect on what contributed to the original design. Spending time under that metaphorical hood may lead to increases in both knowledge and resources.

My hope is that the points made in Nerken's approach help you think about how you can integrate grief concepts into larger identity work when working with addiction.

Model of Family Bereavement and Mourning

Walsh and McGoldrick's (2004) model took a systems approach to bereavement. This model focused on the relational aspects of grief and the family response to bereavement. Open communication around the loss and the emotional response to it were emphasized. Additionally, family members were encouraged to be involved in the grief rituals (i.e. funerals when applicable, other means of detachment or saying 'goodbye,' etc.). The basic premise is that families benefit when they come to terms with loss and move forward as individuals and as a cohesive family unit.

Notably, this approach believed in the continuing bonds theory previously discussed (Klass et al., 1996). As a refresher, continuing bonds theory proposed a transformation of the lost relationship from a physical/alive one to a continued bond that rests on memories and recollections and/or spiritual connections. Further, Walsh and McGoldrick believed that finding or making meaning after a loss was central in coming to terms with what's been lost. Meanings derived from a loss is then woven into "the fabric of life" and integrated into individual and family identities moving forward (p. 9).

This model offered four *Family Adaptational Tasks*. Essentially, if families did not attend to these areas when responding to loss, the chances of dysfunction and family conflict increased (Rothaupt & Becker, 2007; Walsh & McGoldrick, 2004). On the other side of that, if these areas were attended to following loss, there was a greater chance for adaptation (in the short- and long-term) for family members and the family unit as a whole. Walsh and McGoldrick were clear that these tasks were intended as general guidance, not fixed expectations or a measure of how well someone was grieving. Let's consider each briefly and think about how each task could translate to the addictive context.

Task 1: Shared Acknowledgment of the Reality of Death
This is essentially what it sounds like. All family members must first acknowledge that a loss has occurred and come to terms with the reality of it. This first task is in line with the first task in Worden's (2009) model and the first phase in Marrone's (1999) model; both emphasized the need to acknowledge and accept the permanence of loss.

Walsh and McGoldrick believed that with sudden loss, the need to acknowledge what's been lost may feel quite abrupt. This makes sense. If you're not expecting something, you are likely to be taken aback by it. Consider what it might be like to learn that your loved one has been grappling with an addiction without you knowing; your sense of reality is lost or compromised. Likewise, having a loved one die due to an overdose may feel unreal or shocking, especially if the family was previously unaware of use.

In contrast to sudden death or loss are life-threatening conditions. With gradual losses (i.e. sudden death vs. chronic illness) the acknowledgment may evolve over time. Importantly, the anticipation of loss may be filled with hope; if someone is not yet sure an outcome like death or total loss is guaranteed, they may hang onto the chance for recovery or healing. This feeling routinely presented itself during my clinical work. I would acknowledge the reality of client situations and the level of pain, unhealth, and/or insufficient resources, yet often held hope that all was not lost. It resembled an 'it's not over until it's over' mentality. More than most things, this mentality sustained (and still sustains) me as a helping professional. Being able to simultaneously acknowledge what the client (and I as their counselor) was up against while retaining hope that recovery was possible was critical for showing up to work each day. When working with clients (or families of clients) who are stuck in an addictive pattern and sometimes greatly struggling, please don't forget to probe for hope. Loss or failure (to enter recovery) may be anticipated, yet this does not mean there is no hope left to lean on.

Beyond the anticipation phase, was the terminal phase. Basically, if things did not improve, family members might begin to accept the probability of the impending loss and finally the eventuality of it (aka it's no longer perceived as a matter of whether the loss will occur, but when) (Walsh & McGoldrick, 2004). When loss was viewed as inevitable or a death was accepted as likely, the importance of connection was noted. This is important when translating the model to the addictive context. Lack of healing and likely failure/death made connection more important. Bowen (2002), in fact, urged direct contact and visits with the identified family member/client, and advocated that children attend such visits.

The argument was made that trying to hide the severity of the problem from family members could complicate grief processes. Family members, including children, might be more disturbed with the stories they conjure up than the actual reality of a situation (even a really bad one) (Bowen, 1978, 2002; Silverman, 2000). Death and ultimate loss can be taboo subjects; this may translate to a no-talk rule in some families (Rothaupt & Becker, 2007). Open, honest communication about the facts and circumstances around the death or loss facilitates both acknowledgment and acceptance (Rothaupt & Becker, 2007; Walsh & McGoldrick, 2004). To put it simply, knowing what happened, having the ability to ask questions, and get a sense for what happens makes it possible for family members to accept a significant loss has occurred. Conversely, limiting discussion, failing to communicate openly, and remaining in the dark around what happened to a loved one makes grieving difficult.

All of these points are worthy of consideration when families approach the loss of a loved one to an addictive process (i.e. the member is still living but consumed by the addiction) or to death from an addiction-related cause. Sometimes people operate under the assumption that less information makes things less scary. Rarely does that seem to play out in the way it's intended to. As a counselor and as a regular person in the world, consider the relief in acknowledging reality, even when it's paired with pain. For instance, I remember reading a remarkable obituary of a young man who died from a heroin overdose, I believe he was 23 years old at the time of this death. His mother wrote that her son had many honorable and lovable traits including compassion, a quick wit, a willingness to help and serve others, and many athletic talents. She then also shared that her son struggled with heroin, feelings of inadequacy, impulse control, powerlessness, and more that she believed contributed to his death. She talked about her sadness that the struggle overcame the light in him. It was a beautiful, realistic tribute that balanced both truths—he was loved and loving, and he also struggled.

Acknowledgment of a loss or death may sound fairly simple. When you throw addiction into the mix, however, shame, stigma, uncertainty, judgment, and/or the possibility of healing, however remote, can make the molehill feel like a mountain. Offer empathy and patience to family members as they work to adapt to a changing reality. Weigh the options and talk to the families (children too) about their fears, preferences, and questions about what's happening or happened. Help families weigh if visits and connection with someone struggling with an addiction are more likely to be helpful or hurtful. Each family and situation will differ; talk it out.

Task 2: Shared Experience of the Loss

One element of the first adaptational task was connection with the person dying or becoming lost. Through connection, family members could ask and answer questions, confront the changing reality, and begin to absorb the loss (Walsh & McGoldrick, 2004). This second task extends that and focuses more specifically on rituals that occur after the death or loss. Rituals may include:

- funerals (when applicable)
- visits to graves or other places associated with the lost person

- family gatherings or meals centered on remembrance of the lost loved one
- memorializing family members through pictures or other items
- identifying music, poetry, artwork or other items which serve as reminders of the loss
- storytelling about the experience of loss, in any form
- etc.

One application of this concept in the addictive and recovery realm may be living memorials or memorials to the non-addicted version of a loved one. For example, family members could reflect on the bits they remember and loved about their identified member prior to the addiction. Processing feelings around the addiction's impact on those areas can follow (i.e. One's brother used to be reliable, fun, and interested in the well-being of others and with addiction present, he is unreliable and preoccupied or unconcerned with others). Consider the possibilities here for reflection and insight:

- Family members can be encouraged to remember what they loved about someone prior to the addiction
- Opportunity to mourn the changes in their loved one and exploration of what's been lost over time (i.e. trust, hope, relationships, etc.)
- Finding new ways of loving their family member when addiction is present

Remembering the love, particularly when the behavior of a person has become unloving, may help maintain hope for the family unit and/or cultivating ongoing support for the struggling member.

Worth noting once more was the emphasis this approach put on including what they referred to as the "vulnerable family member(s)" whenever possible (Walsh & McGoldrick, 2004, p. 10). If there is an opportunity for family therapy, encourage it. Possible topics for group reminiscing in that context include stories of past events, relationships, and/or traditions that existed before the addiction entered the picture. Another option includes the discussion of bright spots or moments where family members connected despite the addiction's presence (i.e. shared laughter, expressions of love or concern, seeing glimpses of old personality traits such as a sense of humor, sarcasm, etc.). Many may be prefaced with "Remember when... ." When possible, encourage the family (including the addicted member) to share the experience of loss. Finding ways to connect in times of loss can help members acknowledge what's been lost, assess the impact of such losses, and identify means of coping with the new reality (Walsh & McGoldrick, 2004).

Coping may look different for each member of the family. This is also likely to be true when one considers how different family members will respond to the presence of an addiction. Some members may respond with anger and resentment, others with compassion and concern, yet others with defensiveness and disconnection. For this model, tolerance and patience are called for. Keep in mind that as the counselor, you may also be tasked with encouraging patience within the family, particularly if a variety of conflicting emotional responses are present. All forms of emotional expression can be viewed as attempts to cope with a tenuous situation; value the function of the emotional response and encourage family members to do the same. I think of this as shooting at the same target but firing with different arrows. All emotional responses may be intended to assist in coping with the pain an addiction brings (the target), but anger and compassion can look and feel quite different (different arrows).

Task 3: Reorganization of the Family System

With loss comes change. Finding ways to adapt to the changes is important in the wake of loss. This task is reminiscent of the restoration-oriented activities detailed in the DPM discussed earlier in the chapter (Stroebe & Schut, 1999; Stroebe, Schut, & Stroebe, 2005). Recall that restoration-oriented activities included such things as adaptation to new circumstances or roles and/or lifestyle, managing changing or disrupted routines, establishing new ways of connecting with family and friends, and cultivating a new way of life in the midst of all this adjustment. This third task applied these ideas to the family system.

With restoration (as in the DPM) and reorganization (as in this task), circumstances have changed, and individuals are working to change with them. Increased stability and new routines contribute to a new equilibrium (Stroebe & Schut, 1999; Walsh & McGoldrick, 2004). Consider some examples when addiction is present:

- Children may begin to take on adult roles in the absence of a parent (i.e. food preparation, caring for younger siblings, learning to do household chores, etc.)
- One spouse/partner may take on responsibilities formerly assigned to the addicted member
- New routines may be developed that can flex around the presence or absence of the addicted member
- Emotional support may be sought outside the home rather than within the family unit
- New friendships or relationships may be formed that exclude the addicted member; new alliances may form within the family unit
- Family members may relocate with or without the addicted member

Encourage family members/units to be open to changing roles, routines, and expectations. While reorganization is essential for restabilization, encourage pacing. In short, don't change too much too soon (Walsh & McGoldrick, 2004). In this model, equilibrium comes out of adaptation to role changes; the ability to adapt comes out of flexibility (Rothaupt & Becker, 2007). More specifically, families that hold onto old patterns that no longer work can stall in their efforts to adapt to change. The overarching goal here is to maintain a sense of family cohesion while also remaining flexible (Rothaupt & Becker). Secure, but not fixed.

Task 4: Reinvestment in Other Relationships and Life Pursuits

This task is reminiscent of Worden's (1991, 2009) fourth task which centered on the withdrawal of emotional energy from the lost object/person and reinvesting it into new relationships. This task also stirs questions around the appropriate timeframe for grief and mourning. Should it last weeks? Months? Years? Endure forever? Walsh and McGoldrick (2004) emphasized the variability of grief and gave no specific expectation for a solid timeline. They did point out that a sudden loss might make someone wary of reengaging compared to an anticipated, slow-to-come loss. The idea there was preparedness; if an individual or family had time to emotionally prepare for the loss, they might be better able to absorb it and move on toward reinvestment sooner than someone incurring a sudden, unexpected loss. They also talked about well-intentioned people who may swoop in and suggest moving on to new or other relationships, effectively discouraging a connection with the person who's lost. Remember that Walsh & McGoldrick's model was written around death, so this doesn't perhaps sound unreasonable at a certain point. But what about a person who is still living, yet lost in an addictive cycle? Should they be 'moved on from' or not? That will certainly depend on who you are asking. I strongly recommend asking the family. Help family units talk this out and consider the varying opinions which may be present in the family system.

Consider engaging family members who prefer reinvestment in other relationships paired with disconnection from the addicted member, to examine the possible protective nature of that desire. For instance, is it less painful when they don't have to engage? Can they focus more on their life over their loved ones? Does reinvestment serve as a welcome distraction? If yes, are they prepared to cope if the addicted member makes a reappearance in their life? There is nothing wrong or inappropriate about wanting a break from the pain addiction can bring. Loving someone with an addiction can be downright tiring. Be sure as counselor though, that when validating that, the future is also considered. If reinvestment is acting as a distraction from the distress associated with the addicted member, we want to be sure families are prepared to cope if that distress reenters their life down the line. Walsh and McGoldrick agreed with this recommendation. They also warned that immediate reinvestment after a loss could lead to complications in the replacement relationships due to "blocked mourning" (pg. 14).

This model also considered variables that might influence a family's adaptation to loss. Variables included (Walsh & McGoldrick):

- the manner of death/how someone was lost (sudden vs. gradual)
- ambiguous loss (think of a loved one who is physically absent but psychologically present)
- the family and social network (think resources)
- the state of relationships at the time of death
- prior roles and functioning in the family system (think about how big of a gap will be left in their absence)
- the sociocultural context (think stigma)
- transcendence and spirituality (think continuing bonds)
- the timing of death in the family life cycle (think about premature losses like early death, concurrent stressors at the time of loss, and historical elements like prior trauma)

Ultimately, this model highlighted a need to consider the family systems response to loss and served as an important reminder that loss doesn't occur in a vacuum and people don't often mourn in isolation.

References

Bowen, M. (1978). *Family therapy in clinical practice.* London: Aronson.

Bowen, M. (2002). *Family therapy in clinical practice.* London: Aronson.

Klass, D., Silverman, P. R., & Nickman, S. L. (Eds.). (1996). *Continuing bonds: New understandings of grief.* Washington, DC: Taylor & Francis.

Manning, D. (1984). *Don't take my grief away: What to do when you lose a loved one.* New York, NY: Harper & Row.

Marrone, R. (1999). Dying, mourning, and spirituality: A psychological perspective. *Death Studies, 23,* 495–519.

Nerken, I. R. (1993). Grief and the reflective self: Toward a clearer model of loss resolution and growth. *Death Studies, 17,* 1–26.

Rothaupt, J. W., & Becker, K. (2007). A literature review of western bereavement theory: From decathecting to continuing bonds. *The Family Journal: Counseling and Therapy for Couples and Families, 15*(1), 6–15.

Schaefer, J. A., & Moos, R. H. (2001). Bereavement experiences and personal growth. In M. S. Stroebe, R. O. Hansson, W. Stroebe, & H. Schut (Eds.), *Handbook of bereavement research: Consequences, coping, and care* (pp. 145–167). Washington, DC: American Psychological Association.

Self-concept. (2020). In *Oxford Online Dictionary.* Retrieved from https://www. oed.com/view /Entry/175153?redirectedFrom=self-concept#eid

Silverman, P. R. (2000). *Never too young to know: Death in children's lives*. New York: Oxford University Press.

Stroebe, M. S., & Schut, H. (1999). The dual process model of coping with bereavement: Rationale and description. *Death Studies, 23*(3), 197–224.

Stroebe, W., Schut, H., & Stroebe, M. S. (2005). Grief work, disclosure, and counselling: Do they help the bereaved? *Clinical Psychology Review, 25*, 395–414.

Walsh, F., & McGoldrick, M. (2004). Loss and the family: A systemic perspective. In F. Walsh & M. McGoldrick (Eds.), *Living beyond loss: Death in the family* 224(pp. 3–26). New York, NY: W W Norton & Co.

Worden, J. W. (1991). *Grief counseling and grief therapy: A handbook for the mental health practitioner* (2nd ed.). New York, NY: Springer.

Worden, J. W. (2009). *Grief counseling and grief therapy: A handbook for the mental health practitioner* (4th ed.). New York, NY: Springer.

Considering Ben in the Context of Models and Theories of Grief and Loss

You may recall, at the end of Chapter 2, Ben's losses were briefly explored. In this section, I want to provide the reader with options for loss identification with clients so that the ideas of loss and grief can be incorporated into treatment conversations early on. I'll also describe the theoretical approach I used while working with Ben.

The easiest way I have found to begin these conversations is with a so-called 'loss-list.' This is exactly what it sounds like: a list of losses identified by the client with help from the counselor as needed. Helgoe (2002) mentions this idea briefly in his book; for me, it starts to cement the idea that losses have occurred and that those losses are deserving of grief. In short, this simple exercise is the first step toward recognition that loss may have played a part in one's addiction and that it may also play a part in one's recovery.

For Ben, we categorized the losses into two categories: primary losses and secondary losses. As a quick refresher, primary loss refers to the initial loss. It's what comes first, the headliner. For example, if I lose my freedom due to arrest and incarceration, that could be considered the primary loss. Secondary losses come in the wake of the primary loss. Consider this example of a primary and secondary loss list:

Primary Loss = Freedom

Secondary Losses:

- The freedom to choose
- Self-respect
- The respect or trust of others (i.e. think possible criminal record)
- Time (e.g., time living life outside vs. in jail or prison)
- Money (e.g., lost income, legal fees, fines)
- Custody of children
- Coping strategies; some coping tools are not readily available during incarceration (e.g., substances, quiet, preferred people, art materials)

Helping clients get a sense of both primary and secondary losses can inform treatment. Remember that the secondary losses can be as or more impactful than the primary loss and that order does not necessarily equal importance. In this example, if the secondary loss of custody is identified as a major stressor, and reunification as a goal, time and energy can be directed there. Notice that in discussing one secondary loss, others are looped in. Part of addressing the loss of custody may involve the loss of trust, financial considerations, length of sentence (i.e. loss of time), and the freedom to choose. The loss of custody conversation involves more than the simple loss of custody. Validate the complexity of loss and help clients begin to process all the moving parts. Developing primary and secondary loss lists can help examine the scope of loss, providing a visual sense of the domino effect that's occurred. Losing one thing often prompts the loss of others (knock over one domino, another is likely to fall).

Back to Ben. He had a few notable primary losses: heroin (when sobriety or recovery attempted), his arrest/legal involvement, the loss of his mother, and the death of his father. Following the cancer diagnosis and eventual death of his father, he attempted to stop using heroin. His loss list for the substance resembled the following:

Primary Loss = Heroin

Secondary Losses:

•   Loss of a primary coping skill

Notice how Ben's loss list is far shorter than the example provided previously (around the loss of freedom). Take note that the length of a loss list does not matter. Ben's short list is as meaningful as the longer one offered in the example. Let me explain. Heroin was his primary means of coping with negative emotions. There were several layers to this one secondary loss. For Ben, heroin use was more about the absence of things than the presence of a high. Try and appreciate the magnitude of loss here. In losing his primary coping skill, he lost:

•   the ability to distract, disconnect, or numb the parts of his world that hurt
•   the calming procedural elements of preparing the heroin for injection, were also lost
•   control (i.e. the ability to change his physical and emotional state on demand)

Now pair this one primary loss, heroin, with another primary loss, the death of his father.

Consider the loss list for Dad here:

Primary Loss = Dad's death

Secondary Losses:

- loss of support; his father was a central supportive figure
- loss of family/sense of belonging; the idea that he was alone in the world became prominent following his father's death
- loss of self-respect/self-worth
  - regret and guilt factored in here, particularly the stress he thought he added to Dad's life
  - he also questioned if he was a burden to Dad which led to questioning his self-worth
- redemption
  - with his dad's death, he lost the chance to prove to his Dad that he was capable of more (i.e. improved health, recovery, professional success, having a family of his own)

Recall that Ben's attempt for sobriety occurred shortly after his father's death. In short, he had a lot to cope with and no way to do it; his main means of coping (heroin/numbing) was off the table. The interaction of losses can be significant; be sure to help clients make those connections and don't fail to appreciate them as a counselor. One loss can compound another, and that interaction can influence available options, specifically coping skills. In Ben's case, his sobriety attempt (i.e. loss of heroin) influenced his ability to cope with the death of his dad. He was attempting something perceptively healthy (recovery), but it complicated his emotional survival in the short term. It was a frustrating irony.

Additional losses in Ben's story included his arrest and subsequent criminal record and the early abandonment by his mom. I saw value in exploring those as well, but Ben did not. He believed the loss of his father and the loss of his substance/routine were most relevant to his recovery efforts so that's where we spent our time. Remember that the client is the driver of their car; a loss can be present, but it does not mean it demands exploration. Listen to your clients and let them guide you.

In exploring these two losses and the secondary impacts with Ben, I used the DPM as a theoretical framework to guide our discussions (Stroebe & Schut, 1999; Stroebe, Schut, & Stroebe, 2005). What attracted me to this model was the rejection of the grief-work hypothesis. Recall that this idea advocated for the confrontation of emotion in order to fully grieve (aka detach from the lost object). So, if someone was suppressing their loss, they weren't seen as engaging in grief. From where I sit, suppressing one's pain in response to a loss qualifies as grief.

Ben teeter-tottered back and forth between acknowledgment and suppression of his pain; working to let the pain in at times and running from it at others. Sometimes the running was literal; after sessions centered on the loss of dad, he would sometimes not show up for the session. Remember the interaction of Ben's two primary losses: heroin and his dad's death.

Ben knew his Dad was gone and he knew heroin was not a healthy means of coping, but it was an effective one that allowed him to escape reality. At times, counseling felt too "real" and he found ways to escape/avoid it (i.e. no-show). Avoidance is a coping skill, perhaps not a preferable one for counselors who typically like to engage, but it's a coping skill, nonetheless. Remember that.

The DPM also viewed avoidance as a coping skill. In Ben's case, one primary loss (and accompanying secondary losses) got in the way of coping with another. He was not yet prepared to face the totality of his pain. He simply could not yet cope effectively. Basically, the grief-work hypothesis wasn't a good fit. Our most frequent conversations centered on the interrelatedness of his losses and working our way through the secondary losses, exploring the pain attached to each, the ways he would distract from (i.e. avoidance or drug use) or devalue that pain (i.e. "I deserve it," "Other people have it worse" type statements) and ultimately working to increase his ability to live with that pain. The emphasis on secondary losses in the DPM reaffirmed the theoretical fit.

I would often celebrate the session after a no-show when he came back. For readers who know me personally, you can imagine what that celebration might have entailed. For readers who don't, I'm not embarrassed to tell you that glitter, cards, and cookies (shared during session) were sometimes involved. I wasn't only celebrating his return; I was celebrating his avoidance. No-show for a session, without also using heroin, was a far healthier version of escape. He was not only developing new awareness and coping skills; he was using them! Think about it. He would notice the rising emotions prior to the session, assess his ability to cope, and act accordingly. If he felt capable that day, he would attend a session. If he did not feel capable of coping, he would no-show.

The increase in insight and the corresponding behavioral response was worth celebrating and as I write this I'm smiling because it was an absolute revelation for Ben—things aren't always as they seem. Take small steps as big successes sometimes; they fuel hope (for counselor and client alike). Reframing became prominent in our sessions and he took to it.

Over time, reframing was likely the most useful intervention for him. He learned how to dispute his thoughts and gained more power over how his actions, the actions of others, and the world at large impacted him emotionally. Rational Emotive Behavior Therapy and the ABCDEs from that approach were a hit (Ellis & Ellis, 2011).

References

Ellis, A., & Ellis, D. J. (2011). *Theories of psychotherapy. Rational emotive behavior therapy.* Washington, DC: American Psychological Association. Retrieved from https://psycnet.apa.org/record/2010-21512-000 on February 27, 2020.

Helgoe, R. S. (2002). *Hierarchy of recovery: From abstinence to self-actualization.* Center City, MN: Hazelden.

Stroebe, M. S., & Schut, H. (1999). The dual process model of coping with bereavement: Rationale and description. *Death Studies, 23*(3), 197–224.

Stroebe, W., Schut, H., & Stroebe, M. S. (2005). Grief work, disclosure, and counselling: Do they help the bereaved? *Clinical Psychology Review, 25,* 395–414.

Part III

Resilience and Wellness

16 Resilience and the Importance of Relationship

Defining Resilience: An Overview

Interestingly, the concept of resilience has its origins in physics, not counseling. In physics, resilience is the "ability of an elastic material to absorb energy (i.e. from a blow) and release that energy as it springs back to its original shape" ("Resilience," 2020, p. 1). The idea that a person can rebound after a blow or regain their so called-original shape or self is central to any change effort. It's not hard to see why this concept has been adopted in the counseling field.

In translating this idea to counseling, it's worth considering whether or not the idea of 'bouncing back' is the aptest analogy. Jay (2017) argued that resilience wasn't so much a bounce back, but a battle, one that can last for years. She argued that resilience is not an innate trait, rather something that's acquired. Werner (1995), a psychologist, understood resilience as positive developmental outcomes despite high-risk, sustained competence while under stress, and recovery from trauma and adversity. Luthar (2006) defined it as a positive adaptation despite adversity; both elements—significant adversity and positive adaptation—were considered the hallmarks of resilience. Resilience, for many, isn't something that can be objectively measured, but instead inferred through the presence of these two things (adversity and positive adaptation) (Fleming & Ledogar, 2008; Luthar, 2006; Masten, 2001; Sroufe, Egeland, Carlson, & Collins, 2005; Yates, Egeland, & Sroufe, 2003).

Hunter (1999) understood resilience on a continuum—Less Optimum Resilience was one end of the continuum and Optimum Resilience was the other. A client who relies on a substance like alcohol to cope with trauma memories has the adversity but is lacking the positive adaptation (alcohol can be used as a coping tool, but it will not support overall health). This would land them more toward the Less Optimum end whereas an individual who has a traumatic history and has worked to reframe their experience to one that allows for self-forgiveness and compassion would fall more toward Optimum Resilience. In brief, Less Optimum resilience included maladaptive behaviors like violence, high-risk behaviors (i.e. drug use), and social and emotional withdrawal (Fleming & Ledogar, 2008;

Hunter, 1999). The idea that maladaptive behaviors can qualify as resilient is significant (more on that later).

Some researchers believed resilience was the same thing as positive coping, adaptation, and persistence (Greene, 2002) and that the terms could be used interchangeably. Other researchers (Fergus & Zimmerman, 2005) believed that resilience was distinct and that it was confused with other things such as positive adjustment, coping, and/or competence. Fergus and Zimmerman argued that positive adjustment was the product of resilience and that the process of overcoming adversity was resilience itself. This aligns somewhat with the earlier point that the existence of positive adaptation infers the presence of resilience (Luthar, 2006). They further argued that coping with or avoiding adverse situations altogether were also products of resilience. From their view, a person doesn't become resilient by coping or avoiding, rather they are able to cope or avoid because they are resilient. Competence was viewed as an asset and protective factor—an internal, individual characteristic a person either did or did not possess. More competence likely meant healthier responses to adversity.

Resilience Models and Influencing Factors

Three primary models of resilience exist: The Compensatory Model, The Protective Factor Model, and The Challenge Model. All are intended to describe the role of stress on a person's ability to positively adapt to adversity (Ledesma, 2014).

The Compensatory Model viewed resilience as something that mediates or defuses exposure to risk factors (Ledesman, 2014). This is basically saying that if you take a person's resilience and break it down into component parts, pieces of it will compensate for the impact of negative experiences. It's like having a band-aid after you cut yourself; the band-aid compensates for the broken skin. It makes a problem less problematic by filling in gaps. This model called those component parts of resilience *compensatory factors*. Importantly, the band-aid doesn't heal the wound, but it raises the chances of healing, nonetheless. Compensatory factors can have a direct effect on the outcome of adversity independent of the risk factor. Researchers have identified several compensatory factors (Fleming & Ledogar, 2008; Ledesma, 2014; Ungar, 2004; Werner & Smith, 2001):

- active approaches to problem-solving
- ability to perceive negative experiences in a positive light during period of stress
- the ability to attract attention and help from others
- maintenance of a positive view on life
- optimism
- empathy
- insight

- intellectual competence
- self-esteem
- direction or mission
- determination and perseverance

The Protective Factor Model of resilience (O'Leary, 1998) talks about the interaction between protective and risk factors. Protective factors reduce the likelihood of negative outcomes and buffer risk (Bonanno, 2004; Ledesma, 2014; Ungar, 2004).

Protective factors can reduce the chances of a negative event derailing someone's life (i.e. the ability to self-regulate might prevent someone from engaging in physical fights). The presence of protective factors doesn't remove the fight, they simply prepare someone to respond in healthier ways. The next section discusses these constructs in more depth.

Risk and Protective Factors

Inherent in conversations about resilience are discussions of risk and protective factors. Protective factors are biological, psychological, family, or community/cultural characteristics that either lower a person's risk of negative outcomes or acts as a buffer against adversity (National Research Council & Institute of Medicine, 2009). Examples of empirically supported protective factors include (Bonanno, 2004; Fleming & Ledogar, 2008; Olsson, Bond, Burns, Vella-Broderick, & Sawyer, 2003, pp. 5–6; Ungar, 2004):

- emotional management skills
- intrapersonal reflective skills
- problem-solving skills
- planning and decision-making
- foundational sense of self
- self-esteem
- self-efficacy
- internal locus of control
- sense of humor
- hopefulness
- strategies to deal with stress
- academic or other success
- attachment to others
- developed language
- robust neurobiology
- prosocial attitudes
- tolerance for negative affect
- enduring set of values
- malleability and flexibility

- fortitude/conviction/tenacity/resolve
- cohesion and care within the family
- non-blaming attitudes in the family
- marital support
- talent or hobby valued by others
- material resources
- supportive peers
- responsiveness to others
- positive temperament (i.e. glass half full vs. half empty)

Note that some researchers distinguish between *assets* and *resources* when considering protective factors. *Assets* are positive factors that exist inside someone whereas *resources* are positive factors that exist outside someone (Fergus & Zimmerman, 2005). This distinction is meant to clarify that resilience is not solely determined by individual traits; a host of external factors also determines one's level of resilience (i.e. social environment, family, etc.) (Bonanno, 2004; Bonanno, Wortman, & Nesse, 2004; Fergus & Zimmerman, 2005; Ledesma, 2014).

Risk factors are essentially the opposite of protective factors. Risk factors are biological, psychological, family, or community/cultural characteristics that are connected to increase the risk of negative outcomes or adversity (National Research Council & Institute of Medicine, 2009). The idea here is that the more protective factors equal more resilience (Bonanno; Bonanno et al., 2005; Fergus & Zimmerman; Fleming & Ledogar).

The Challenge Model asserted that when a risk factor is not too extreme, it can increase a person's adaptation (Ledesma, 2014; O'Leary, 1998). This is akin to the idea that what doesn't kill you makes you stronger. By overcoming one challenge, a person can be better prepared for the next. Using this model as a foundation, Richardson (2002) came up with the idea of *resilient reintegration*. Resilient reintegration refers to growth or insight that comes out of adversity; it's the idea that people can grow from pain and use that growth to fuel future efforts (Ledesma, 2014; Richardson, 2002). Richardson saw this as the ideal outcome of stress or adversity. One element of this was identification. Following adverse situations or outcomes, one had to first identify their resilient qualities that allowed them to survive. This idea was grounded in the belief that people are stronger and more resilient than they're aware of and that misfortune can bring those qualities to the surface. Negative circumstances can lead to the discovery of inner strength we didn't know existed.

Richardson (2002) saw resilient reintegration as evolution or extension of resilience theory. He viewed earlier ideas as descriptive, specifically describing resilience as a list of strengths, resources, or assets that aided survival. The idea of resilient reintegration was applied more to nature; a means of helping people translate those strengths, resources, and assets into growth following life disruptions (Ledesma, 2014). Some researchers (HeavyRunner &

Marshall, 2003; Mills & Shuford, 2003) believed that resilience and a resilient outlook were innate qualities, present in everyone from birth. The task then was to empower people to discover and adopt them.

This is one area where I see research and counseling converging. Helping clients look within and reflect on who they are, what they have lived through, *how* they have survived, and what they hope for the future is in our clinical wheelhouse. Be sure to discuss both healthy and unhealthy coping measures—think effectiveness over health. Help clients explore their survival strategies and discover their resilience within them. Also remember, we're playing the long game; we're trying to help clients in the present and into the future. Long-term benefits come when resilience prompts new learning such as new perspectives or skills (Carver, 1998; Ledesma, 2014). For example, learning emotional regulation skills, gaining knowledge of resources available and how to access them, and/or straight content knowledge (i.e. differences between recovery vs. sobriety). The idea here is that when people acquire and master new skills, they are better prepared to meet and respond to future problems. Part of resilience is navigating problems in the present and then applying that learning to the future (Carver, 1998; Ledesma, 2014). These ideas draw on internal and self-factors to resilience. Most notably, building a sense of coherence, the use of personal resources, coping ability, cognitive resources, a sense of control, insight, empathy, and perseverance (Ledesma, 2014; Ungar, 2004). Ultimately, resilience facilitates thriving.

Thriving has been defined a number of ways. Nishikawa (2006) defined it as a person's positive transformation out of negative events. Ickovics and Park (1998) defined thriving as an effective mobilization of resources (individual and social) when responding to risk that leads to positive outcomes (mentally, physically, and/or socially). Yet another definition from Carver (1998) centered on decreased reactivity to and faster recovery from future stressors. A combination of these definitions understands thriving as a positive transformation, achieved through mobilization of resources, with the future benefit of reduced stress and resilience leading to positive mental, physical, and social outcomes (i.e. confidence, skill acquisition, sense of security in relationships, etc.).

Let's focus on two internal factors that have been associated with positive outcomes from stress events: optimism and hope. Individuals with the highest levels of hope and optimism are documented to be those who expect positive outcomes and who believe they have the ability to set and meet their own goals (Fleming & Ledogar, 2008; Ledesma, 2014; Matsen, 2005, Ungar, 2004). Putting all these together, optimism + hope + positive expectations + semblance of personal control = growth out of adversity (aka increased resilience/thriving). *To foster resilience, we need to foster hope.*

Considering the strong influence of external factors to resilience, one variable consistently stands out as a contributor: *relationships* (Ledesma, 2014; Matsen, 2005). Counselors have an opportunity to directly influence a central factor in resilience when working with clients: the relationship. In the counseling field, there has been exhaustive research documenting the importance of the therapeutic relationship and alliance (Bordin, 1979; Cronin, Brand, & Mattanah, 2014; Laska, Smith, Wislocki, Minami, & Wampold, 2013; Lynch, 2012; Summers & Barber, 2010; Wampold, 2001, 2015; Wampold & Imel, 2015). Relationships matter, and as helping professionals, there's a golden opportunity to contribute to the resilience of the people we work with. Let's now focus on ways to form the therapeutic alliance and think about how to cultivate an external protective factor via the counseling relationship.

Strategies for Building the Therapeutic Alliance

Summers and Barber (2010) outlined several strategies for building the therapeutic alliance. There's no magic here, just simple behavioral strategies and perspective-taking. First, provide a brief explanation of the therapy and what clients can expect when they come to a session. Do not let the simple nature detract from the importance. Knowing what to expect from your environment and the people in it is something that might feel unfamiliar, particularly when addiction has been part of life. This could sound something like:

> I'm glad you're here and I want to give you a sense of what to expect from me and our time together. I have no interest in forcing you to change; that's something for you to decide and ultimately act on. I do have interest in helping you meet your goals and finding a less stressful life. This means that I'm not going to tell you what to do or give you a laundry list of what has worked for others. I want to know you and your life, your losses, your challenges, *and* your successes. I want to help you find a path that will work for *you*. Part of this process will be exploring different areas of life like relationships, losses, coping abilities etc. and understanding your addiction through them. I'll be interested in what works/worked for you about use (or the addictive pattern) and what didn't. You're the drive here and I'm more of a navigator going along for the ride. Your job is to tell me the destination, what you hope for, obstacles you see, and how the car is functioning, and ultimately steer/choose the direction. My job is to help navigate so you arrive safe at your destination. I won't judge you or shame you for going the wrong direction or crashing the car. I will celebrate with you when things go right. And lots of things will go right (for example you're here today). I encourage you to be patient with me, but more importantly, with yourself. I'll have realistic expectations around how hard this change might be, and I'll have faith in your ability to do it anyway. I hope you can join me in that in time.

This example is of course what *I* might say. I encourage you to incorporate your own perspective, truths, and flavor into your version. The point though is to set the stage and then follow-through. However you purport to be, be that way. Do not say things you don't intend to or can't follow-through. For instance, if I say I will not shame them for going in the wrong direction, I should not respond with disappointment or disapproval if they lapse or relapse. Likewise, I should not be working at a clinic that will discharge someone for lapsing or relapsing. Think this through and state your truth. Just be sure you know what that truth is. I strongly encourage self-reflection on your helping style before engaging in this type of discourse.

Be clear about client goals and develop an understanding of what you'll be working on. If clients are interested in avoiding jail versus understanding themselves better, that's worth knowing. I would argue the former (jail) can be partly addressed by the latter (greater self-understanding), but a conversation between counselor and client should be had around goals. Be sure you're working to meet their needs, not your own. Summers and Barber (2010) cautioned providers to watch for too much pleasure or too much anxiety on their part. Becoming overly invested in the outcomes of our client's work can be unhelpful. Remember that clients are the ultimate deciders and they are responsible for their decisions. As helpers, we are responsible for our reactions; keep a close eye on your reactions (what you say and do) if you notice strong emotional responses to clients.

The next recommendation centers on maintaining curiosity and self-awareness in the relationship (Summers & Barber, 2010). Specifically, this refers to knowing your blind spots as a counselor as well as that of your client. Think of blind spots while driving; they're areas that you can't see well but they might hold something of consequence. Just because you can't see clearly doesn't mean there isn't something there worth noticing.

Work to become aware of areas of content or emotion you tend to avoid; work to also notice which areas your clients steer away from. Don't give up when you feel confusion or frustration in session. Encourage your clients to take a second look as well. One of my favorite lines as counselor is "Guess." For example, if I ask someone what hurt the most, I may get "I don't know" or "it's hard to pin it down" in return. Ask for a guess. More often than not, when a question seems unanswerable, people will still venture a guess. After all, a guess can't be wrong. Maintaining curiosity and self-awareness conveys to the client that there is something to be learned or discovered (curiosity) and what we know about ourselves can help us find answers or options of which we were previously unaware (self-awareness).

Next, have faith that "warmth, enthusiasm, support and empathic skepticism about client's coping strategies" will spark client interest (Summers & Barber, 2010, p. 87). Rather than dismissing addictive behaviors or patterns as maladaptive coping, shift instead to understanding the adaptiveness. Remember that coping can be effective *and* unhealthy. Take a curious, empathic stance. Be curious about both sides; what made something worthwhile even though there were downsides? Explore the function of use or behavior (i.e. what it was intended to do), whether or not it worked, and inject hope that if they found one way to cope, they can ultimately find others. Notice the absence of shame. Making people feel bad will likely never prompt them to do good. Positive emotional engagement (interactions that feel good) are important between counselor and client; curiosity, empathy, and a belief that behaviors were meaningful/ purposeful can add to such interactions.

Find what's likable in your client and tell them that every now and again (Summers & Barber). Work to be a reminder of what's good and worth saving in them; work not to be a reminder of what feels broken. Remember earlier that optimism and hope are two internal factors associated with positive outcomes from stress events. People who expect positive outcomes and believe they're capable of setting and meeting their goals have the most optimism and hope.

As counselors, we have a lot of power here to reflect back to the client their strengths, particularly in times of stress. We can contribute to their ability to notice their ability to endure hardship and remind them that there is tremendous hope in survival alone (after all, if you're alive you have options). Encourage clients to expect something good to happen and be flexible in how you define "good." One of my favorite client memories is a younger man I worked with. He was 19 years old at the time and had been injecting cocaine seven to eight times a day. We mutually agreed that he would try to stop using one day of the week; so, the goal was to use for six days, not all seven. The following week he came in and reported using all seven days. The only difference he noted was using six times three of the days, rather than his typical seven or eight. I nearly fell out of my chair with excitement and he looked at me like I was weird. I'll explain my response to you as I did to him:

> If you add up all the times you didn't use, that almost equals a whole days' worth of use! Three days with 1 to 2 less times per day equals 3 to 6 less incidences of use. That's a big deal and we're going to celebrate. It might not have come in the package we were hoping for, but it still came. You found a way to cope without cocaine during those moments. That's important and we're going to get to the bottom of it. Tell me what was different when you didn't use. Let's explore what you did that was different and try to build on it or at least recreate it.

That last bit is touching on the idea of *exceptions* inherent in Solution Focused Therapy (De Jong & Berg, 2013). If you're not familiar, I encourage you to look it up; it's a helpful concept when working with progressive change. Help clients celebrate their progress, however small. Hope doesn't have to come in big packages.

See the best in your clients and believe in their capabilities. Have empathy for their struggles and also hold them accountable for how their behavior impacts others. Part of change is recognizing what's not working; part of counseling then is helping identify that. Remember balance is key. If we only have support and no acknowledgment of reality, we are working with half the equation. Help clients acknowledge their reality and help them learn to live within it or to reshape it into something more tolerable. Summers and Barber (2010) advised helpers to "ally with the healthy side of the patient, that is, the part that is distressed by what he or she is doing, feeling, and experiencing" (p. 89). That sentiment is reminiscent of Motivational Interviewing in some ways (Miller & Rollnick, 2013).

Any statements you make which touch on the idea of resistance should be paired with empathic comments acknowledging that the client is in pain (of some sort) (Summer & Barber, 2010). For example, a client who sits silently and refuses to speak to the counselor could be labeled "resistant." Consider some responses that both acknowledge the resistance (sometimes implicitly) and the pain:

> "I can see that you're not sure engaging with me is going to be worth it. You're in a tough spot right now and I appreciate you coming in at all."
> "You've got a lot to sort through and there are no easy answers."
> "Each time you try to get up and take a step forward, something else knocks you down."
> "You've lost a lot. I don't expect it'll be easy to talk about. Let's take this slow."
> "I know this isn't easy."
> "When we're faced with the unknown, it makes sense to protect ourselves."

Gentleness can go a long way in helping someone feel understood; direct confrontation is sometimes overrated.

Ruptures to the alliance are going to happen. When they do, try your best to notice them or ask your client what happened, try to understand your role in what went wrong and account for it—apologize. Once there's an understanding of what happened and apologies have been made, try to connect the instance to any patterns that have emerged in your work with that person (i.e. telling the counselor they're wrong might reflect a pattern of shutting down any perspectives that don't match their own) (Summer & Barber, 2010).

Recall that resilient reintegration is the idea that people can grow from their pain and use that growth to seed future efforts (Richardson, 2002). For that to happen though, one must first identify the resilient qualities that allowed them to survive and then translate those strengths into healthy action. Building a strong alliance that embodies curiosity, accountability, hope, and patience while holding a belief in the capabilities of clients to overcome hardship can help clients translate their strengths and resources into growth and ultimately recovery.

Tips for Fostering Resilience

Practically for counselors, one component in fostering resilience is simply noticing its presence. Looking for the adversity in a client's story, not often hard when addiction and/or loss are involved and examining how they've adapted to support life/health despite them. Once people's stressors have been identified, they need to be validated. Part of becoming resilient is recognizing that what you've battled or are currently battling is legitimately stressful (aka don't minimize client problems and encourage clients to avoid doing so) (Jay, 2017). Recognizing and validating ambiguous and nonfinite losses may be especially important as the world has a tendency to deny their existence and/or impact. The same is true for disenfranchised and unconventional grief (refer back to Chapter 2 if you need refreshing on these terms).

Once a loss or grief process experience has been validated, counselors can help clients look for evidence of existing resilience (Jay, 2017). This comes back to noticing what has already been survived. I've said it a few times already in this text, but if people can learn into unhealth they can learn into health. Same is true for survival; if they can survive an addiction, there's a good chance they can survive recovery. There's no saying this will be simple, but don't hesitate to notice the strengths and qualities that have helped clients endure. Notice them and lean on them when working toward or within recovery. Once there's a sense of the client strengths, try to mobilize them into action (in this case, behaviors) (Jay). Helping clients assess what control they do have or what their options might be, however limited, can spur active efforts to try some of those options out.

Awareness + self-efficacy (both protective factors) = behavior change; that's one of my favorite ideas from Motivational Interviewing (Ledesma, 2014; Miller & Rollnick, 2013). Its applicability is wide in the counseling world and it fits here too. If clients believe they are capable and have available options, there's a chance they'll access them. Foster resilience through strength and resource identification. Be sure to value the role of the relationship as well. Having supportive relationships is an important element of resilience as previously noted. We have a wonderful opportunity to support client resilience through our interactions and relationship with them.

Important Reminder for Counselors and Counselors-in-Training

For the readers who are, or who are training to be, helping professionals, I strongly encourage you to think about how you define what constitutes "bouncing back" from a blow. I also encourage you to consider the alternate view that resilience is more of an ongoing "battle," and importantly, a battle that can be won (Jay, 2017). Taking definitions of resilience from the research and applying them to your clinical practice is critical; this can't just be some buzz word we throw around in a counseling session. It's worth so much more than that.

As a counselor myself, my understanding of resilience has slowly evolved from that of a positive adaptation which supports health (as some researchers have noted) more toward sheer adaptation to adversity. More specifically, I have learned to see the survival value inherent in a variety of behaviors, whether they support optimal health or not. A person who leans on heroin to cope with their trauma is quite resilient in my mind; they've found a tool that allows for survival, however unhealthy, they have adapted, and they are alive. If one can adapt to adversity through negative means, it remains possible they can learn to adapt through positive (aka healthy) ones. The idea of resilience conveys hope that change is possible. Find the strength in how clients have survived and adapted to adversity and help them to realize and appreciate their resilience.

References

Bonanno, G. A. (2004). Loss, trauma, and human resilience. *American Psychologist, 59*, 20–28.

Bonanno, G. A., Wortman, C. B., & Nesse, R. M. (2004). Prospective Patterns of resilience and maladjustment during widowhood. *Psychology and Aging, 19*, 260–271.

Bordin, E. (1979). The generalizability of the psychoanalytic concept of the working alliance. *Psychotherapy: Theory, Research and Practice, 16*(3), 252–260.

Carver, C. S. (1998). Resilience and thriving: Issues, models, and linkages. *Journal of Social Issues, 54*, 245–266.

Cronin, E., Brand, B. L., & Mattanah, J. F. (2014). The impact of the therapeutic alliance on treatment outcome in patients with dissociative disorders. *European Journal of Psychotraumatology, 5*. doi: 10.3402/ejpt.v5.22676.

De Jong, P., & Berg, I. K. (2013). *Interviewing for solutions* (4th ed.). Brooks/Cole: Pacific Grove.

Fleming, J., & Ledogar, R. J. (2008). Resilience, an evolving concept: A review of literature relevant to Aboriginal research. *PubMed Central Canada, Pimatisiwin, 6*(2), 7–23.

Greene, R. R. (Ed.) (2002). *Resiliency: An integrated approach to practice, policy, and research*. Washington, DC: National Association of Social Workers Press.

HeavyRunner, I., & Marshall, K. (2003). "Miracle survivors": Promoting resilience in Indian students. *Tribal College Journal, 14*(4), 14–19.

Hunter, A. (1999). Adolescent resilience. *Journal of Nursing Scholarship, 31*(3), 243–247.

Ickovics, J. R., & Park, C. L. (1998). *Thriving: Broadening the paradigm beyond illness to health*. Quarterly Publication for the Society for the Psychological Study of Social Issues. Blackwell Publishers.

Jay, M. (2017). *Supernormal: The untold story of adversity and resilience.* New York, NY: Hatchette Book Group.

Laska, K. M., Smith, T. L., Wislocki, A. P., Minami, T., & Wampold, B. E. (2013). Uniformity of evidence-based treatments in practice? Therapist effects in the delivery of cognitive processing therapy for PTSD. *Journal of Counseling Psychology, 60*(1), 31–41.

Ledesma, J. (2014). Conceptual frameworks and research models on resilience in leadership. *SAGE Open.* doi: 10.1177/2158244014545464.

Luthar, S. S. (2006). Resilience in development: A synthesis of research across five decades. In D. Cicchetti & D. J. Cohen (Eds.), *Developmental psychopathology: Risk, disorder, and adaptation* (pp. 740–795). New York, NY: Wiley.

Lynch, M. M. (2012). *Factors Influencing Successful Psychotherapy Outcomes.* Retrieved from Sophia, the St. Catherine University repository website: https://sophia.stkate.edu/msw_papers/57

Masten, A. S. (2005). Ordinary magic: Resilience processes in development. *American Psychologist, 56*(3), 227–238.

Miller, W. R., & Rollnick, S. (2013). *Motivational interviewing: Helping people change* (3rd ed.). New York, NY: Guilford Press.

Mills, R. C., & Shuford, R. (2003). *Health realization: An innate resiliency paradigm for school psychology.* Presented at the Hawaii International Conference on Education, Waikiki, HI, January 7–10, 2003.

National Research Council (US) and Institute of Medicine (US) Committee on the Prevention of Mental Disorders and Substance Abuse Among Children, Youth, and Young Adults: Research Advances and Promising Interventions. (2009). O'Connell, M. E., Boat, T., & Warner, K. E., (Eds.). *Preventing mental, emotional, and behavioral disorders among young people: Progress and possibilities.* Washington (DC): National Academies Press (US). Retrieved from https://www.ncbi.nlm.nih.gov/books/NBK32775/ doi: 10.17226/12480.

Nishikawa, Y. (2006). *Thriving in the face of adversity: Perceptions of elementary-school principals.* La Verne, CA: University of La Verne.

O'Leary, V. E. (1998). Strength in the face of adversity: Individual and social thriving. *Journal of Social Issues, 54*, 425–446.

Olsson, C., Bond, L., Burns, J. M., Vella-Broderick, D. A., & Sawyer, S. M. (2003). Adolescent resilience: A concept analysis. *Journal of Adolescence, 26*, 1–11.

"Resilience." (2020). *Merriam-Webster.com Dictionary*, Merriam-Webster. Retrieved on February 20, 2020 from https://www.merriam-webster.com/dictionary/resilience

Sroufe, L. A., Egeland, B., Carlson, E., & Collins, A. (2005). *The development of the person: The Minnesota study of risk and adaptation from birth to adulthood.* New York, NY: The Guilford Press.

Summers, R. F., & Barber, J. P. (2010). *Psychodynamic therapy: A guide to evidenced-based practice.* New York: The Guilford Press.

Ungar, M. (2004). A constructionist discourse on resilience. *Youth & Society, 35*, 341–365.

Wampold, B. E. (2001). *The great psychotherapy debate: Model, methods, and findings.* Mahwah: Lawrence Erlbaum Associates.

Wampold, B. E. (2015). How important are the common factors in psychotherapy? An update. *World Psychiatry, 14*(3), 270–277.

Wampold, B. E. & Imel, Z. E. (2015). *The great psychotherapy debate: The research evidence for what works in psychotherapy* (2nd ed.). New York, NY: Routledge.

Werner, E. (1995). Resilience in development. *Current Directions in Psychological Science, 4,* 81–85.

Werner, E. E., & Smith, R. S. (2001). *Journeys from childhood to midlife: Risk resilience and recovery.* New York, NY: Cornell University Press.

Yates, T. M., Egeland, B., & Sroufe, L. A. (2003). Rethinking resilience; A developmental process perspective. In S. S. Luthar (Ed.), *Resilience and vulnerability: Adaptation in the context of childhood adversities* (pp. 243–266). New York, NY: Cambridge University Press.

17 Considerations for Counselor Wellness

Before closing out the book, I think it's important to take some time to appreciate the impact of client losses on counselors. Providing support to others can be taxing. Listening to stories of hardship, loss, and grief can take a toll, particularly when efforts to empathize are present. The effort to empathize moves the interaction from passive listening to active, empathic engagement. There's more emotional skin in the game. Some client losses and/or addictions will pair with traumatic events and researchers have consistently noted that can take a toll on the psychological well-being of the helper (Adams, Boscarino, & Figley, 2006; Figley, 1995, 2002a, 2002b; Ohaeri, 2003; Sabin-Farrell & Turpin, 2003).

Definitions

Several terms exist to describe the negative impact of chronic exposure to client psychological trauma: *vicarious traumatization* (Pearlman & Saakvitne, 1995), *secondary traumatic stress* (Stamm, 1995, 1997), and *compassion fatigue* (Figley, 1995). Vicarious traumatization (VT) refers to the "emotional residue of exposure" to stories of the pain, terror, and fear inherent in trauma (American Counseling Association, 2020, p. 1). Secondary traumatic stress (STS) is the "emotional duress" that comes from hearing the trauma narratives of another (The National Child Traumatic Stress Network, 2020, p. 1). Compassion fatigue (CF) is mental and physical exhaustion, emotional withdrawal, apathy, or indifference toward the suffering of others due to frequent exposure to such suffering (Figley, 1995; Gentry & Dietz, 2020; Smith, 2009). Put simply, empathizing with client suffering too much can lead to a lack of caring. Overexposure dulls the response. Think of a sponge; if it's been drenched in water it can't absorb anymore.

As you can see, these concepts tend to bleed into one another and are often used interchangeably, but importantly they can all lead to burnout (Kearney, Weininger, Vachon, Harrison, & Mount, 2009). Burnout is characterized by emotional and physical exhaustion, depersonalization (when one loses their sense of identity), cynicism, detachment from the job, and a feeling that nothing is being accomplished (Kearney et al., 2009).

Symptoms

When working with addiction and addiction-related loss, keep an eye out for symptoms for any or all of these states. The American Counseling Association (2020, pp. 1–2) lists the following symptoms of vicarious trauma (notably, such symptoms are also tied to STS and CF):

- Having difficulty talking about their feelings
- Free-floating anger and/or irritation
- Startle effect/being jumpy
- Over-eating or under-eating
- Difficulty falling asleep and/or staying asleep
- Losing sleep over patients
- Worried that they are not doing enough for their clients
- Dreaming about their clients/their clients' trauma experiences
- Diminished joy toward things they once enjoyed
- Feeling trapped by their work as a counselor (crisis counselor)
- Diminished feelings of satisfaction and personal accomplishment
- Dealing with the intrusive thoughts of clients with especially severe trauma histories
- Feelings of hopelessness associated with their work/clients
- Blaming others

It's also important to keep tabs on symptoms of burnout. They include (Mosadeghrad, 2014; Rozman, Grinkevich, & Tominc, 2019):
Physical symptoms:

- Exhaustion
- Fatigue
- Headaches
- Sleep disorders
- Loss of energy
- Nonspecific pain
- Reduced attention span
- Raised blood pressure
- Chest pains
- Gastrointestinal disorders

Emotional symptoms:

- Apathy
- Feelings of meaninglessness
- Depressed mood state/lack of enjoyment at and outside of work
- Anxiety
- Irritability
- Loss of confidence

- Tension
- Sadness
- Feelings of dread (related to work)

Behavioral symptoms:

- Reduced reaction times
- Reduced work capacity
- Less work motivation
- Difficulty concentrating
- Lacking patience with coworkers (tied to irritability)
- Reduced engagement in pleasurable activities outside of work

Responding to Vicarious Trauma, Secondary Traumatization, and Compassion Fatigue

The National Child Traumatic Stress Network (NCTSN, 2020) offered strategies for organizations and individuals in responding to VT, STS, and CF. On the organizational level, they stress the importance of adequate clinical supervision. I could not agree more that counselors need their own support when working with client pain. With addiction comes loss and with loss often comes pain. Assume that this is relevant in the addictions sphere; it is. Balanced caseloads (i.e. not all trauma or severe hardship in every client), supportive workgroups or coworker networks, measures that ensure the physical safety of staff and flextime schedule when possible are also suggested. Further, the importance of training around STS for all staff, not just counselors, and an ongoing assessment of staff needs, risk, and response/resiliency are encouraged.

My takeaway from all of these is that organizations and leadership must recognize and appreciate that this work is hard, and it will have an impact. For staff to fare well, they need support and cannot be expected to take on more water when their sponge is clearly full. Advocate for yourself as a counselor. Notice what you are feeling, try to identify what you need, and speak your truth. In advocating for your wellness, you're also advocating for your client's wellness.

On the individual level, using supervision to process client cases, stories, and any symptoms experienced is important (NCTSN, 2020). Maintaining and enhancing self-awareness of STS and working toward a healthy work-life balance is also crucial. Part of that includes taking care of one's body through nutrition and exercise, maintaining and forming relationships/meaningful connections in and out of work, and continued training on how to manage the risk of STS and caring for oneself when encountering client trauma and pain. One suggestion that I particularly like is a self-care accountability buddy system. This builds on the importance of connection. Have someone who checks in on you and who you check in on.

Remember to practice what you likely preach to clients: try to avoid isolating with the pain. Have built-in connections that are centered on wellness and the knowledge that sometimes maintaining wellness is hard.

Examining your Own Responses to Loss

Ultimately, as counselors working with loss, take the time to examine your own reactions to loss. If you're going to work with someone else's reactions to loss, you first need to understand your own. Think and reflect on the following:

- What do you *do* when you lose something? (i.e. isolate, reach out for support, conceal what you're feeling, share it with the world, throw yourself into work, eat, use alcohol or drugs)
- What do you *feel* when you lose something? Which emotions come up? (i.e. relief, terror, sadness, excitement, dread)
- What *thoughts* run through your mind? (i.e. I'm alone, the world is better, worse, unchanged…)
- Do any of these thoughts, feelings or behaviors shift or change depending on what's been lost (i.e. relationship, identity, object) or how something's been lost (i.e. by choice or by chance)?
- What does that mean that your reaction changes when the loss or loss circumstances change?
- How do you cope?
- Do you reach out or look within?
- Do you try to welcome the pain/emotions or distract from them/dull them?
- Do you want others to know the extent of what you're thinking or feeling (i.e. do you want to be known in your loss?) or do you want to hide away and ride it out alone?
- Do you ever feel shame or guilt around losses? If so, which and why?
- Are you resilient? If so, what's contributed to it? What are you still working on?
- Who supports you and what do they do or say that feels supportive?
- What are the ways in which people try to support you but fail? (i.e. platitudes such as "it'll be okay" are often intended to be helpful, but often feel empty)
- Do you try to hang onto memories, forming a continued connection or bond or do you try to move on from them, leaving the past in the past?
- How do you remember? (i.e. telling stories, memorial items such as photographs or personal items, literal scars or remnants of a physical wound, dates such as anniversaries, etc.)
- *Why* do you remember? (i.e. not to forget what you once had and what you've now lost, to learn from it, to notice how far you've come,

to feel something—happiness, anger, relief, sadness, etc., or any another reason)
- Do you think your way of grieving is the right/correct way? Are you able to separate how you grieve from how others respond to loss?
- Do you believe in the validity of nonfinite and/or ambiguous loss?
- Do you see the pain and value inherent in disenfranchised and unconventional grief?
- What do you still need to learn about loss, grief, and how they relate to addiction? Are you willing to have these conversations with clients and allow them to inform you? If not, what's holding you back?

There's so much to be learned from loss. Out of pain can come growth. Look for the lessons—for your clients and yourself. Find the presence in the absence and continually search for new meanings in the experiences of grief, loss, addiction, and recovery.

References

Adams, R. E., Boscarino, J. A., & Figley, C. R. (2006). Compassion fatigue and psychological distress among social workers: A validation study. *American Journal of Orthopsychiatry, 76*(1), 103–108.

American Counseling Association. (2020). *Vicarious trauma (fact sheet).* Retrieved on February 27, 2020 from https://www.counseling.org/docs/trauma-disaster/fact-sheet-9---vicarious- trauma.pdf

Figley, C. R. (Ed.). (1995). *Brunner/Mazel psychological stress series, No. 23. Compassion fatigue: Coping with secondary traumatic stress disorder in those who treat the traumatized.* Brunner/Mazel. Retrieved from https://psycnet.apa.org/record/1995-97891-000 on February 19, 2019.

Figley, C. R. (2002a). Compassion fatigue: psychotherapists' chronic lack of self-care. *Journal of Clinical Psychology, 58*, 1433–1441. doi: 10.1002/jclp.10090.

Figley, C. R. (2002b). *Treating compassion fatigue.* New York, NY: Brunner-Routledge.

Gentry, E. J., & Dietz, J. J. (2020). *Professional resilience: Prevention and resolution of burnout, toxic stress, and compassion fatigue.* Parker, CO: Outskirts Press.

Kearney, M. K., Weininger, R. B., Vachon, M. L., Harrison, R. L., & Mount, B. M. (2009). Self- care of physicians caring for patients at the end of life: "Being connected…a key to my survival." *Journal of the American Medical Association, 301*(11), 1155–1164.

Mosadeghrad, A. M. (2014). Occupational stress and its consequences: Implications for health policy and management. *Leadership in Health Services, 27*(3), 224–239.

Ohaeri, J. U. (2003). The burden of caregiving in families with a mental illness: A review of 2002. *Current Opinion in Psychiatry, 16*, 457–465.

Pearlman, L. A., & Saakvitne, K. W. (1995). *Trauma and the therapist: Countertransference and vicarious traumatization in psychotherapy with incest survivors.* New York, NY: W. W. Norton & Company, Inc.

Rozman, M., Grinkevich, A., & Tominc, P. (2019). Occupational stress: Symptoms of burnout in the workplace and work satisfaction of the age-diverse employees. *Journal of Management, Informatics, and Human Resources, 52*(1). Retrieved on February 27, 2020 from http://organizacija.fov.uni-mb.si/index.php/organizacija/article/view/930

Sabin-Farrell, R., & Turpin, G. (2003). Vicarious traumatization: Implication for the mental health of health workers. *Clinical Psychology Review, 23*, 449–480.

Smith, P. (2009). *To weep for a stranger: Compassion fatigue in caregiving.* Healthy Caregiving, LLC.

Stamm, B. H. (1995). *Secondary traumatic stress: Self-care issues for clinicians, researchers, and educators.* Lutherville, MD: Sidran Press.

Stamm, B. H. (1997). Work-related secondary traumatic stress. *PTSD Research Quarterly, 8,* 2, Retrieved on February 27, 2020 from http://www.ncptsd.org/publications/rq/rq-lrst.html

The National Child Traumatic Stress Network (NCTSN). (2020). *Secondary traumatic stress.* Retrieved on February 27, 2020 from https://www.nctsn.org/trauma-informed-care/secondary-traumatic-stress/introduction

Appendix A

Adult Attachment Style Descriptions

Secure

Secure attachments in childhood are fostered by an early, ongoing emotional attachment to an adult. The adult is in touch with the needs of the young child and is sensitive and responsive to their needs. Consistency is key and this attachment relationship transforms over time to become a secure base from which to explore the world. Independence is fostered through this secure exploration. The security in this secure attachment rests on perceived and actual safety, attention, and soothing.

In adulthood, these secure attachment patterns are repeated. Individuals have a strong sense of identity and a firm self-concept. Close relationships are sought and relationships are emotionally invested. They view themselves in a largely positive light and see others in the same way. Balance predominates this attachment orientation and people are both independent and able to engage/invest in and rely on their relationships with others.

Insecure-Dismissing/Avoidant

Insecure-dismissive/avoidant attachments in childhood are fostered by emotionally absent or unavailable adults. The adult is not attuned to the child and has little to no sensitivity or responsiveness to the child's needs. A distressed child might be encouraged to suppress or contain the emotion, rather than acknowledging, accepting, and expressing it. Independence and caring for oneself is encouraged and children that embody this style can present as small adults. Children learn not to seek out adults when in pain or distress and foster a deep sense of independence to the point of avoiding others when social support might otherwise be indicated.

In adulthood, these avoidant attachment patterns can persist and become dismissive in nature. People spend time alone and prefer that to interpersonal interaction. Relationships and emotional investment are a low priority and largely seen as unimportant. These people are thinkers and rely on their ability to think-through situations rather than feel-through them. They can appear quite cognitive and emotionally vacant. When problems arise, they will generally withdraw and distance themselves (aka avoid).

Balance is missing here and operate largely internally and alone; others do not factor in because they are not invited (Levy, 2017).

Insecure-Preoccupied

Insecure-preoccupied attachments in childhood are often referred to as ambivalent/anxious. Such attachment patterns are fostered through inconsistent attunement. Sometimes parents will be connected and caring and at other times insensitive and invasive. These contrasting presentations and responses produce confusion and insecurity in children due to their unpredictability. Suspicion of adults can also arise, and children can find it difficult to trust. Concurrently though, they may cling, quite literally, and constantly seek validation and connection.

In adulthood, this ambivalent/anxious pattern is renamed insecure-preoccupied and is characterized by insecurity and a negative view of self. People are often self-critical and seek external validation of their worth; even after they get it though, the self-critiques and low self-worth remain. A strong fear of rejection and abandonment predominate and worry along with a lack of trust fans the flames of fear. Clinginess and consistent dependence on others, particularly partners, highlight the imbalances. Insecurity, self-doubt, and turning to others to relieve both—with no success—are characteristic here.

Insecure-Fearful

Insecure-fearful attachments in childhood are fostered by scary caregivers. Abuse can fuel this attachment pattern and the child can genuinely fear for their lives when faced with physical, emotional, or sexual abuse. High levels of aggression can also spur this fear and fear response. The child's brain tells them to run and find safety, but the attachment figure to whom they might run is the person they are running from. The adult and their behavior are the source of distress and emotional dysregulation. Dissociation is a common result, with children essentially psychologically retreating. This level of detachment separates them from their current reality.

In adulthood, this insecure-fearful pattern is characterized by fear and avoidance. Continued detachment from feelings during times of stress, even great stress, is common; as a result, they have a disconnected, fragmented sense of self. Relationships are sought and preferred until they reach the point of emotional investment or intimacy. This emotionality presents as a threat and the brain responds to the vulnerability with reactions from the past. Unfortunately, the person is not always able to make the connection that present feelings are rooted in the past. This disconnect is significant and is a trauma response based on survival. Balance is missing here too and relationships can be confusing or disrupted. Such individuals struggle to connect with themselves and with others (Levy, 2017).

Reference

Levy, T. (2017). *Four styles of adult attachment*. Evergreen Psychotherapy Center Attachment Treatment & Training Institute. Retrieved on November 13, 2018 from https://www.evergreenpsychotherapycenter.com/styles-adult-attachment/

Appendix B

Expanding the Emotional Conversation Activity

This activity can be useful when a client is repeating a certain word or phrase when describing how they feel and are unable to expand or elaborate on that emotional experience. For example, phrases such as, *"This sucks," "This hurts," I'm stuck," "I just want to move on," "I don't want to let go,"* may be repeated over and over again in sessions, yet counselor and client may both struggle to fully understand the feelings being expressed. This repetition persists even with the counselor's efforts to reflect back different options or depths of emotion or experience. When this happens, sessions can feel like they've stalled. Here's one option for getting back on track and learning what's behind and within such words or phrases.

1 Get out a blank piece of paper (scrap paper works just fine). Start by writing the word or phrase on the top of a blank sheet of paper. For this example, we'll use "I just want to move on."
2 Next, ask the client to complete the following sentence: *"When you just want to move on, you also feel* _____?" or *"You want to move on and you can't. Complete this phrase," "When I feel stuck, I also feel* _____."

    Some answers I have heard from clients filling in the blank for this phrase include:

- Stuck
- Frustrated
- Lost
- Sad
- Hurt
- Annoyed
- Hopeless
- Tired
- Tired of thinking about it
- Over it/done
- Like I'm rehashing the past and getting nowhere
- Like others only see me as what I used to be

Once you have a list—and it can be two things or 20—either is valuable, move on to step 3.

3 Ask the client to read over the list and note any connections between the words they've come up with.

- For example, lost and sad might fit together, meaning they co-occur. Tired and annoyed might go together. Over it/done and feeling like others only see me as what I used to be....

Clients can draw lines noting connections between items, color code them, or simply group them together in a separate list. Have them stop when they feel like they've noted what connections exist.

Next, ask them to talk about the connections they've made.

- Why do certain things go together? Do any stand alone?
- Do some feelings seem to come up more frequently than others?
- Have they noticed these connections before?
- What thoughts or feelings (or overall reaction) do they have looking at their list?

Once you and the client have discussed connections and reflected on the patterns, move on to step 4.

4 Have the client rank the pairings that bother them the most. I typically say, "Now I want you to rank them. Rank them in order of how much you want them gone. So, number 1 will be the feeling that bothers you most. Give me the top three or four."

5 Ask the client to explain their rankings. For example, what about number 1 is most bothersome? Which items made it to the bottom of the list (lower priority/least bothersome)? Consider the rankings/ priorities when setting goals with your client.

6 Finally, reflect on where you started just minutes prior. In this example the phrase *"I just want to move on."* was repeated without elaboration numerous times. Acknowledge that moving forward, when that phrase comes up, you and they will have a better sense of what is being expressed. When the client says, *"I just want to move on,"* they are also saying they feel tired, annoyed, hopeless, frustrated, hurt, etc.

Point 6 closes out the activity and makes the point that our words often carry more meaning than we realize. This activity is aimed at revealing what's beneath the surface.

Appendix C
Letter Writing Activity and Examples

Letter writing can be used as a tool to encourage client reflection. The idea here is for the client to identify a recipient, write a brief (or long) letter to it/them expressing things that have and have not yet been shared. These are intended to be emotion-centric letters and can be a helpful way to get a sense for what the client is thinking and feeling. Depending on the variation used, these may resemble Dear John letters—goodbye letters that finalize a breakup by outlining the reasons for the split. Such letters can be used in individual or group modalities. Consider some options and note the examples of completed letters that follow:

- Dear heroin (or other behavior/substance)
- Dear anxiety (or other state of feeling)
- Dear mom
- Dear kids
- Dear addict self (written from the perspective of the recovery self)
- Dear future/recovering self (written from the perspective of the addicted self)
  - Clients can also draft responses to these letters; for example, have the client write to their past 'addicted' self and then respond from their 'recovering' self.
- Dear dog (or another non-human companion)
- Dear boss/employer
- Dear God (or other higher power)

NOTE: Even if the recipient is an actual living person, these letters are NOT sent; they are for therapeutic use only. Be sure this point is clearly communicated to the client. If a client decides they want to send the letter, have a conversation, and talk it out. There may be benefits, there may be harm. Help your client sort that out before they take any action.

Examples

Dear addicted self,

I hate you sometimes. You make terrible choices and in trying to escape pain, you create it. You know you do stupid things and yet you keep doing them. When will it be enough? When will you change? I can't keep asking these questions and wondering if the time will ever come. I need to know, is there even hope? Can you get out of this or are you permanently stuck? I know it's hard and I know you're trying, but I wish change was happening faster. Some people have given up on you and think you're worthless and, to be honest, sometimes I think that too. Those are hard days. Looking in the mirror and seeing parts that feel worthless. Keep trying. Just keep trying.

Sincerely,
The rest of me

Dear heroin,

You've screwed me over so many times. You've taken my looks, my money, my family (some of them anyway), my hopes, and trust. What hurts the worst is how I have lost myself to you. I don't know who I am without you anymore and sometimes I'm not even sure I want to know. How messed up is that? You're terrible and amazing all at once and most times both of those—your awful parts and your amazing ones—come together. You take away my pain and then you bring me more. I hate you and I love you. I want you gone, and I also think I'll miss you. I'm not sure what to do with that.

Sincerely,
Someone who's trying

Dear kids,

I'm so sorry that I've got you mixed up in this life. I wanted so much better for you and it hurts my heart that you see me this way. I hope that you can also see the other parts of me. The parts that are trying and the parts that love you so much (even when I don't show it as much as I should). I'm excited that I'm working on getting better and I want you to know how much I want that for all of us. You deserve more than me and I'm going to get closer to the 'good' parent I want to be. I promise. I'll get there. Please don't give up on me. But if you do because it gets too hard, I'll still love you. You deserve to know that too.

Sincerely,
Mom/Dad

Dear baby (infant loss due to pregnancy loss),

I'm hurting so badly and I wish you were here. I'm so scared. I want these feelings to just go away and I'm trying to stay strong and not use. But I want to so much. Every time I see a reminder of you or what I had and lost, I die a little inside. It hurts so much that you're gone. I miss you. I'm so sorry.

Sincerely,
Mom/Dad

Dear future self/recovery self,

I can't wait to meet you. I have so many hopes of who you will be. I hope you'll be smarter and not make dumb decisions. I hope that you'll be patient with yourself and realize you don't have to be perfect to be good. I hope you notice that what other people think and do doesn't have to impact you as much as it does now. I hope you notice you are strong and appreciate that you've survived. I hope you love yourself and I hope you love others. I hope you show that love too, not just get caught up in your head. I hope you can get a job and not one just to pay the bills (but that's important). I hope you like things and feel things and know what to do with both of those. To be honest, I have no idea who I am right now and am working on that. But I hope that you've figured it out. I hope that when you look back at who I am (your past self) that you don't hate me and that you forgive and understand.

Sincerely,
You

Dear dog,

I'm so grateful for you. You love me no matter what and have never given up on me. You are the only thing in my life that has never failed me. I hope that I love you enough and that you know how much you mean to me. You're the best dog ever.

Sincerely,
Your human

Epilogue

I did it! We can do hard things and so can our clients. Always remember that.

Index

Printed in the United States
By Bookmasters